Lake of Widows

Liza Perrat

Copyright © 2024 by Liza Perrat

The moral rights of the author have been asserted.
All rights reserved. No part of this publication may be reproduced, distributed, or transmitted in any form or by any means, including photocopying, recording, or other electronic or mechanical methods, without the prior written permission of the publisher, except in the case of brief quotations embodied in critical reviews and certain other non-commercial uses permitted by copyright law. For permission requests, write to the publisher, addressed "Attention: Permissions Coordinator," at the email address below.

Cover design: JD Smith.
Perrat Publishing.
All enquiries to info@lizaperrat.com
First printing, 2024.
ISBN E-book: 979-10-95574-12-5
ISBN Print book: 979-10-95574-13-2

Lake of Widows is dedicated to my
wonderful family, near and far.

Prologue

Adrienne
April 1966

The twins are twelve years old today, almost teenagers! To celebrate Antoine and Martine's birthday, I've planned a family outing in the Parc de la Tête d'Or, one of the largest parks in the whole of France.

The picnic basket waiting beside the door, I bustle around the flat, tidying, and clearing away breakfast.

'Don't forget your raincoats,' I call to the twins, but they don't answer, and I have to ask my husband three times to please get dressed.

As soon as we are in the Citroën, driving to the park, the twins start up their usual bickering.

'Ow, Antoine hit me,' Martine whines.

'Did not,' her brother grunts.

When I discovered I was pregnant with twins, I'd feared double trouble. But people said twins were easier — having grown together inside me, they'd be friends for life. But Antoine and Martine have despised each other right from their initial battle at the door of my womb to be first into the world.

'What are we supposed to do at the boring park?' Martine says, in that moany manner she's adopted. 'We're too old for that stupid Guignol puppet show. And you *do* know I'm missing out on playing the Monkees' songs with my friends this afternoon?'

'Try and enjoy the day,' I say, wishing Emile would agree with me, but my husband remains wordless. Though I suppose it's important he concentrates on driving.

The closer we get to the park, the more the twins argue. Tears well, that familiar lump blocks my throat, and I swallow hard.

'I'm s-sure it will be f-fun,' I stammer, swivelling around and flashing them a smile.

But the day only gets worse, starting with a rain squall that soaks us all.

'Couldn't you have planned an indoor venue?' Emile says, as we huddle, wet and shivering, beneath a tree. He frowns at me. Or the rain. Or both.

'How could I know it would rain this much?' I say.

'After my busy week, this is the *last* thing I need,' Emile goes on. 'You'd see if you swapped places with me, Rien. You'd realise how hard I work to provide for you and the twins.'

'I know, and I *do* appreciate that, but could you please stop calling me "Rien"? It makes me feel as if I'm worth nothing.' Emile smiles and plants a wet kiss on my brow.

'It's only a joke, *chérie*. I've told you countless times, "Rien" is simply a shortened form of "Adrienne". Don't you get that?'

I sigh, and regret, once again, being oversensitive.

'You know Maman can't take a joke, papa,' Antoine says, with an exaggerated eye roll.

'That's not true, I *love* jokes,' I say, though I have to admit that lately, there is more and more of Emile's humour that I don't understand. Perhaps I am simply too stupid, too uneducated — unlike my husband with his medical degree — to grasp normal humour.

'Well, maybe you've just lost your sense of humour today, *notre petite maman*?' Emile says.

I clamp my lips to avoid shouting at Emile. Calling me "our little mother" is almost as bad as calling me "Nothing".

'Oh no, I've offended you again.' Emile grins at the twins as if urging them to agree with him. 'I'm sorry, but you're so touchy, *chérie*. Perhaps it's the strain of organising the birthday outing?'

'The *strain*? Why would the twins' birthday be a strain?'

Martine stamps a foot. '*Oh là là,* stop your jabbering!'

'Let's all calm down,' Emile says. 'It's stopped raining, so why don't we go and see those lions in the zoo, then row a boat across the lake? And I'll buy everyone the biggest birthday ice-cream ever. How does that sound?'

'But I packed a picnic …' My voice trails away, and I trudge off after them, beneath that sky swollen with grey clouds, and a lone bird wheeling overhead, cawing and battling the wind.

My legs ache, my chest is tight, my head throbs, and I have no idea why I am so upset and foul-humoured.

~

That evening, in a last bid to salvage the disastrous birthday outing, I cook the new meatloaf recipe that is popular in America, so everyone in France wants to try it. I set the table with a linen cloth, the nice Limoges plates and silver cutlery.

'That was actually quite tasty,' Emile says with a smile, as he pushes away his empty plate. 'Thanks, *chérie*, and I hope you're feeling better?'

'I'm fine thank you,' I say, as the twins sidle off to their bedrooms without a word. I don't know if they liked the meatloaf, and I don't dare ask.

'Why am I *so* exhausted, Minou?' The cat miaows and weaves through my ankles as I clear away, while Emile sits in his armchair perusing the newspaper. 'Maybe I'm lacking something in my blood, and I should see the doctor?'

But it's not only my body. My mind too, has become so heavy with this fatigue I can't shrug off. Even though Emile is a psychiatrist, not a general practitioner, I have mentioned this tiredness to him.

'Lie down and have a rest, *chérie*,' is always his answer.

But I doubt a rest would fix things. No, it runs deeper; something that is gnawing at my very core.

I trudge about finishing last-minute jobs — wiping out gunk from the kitchen sink, closing shutters, and moving shoes from the doorway so I won't trip over them in tomorrow's dim dawn light. I tiptoe around so as not to disturb them all, tightening the leaking bathroom tap so the drip-drip noise won't keep us awake. I pick up a dirty sock and fling it into the washing basket.

'A good wife doesn't complain,' Emile's mother always says. 'No husband likes a complaining wife, especially a husband who works so hard for his family.'

Yes, Emile *does* work hard for us, so I have no reason to complain, or feel this awful. If my husband beat me or ran around with other women, I could complain. But he doesn't do any of those things. Instead, Emile buys me everything a wife could possibly want. So, whatever is wrong with me?

I'm sorry, mother-in-law. I'm sorry, Emile.

Part I

June – September 1970

Adrienne & Blanche

~

1

Adrienne

Emile strode into the kitchen, kissed my cheek and peered over my shoulder.

'What's that divine smell, *chérie?*'

'My special lemon chicken for dinner tonight,' I said, stirring the sauce simmering on the stovetop. 'The twins' favourite.'

'Aren't you overdoing the butter?' He planted a friendly slap on my backside. 'Only thinking of your figure, Rien.'

Emile started calling me 'Rien' at a medical dinner with his colleagues and their wives several years ago. My husband had laughed hysterically, his infectious cackle making everyone else laugh too. I'd given them all a weak smile and hid my embarrassed blush.

And still I flinched as he sat down to his *entrée* of *salade composée*. With only an hour to spare from his busy psychiatric practice, I always had Emile's lunch ready when he walked in the door, along with a half-glass of his preferred Bordeaux wine, not a trickle more or less.

I turned off the stove and sat beside him to eat. Hair neatly combed, sideburns trimmed to precision, shirt and trousers still uncreased, my husband looked groomed and handsome even in this June heat.

Like every lunchtime, before Emile arrived, I'd hurriedly brushed my hair and smeared on lipstick, but still I was conscious of my haggard appearance: flushed cheeks, stained house apron, and limp hair strands sticking to my sweaty brow.

'Why are you cooking for the twins? Antoine and Martine won't be home this weekend,' Emile said, mopping up the vinaigrette dressing with a chunk of baguette. 'You know they haven't been home in *months*. In fact, I doubt we'll see them the entire summer.'

'My children aren't coming home the *whole* holidays?' The blood drained from my face, my fork clattering onto my plate. 'But why?'

'Martine mentioned plans to spend the summer with friends at some family beach home on *la Côte d'Azur*.'

My shock and dismay were so deep I didn't even think to ask how Emile knew that, and I did not.

'But they've never had holidays with friends before.'

'It appears to have escaped you, Adrienne, but our children are *sixteen* now. They've made new friends at boarding school, and have better things to do than come home to you moping about how tired you are.'

'Well, if you hadn't sent them off to that school — without even consulting me — I might not be so *mopey*.'

I took a deep breath, swallowing my frustration and sadness, as I served Emile his pork cutlet and potatoes. I was no longer hungry.

'I know you believe it was the right thing, sending our children away,' I said, 'but I miss them so much. And I'm barely allowed to see them.'

In that moment, I recalled their twelfth birthday, four years ago, and how I'd yearned to be away from them all for a few moments — the jokey husband and the hostile pre-adolescents. But now, I'd give anything to have them back home.

I'd never complain about them dawdling in late on these long summer evenings, or Antoine hanging around with those dubious friends, finally dragging himself home after dark, and stinking so badly of Gauloises and body odour that I struggled not to gag. And I'd never mention Martine's musk-scented *eau de toilette* that clogged my throat every time she wafted into my kitchen.

'Boarding school was the *only* decision,' Emile said, jabbing his meat knife at me. 'My children must have the best education if they're to have a decent life.'

'I know but …'

Emile stood up, his chair scraping on the tiles sending goose bumps down my spine. 'No buts, *notre petite maman*. Trust me on these things, I do know best. Anyway, see you tonight, *chérie*.' He kissed my cheek, grabbed his Citroën keys and marched out the door as briskly as he'd marched in an hour earlier.

Once the flat was blissfully silent again, I sipped my cup of tea, stroking the cat stretched across the chair beside mine.

'I should go and get those groceries, eh, Minou? But it's *so* hot.' I glanced outside at the blazing sun, trying to muster the energy to leave our cool, marble-floored apartment with its efficient ceiling fans. 'Besides, food shopping seems so pointless without the twins.'

Another stab of misery pierced my heart as I filled Minou's water bowl, hung my apron on its hook and folded the shopping list into my handbag. I took the meat from the fridge's freezer compartment. I would cook the chicken for that lemon sauce anyway, in case the twins *did* come home.

I waited for the lift, running a palm across the cherub and animal carvings that decorated our front door. How overdone and fussy it looked, I thought, as if seeing that elegant wooden door for the first time. Like the woodcarver hadn't known when to stop.

'Think of our home as your *château*,' Emile had said when he'd purchased our spacious top-floor apartment in the most expensive suburb of Lyon. 'And you, *chérie*, are the *châtelaine*.' I'd clasped my hands together, excitedly planning how I'd decorate my castle.

Before I stepped out of the lobby into the city heat and dust, I glanced at the gilded barometer-thermometer.

'Louis XVI period,' the real estate agent had boasted.

Twenty-three degrees.

Only twenty-three? Why do I feel so hot? A change of life hot flush? No, no! Mid-thirties is far too young.

As I trudged along to the bus stop, I put it down to that exhaustion I'd been feeling these past weeks. Or months. Or was it years? Waiting for the bus, I knew I should walk to Carrefour. The supermarket wasn't that far.

'Bit of exercise will do you good,' Emile would say, but as I sat on the bus blotting a handkerchief against my moist brow, my bottom sliding on the sweat the previous passenger had left, I convinced myself it was far too hot to walk anywhere, especially lugging heavy shopping bags.

On days like this, I wished I'd been brave enough to insist that Emile teach me to drive.

~

As usual, I ended up choosing a trolley with a wonky wheel, and I puffed and sighed up and down the Carrefour aisles, forcing it in the right direction.

The more I filled the trolley, the worse it wobbled, and I almost slammed into a cluster of housewives gathered before the row of televisions. They likely weren't interested in purchasing a set, but it was a good place to chat, and watch whatever program was showing. I caught snatches of a newsreader's words:

... two schoolgirls and two civilians were killed by shells from Jordan and eight Arab guerrillas were pursued and killed in other incidents.

The world out there was becoming so dangerous. I shivered, the trolley almost snagging the heels of a shuffling old woman. I thought of moving everything to a working one, but that would be more trouble than it was worth, tramping back the entire length of Carrefour to where the trolleys were stored.

Besides, I'd ticked everything off my list, except that brand of *Madeleines* Antoine loved. Not that my ravenous son even tasted anything, simply gobbling down the cakes. Maybe I'd pick up a bottle of that musk-scented *eau de toilette* too, and surprise Martine.

On I plodded, ignoring Emile's words that my children would not be home this weekend, and trying to relax to the background music.

It was the same music as every Friday — that classic supermarket jingle my husband said was supposed to lull you into purchasing more items. Something about brain-wave patterns hidden in the musical compositions. But rather than enticing me to buy more items, the music only irritated me, the grating sound making me want to leave Carrefour and the stupid trolley that second, and rush home to my quiet, fan-cooled haven.

I finally found the *Madeleines* and the perfume and, my shoulders almost wrenched from their sockets, I manoeuvred the trolley to the shortest checkout queue.

I waited behind a stylish woman with a roll-up hairdo, kohl-rimmed eyes and high heels. Her fitted frock showed off a slim, curvy figure, and I tried to think back to when I'd been slim and curvy.

A sweet, rosy-cheeked boy of about seven years old sat hunched up in the stylish woman's trolley, surrounded by groceries. I thought he was a bit old to be sitting in a trolley, but as he curved his chubby little fingers into a wave and gave me the cutest grin, he reminded me of my twins, who'd been as adorable at that age. I smiled and waved back, wondering why the boy wasn't at school. Perhaps he was unwell, the red cheeks from some slight fever.

I reminded myself he wasn't my child to worry about — that I no longer had to worry about small children at all — and shifted my gaze to the magazine rack. The covers were filled with fashion images from Paris, London and New York, mostly girls with perfect bodies wearing swimsuits. At one time, I could've been one of them and, for a fleeting moment as I plucked the latest *Cosmopolitan* from the rack, I yearned for my pre-pregnancy body.

It was almost the stylish woman's turn at the checkout, and I was about to place the magazine in my trolley — unlike some women who read it right through whilst waiting their turn, then shoved it back, which is almost like stealing — when I heard the words. They came from the sweet seven-year-old.

'Why's that lady got a fat potato bum?'

'Pierre, hush!' the stylish mother chided, frowning at the child, and refusing to meet my horrified stare.

'Fat potato-bum, fat potato-bum,' Pierre chanted, fixing me with a wicked grin. The mother tore open a packet of biscuits and shoved one into Pierre's mouth.

'Fat potato-bum, fat potato-bum,' Pierre went on, spurting biscuit crumbs down his front. He stood up, gripped the trolley sides, and stamped his feet as he sang, 'Fat potato-bum, fat potato-bum.' He stomped on a slab of butter, which squished over other food, but on he went, spitting bits of biscuit, and not stopping for a breath.

'Pierre, that's *enough*.' His mother's face turned crimson as she slapped the ugly, snotty-nosed kid on his own — skinny — bum. 'Sit down and shut up, right now!'

I couldn't move. I was nailed to the ground, my fingers clasping the wonky trolley. As the revolting child's mother unpacked her groceries, she threw me a furtive glance, obviously hoping that I hadn't caught the demon Pierre's hurtful words.

But I had, and something was shifting deep inside me. A fire igniting in my belly, beginning slowly as flames licked kindling, catching wood, taking hold, burning faster, gaining height, width, strength. And peaking in a red-hot fury.

The fire scalded my chest and arms, the nape of my neck and my cheeks. My legs shook, and I gasped, trying to catch my breath that the vile Pierre had stolen.

Stone-faced, and without conscious thought, I peeled my fingers from the trolley, swivelled around and walked away from the checkout.

'Madame?' The cashier's voice probably, though I didn't turn around. 'Madame, what about your *groceries*?'

I ignored the voice, louder now. I took no notice of all those poison-dart stares piercing me from every angle, aware only of the ache crushing my chest, and the deep agony of hurt and embarrassment.

My feet moved, one in front of the other, but I was no longer walking. I was gliding in a slow, rhythmic line, my gaze fixed on the exit doors. As I drifted out of Carrefour, the cashier's shouty voice and the whispers of other shoppers faded to garbled murmurs.

Until all I heard was silence.

~

How I made it across that busy car park without getting knocked down, I'd never know. I think several cars honked, but I didn't look up or acknowledge anyone.

I was aware only of rods of sun searing my arms and legs, my muscles twisting, sweat trickling down my armpits. But I felt no pain or discomfort. I felt nothing.

I found myself back at the bus stop. Feeling giddy, I sank onto the bench seat. Cracked throat screaming for water, I licked my dry lips, clamped a palm over my racing heart, and breathed deeply.

After a rest and a drink, I'll be all right. I'll go back and fetch my shopping. A quick rest, that's all I need.

But when a bus wheezed to a stop, and the doors screeched open, I stepped up inside it. I didn't know if it was *my* bus, and I had no clue where it was going, I just knew I had to be on it. Shaky fingers fumbled in my purse for my bus pass, praying I had some of the ten journeys left on my card. I couldn't have faced the trouble of buying a new one.

My head resting against the window, I closed my eyes and let the bus jolt and jiggle me where it wanted, as it chugged further away from Carrefour.

I was vaguely aware of people getting on and off at regular intervals.

Bus stops, I suppose.

My eyes snapped open as the great beast of a vehicle swerved around a corner and I almost slid off the sweaty seat. I didn't recognise this street, and all the signs were blurred. I didn't know where I was, though the bus was heading away from town. Away from my home. But still I sat there, my mind pitching and reeling with the bus movement.

If I keep sitting here, I'll be all right. Soon, I'll be all right.

2
Adrienne

I'm searching for something but I don't know what. My brain is filled — bursting — with nothing. If only I could think clearly, could think at all. So much is missing from my mind but I can't even imagine what it might be.

Messages, information, questions, clamour to reach my brain. Who am I? What month ... what year is it? Where am I?

An image fills my mind — a distressed child reaching up her arms to her mother. But Maman's not there and the little girl keeps reaching and crying.

Am I dead? Dying? A car has knocked me down, and I'm lying on the hot tarmac, bleeding from a soon-to-be fatal head wound.

I feel no blood around my head. Dieu merci, it's only a slight concussion. I'll be all right, and soon everything will be back to normal.

But something has happened. What?

A spasm jerks my body, nausea rising like mouldy damp. I swallow the acidy bile. Even thirstier now. If only I could get to my fridge, to my delicate crystal jug of cool water, with lemon slices. I yearn so much for this cold water, but Grandmère's cold, gnarly hand stops me reaching for it.

No drink for you, girl, not until you've cooked your father and me a meal.

I try to tell Grandmère I'd stood for hours in the food queue, but there was barely anything. Those Nazi occupiers take everything.

My heart jolts into my throat. Something is pressing on my chest, and the ache stops me catching my breath. The Gestapo firing a bullet into my chest? No, I'm too young to be a Resistance fighter.

Breathe. Breathe. Thick, hot, musty air in my nostrils. Dying of thirst.

Dizzy from breathing too fast, I focus on slowing my breathing. My life is only this now, controlling my breaths. In, out. Slow, deep.

I lurch forward, and backwards, and a voice jangles through the fog of my mind.

~

'Madame, we've reached the terminus. You'll have to get off the bus.'

'Get off?' My voice a hoarse whisper, I looked around me. Oh yes, I *was* the sole passenger left. Clutching my handbag to my chest, I stood up, legs quivering. I tugged my frock, bunched in wrinkled sweaty folds, back into place, ignoring the bus driver's stare as I stepped outside into that oven-hot afternoon.

Runnels of sweat itching my back, I stared around me at this unfamiliar place, as though I'd landed on some different planet. Then, like distant figures emerging from a desert mirage, things became more defined.

I'm Adrienne Chevalier, thirty-five-years-old, married to Dr Emile Chevalier, and we have sixteen-year-old twins, Antoine and Martine. We live in a lovely apartment with stunning views of the Lyonnais cityscape.

This information was a lifebuoy that I clung to in that stormy sea, afraid that if I let go, I'd drown.

I'm alive. Alive, but lost, and so thirsty! Why am I not at home, the smooth marble floor cooling my feet, the ceiling fan humming as it blows cool air across my face? Why am I standing here, alone, in this ugly, blazing hot bus terminal with not a soul in sight?

Bells tring. Cash registers. Grating music. The Carrefour jingle.

And I remember.

Like every Friday afternoon, I'd gone to buy the groceries. I'd found the last things on my list, Antoine's *Madeleines* and Martine's *eau de toilette*.

So where is my shopping? Did I leave it on the bus?

I turned back, a palm shading my brow from the heat. The bus door was locked, the driver had vanished, and the terminus had that unsettling, ghost-town feel.

First thing, find water.

I looked around me. No taps. No shops. No people. Nothing but a row of empty buses parked diagonally along a hot, deserted tarmac.

Clutching my handbag — *Dieu merci*, I hadn't left that on the bus! — I shuffled toward the main road. I'd know what to do once I got there, and surely I'd find water.

I'd never had a good sense of direction, and didn't know if I was facing north, toward Paris, south, toward Marseille, or east, toward Geneva. Maybe I was facing west, toward ... I couldn't think of a single westward city, only the Atlantic Ocean.

Oh, to sink my broiling body into the cool ocean. That would clear my mind completely. It was this sizzling heat that was making me so confused. I'd heard that could happen. Some kind of mild sunstroke.

Only it wasn't *that* hot. I recalled our lobby thermometer-barometer reading twenty-three degrees. Perhaps it was broken, and giving false readings.

The sun had begun its setting arc, searing my brow like a flaming arrow, and I tented a hand across my face. So I must be facing west, and if I kept walking — even if it was hours, possibly *days*, away — eventually I would reach that refreshing Atlantic Ocean.

Yes, if I keep walking, keep moving from one patch of shade to the next, I'll get to somewhere I want to be.

After about five minutes, one of those Volkswagen van-type vehicles — a Combi? — pulled up. It was a faded red, decorated with swirly paintings of flowers, rainbows and peace signs. A man's face popped out of the window.

'Need a ride?' he said, with a friendly smile, turning down the radio, from which *Raindrops Keep Fallin' on my Head* was blaring.

The sleeves of his wrinkled greyish shirt — possibly once white — were rolled up. A tanned forearm covered in blond hair, beaded bracelets encircling his wrist, rested on the side. His shaggy hair was pulled back in a loose ponytail, and my first thought was that he had the loveliest blue eyes I'd ever seen.

I frowned. 'A ride? Why do you think I need a ride?'

'Because you had your hand stuck out.' He flicked sun-streaked hair strands from his face. 'Like you're hitchhiking.'

'Hitchhiking, *me*? Oh no, I wouldn't …' I took a breath, trying not to stare into those mesmerising eyes. 'I didn't have my hand out, well maybe for a moment, but I didn't mean to … oh I don't know. I'm so thirsty, do you have any water?'

He reached across to the passenger seat and handed me a tattered khaki-coloured water flask. Too thirsty to worry about dirt and germs, I gulped down most of the water.

I sighed in blissful relief, wiped the mouth part, and handed back the flask. 'Sorry, I didn't mean to drink that much, I was parched.'

'No problem, I'm almost home so I can fill up there,' he said, with that lovely smile, so soft, comforting and honest. 'So, even though you are definitely *not* hitchhiking, can I give you a lift? Where are you going, anyway?'

I glanced down at my dusty shoes that cut into my sweaty and swollen feet, wondering where I might be going. I couldn't think of a single place.

'Where are *you* going?' I asked, gazing back into those cornflower-blue eyes. 'It might be the same way I'm going. I don't want to put you out of your way.'

'You're not putting me out. I'm in no rush.' Waving a thin arm, he spoke lazily, as if he really did have all the time in the world. 'I'm on my way home to La Vallée du Bonheur.'

'Your home's called Happy Valley? Oh, that does sound like a nice place.'

He nodded. 'A place of peace, harmony and happiness. I couldn't imagine living anywhere else.'

'Oh, like one of those Kibbutz places? I heard about them on television.'

'Kind of,' he said. 'We *are* based around agriculture, as the early Kibbutz was, but it's more a safe and peaceful world, where everyone helps out, and where we love all our neighbours. At La Vallée du Bonheur we're all equal — man, woman and child.'

'Goodness, that *does* sounds lovely,' I said, unable to imagine such a place.

He stretched a hand out of the window for me to shake. 'My name's Bambou, and I'd be happy to give you a ride anywhere you want to go. Or you could come with me, to La Vallée du Bonheur?'

Bambou? What kind of a name is that?

'I'm Adrienne … Adrienne Chevalier.' As I shook his hand — the rough, earth-stained hand of someone who works the land — nothing like Emile's soft and limp psychiatrist's hand, the more this La Vallée du Bonheur place sounded appealing. Especially on such a hot afternoon.

And, despite his strange name, and my apprehension about getting into a stranger's car, Bambou did have a trustworthy face. It was familiar too, though I couldn't place it.

He kept looking at me, as if waiting for me to say that even though I'd love to go to La Vallée du Bonheur with him I had a husband who'd be expecting me home.

Then again, I *could* go with the good-looking Bambou. A simple nod and he'd open the passenger door and in I'd jump. It would be that easy.

3
Adrienne

As Bambou kept his hypnotic gaze on me, obviously waiting for me to decide if I was coming with him or not, a warning whisper fluttered through my mind.

He looks nice, but he's really a killer, the same as that lunatic, Dr Marcel Petiot, who murdered all those people during the war.

After a moment convincing myself it would be rude to keep Bambou waiting, I clambered up into the Combi. A frisson of fear shook me as I imagined Emile's surprise and horror if he could see his wife climbing into a rusty old van painted with flowers and peace signs, with a scruffy stranger wearing tie-dyed trousers and a grubby shirt.

Bambou smiled again. 'Ready then, Adrienne?'

To mask my nervousness and my utter bewilderment at my brazen boldness, I gave Bambou a firm nod, as he drove off and turned up the radio volume.

'*… yesterday TWA flight 486 … fifty-one passengers … hijacked … ransom,*' the newsreader was saying.

How terrible to be imprisoned in a plane by some madman, not knowing if you were going to live or die. I tried to ignore the wave of panic rolling through me.

Don't be silly, that plane hijacking is far away, in America. Things like that don't happen deep in the countryside of France.

'Let's find something happier,' Bambou said, fiddling with the dial until that popular new song *In the Summertime* came on.

I pulled down the visor against the sinking sun blasting into my eyes, and clutched my handbag on my lap. I wanted to sing along with Bambou, but my nerves kept snapping at my breath, so I hummed quietly, resisting the urge to blurt out, 'No, stop! Please turn around and take me home.'

Bambou didn't ask me anything about my family or where I lived. It was as if I had no past at all, and the old Adrienne was gone. A new, bold and carefree Adrienne was bumping along in that rattly Combi, a blur of trees whizzing past, the hot breath of wind lashing her hair across her face, and swinging the beads dangling from the rearview mirror.

My knuckles turned white, gripping my handbag, and I didn't know whether to chase after that old Adrienne or bid her good riddance.

I was glad Bambou sang, rather than chatted. I wouldn't have had a clue what to say to him, since I couldn't explain any of what was happening to me. Though if Bambou did strike up a conversation, I wouldn't be able to ignore this kind man who'd rescued me.

Rescued me from what?

Oh yes, from such terrible thirst. And from the heat reflecting off the beige earth and the brown Monts du Lyonnais hills ahead.

But it was more than that. As my senses filtered back to me, and I relaxed in his presence, I sensed that Bambou was rescuing me the same way Emile had once rescued me. How Emile's wedding ring on my finger was my escape route from that gruesome childhood — those years after they took Maman away to the asylum, and I was left alone with Papa and Grandmère. The terrible years that, once I married Dr Emile Chevalier, I'd banished to the darkest wedge of my mind.

'Never speak of your mother's sickness,' Grandmère would say, jabbing a bony finger at me. 'Or people will think you're mad too, Adrienne. Madness runs in families, you know.'

The supermarket scene flitted back into my mind, and I saw it all differently. Why hadn't I simply realised – – like any normal person — that what I'd perceived as hurtful and insulting remarks, were only the silly words of a child? Why had I overreacted so badly?

And why couldn't I accept the harsh truth when it was flung into my face like a damp cloth — that not only was my backside too fat, but *all* of me? Why didn't I see this as a sign that I should fix that, instead of making a huge fuss and leaving a trolley full of groceries in the middle of Carrefour?

I should ask Bambou to drive me back to the supermarket. I'd pay for the groceries, haul the bags home, unpack everything and cook the lemon chicken recipe.

But the tiredness overwhelmed me again, so I said nothing, letting my eyes close and rocking to the van's movement, inhaling its sweet-sour odour. How different this was, from Emile's quiet and immaculate Citroën.

Besides, deep inside, I knew Antoine and Martine wouldn't be home for the weekend. Always busy with their new friends, I couldn't even recall the last time they came home, so what was the point in cooking their favourite meal?

The van hit a pothole, startling me back to the present. I opened my eyes to the green-brown blur of fields, and suddenly I didn't care a fig about Carrefour groceries or lemon chicken.

I licked my lips, gasping for another drink. As if reading my thoughts, Bambou said, 'I'll get you a drink as soon as we arrive at La Vallée du Bonheur, something tastier than tepid water from an old flask.'

'Thanks, Bambou.'

'Bambou isn't my birth name, it's my La Vallée du Bonheur name.'

'Such a funny name. Like the tree?'

He laughed. 'When I was a kid, my mother said I grew faster than bamboo.'

That made me smile, and I wondered if I could change my name to something exotic like 'Bambou'. If I was no longer Adrienne, I might be able to forget about Emile's awful nicknames.

As the Monts du Lyonnais hills loomed closer, and I spied a village and a lake in the distance, the countryside began to look familiar.

'Is that Sainte-Marie-du-Lac and lac du Héron?'

Bambou nodded. 'Yes, we swim there, and I get our herbal medicines from a friend who concocts everything herself, Clotilde Bonnefille. The Sainte-Marie villagers call Clotilde, and her girlfriend, Bev, witches, charlatans and fakes.' He laughed. 'But rumour has it they all sneak off to *la maison des sorcières* in secret, preferring her cures to those of the local doctor.'

'Lac du Héron is one of my favourite places,' I said, thinking back to my engagement weekend there with Emile, then our blissful honeymoon.

As I imagined myself swimming in the crystalline lake water, I reefed my gaze from the good-looking Bambou, and let my heavy eyelids close again.

I peel the tight shoes from my red, swollen feet, go to line them up neatly, but leave them as they fall — one lying sideways, the other upside down. I fling my sweat-soaked dress, bra, slip and knickers into a ragged pile on the shore. I wade in, letting out an ecstatic sigh as the refreshing water cools my naked body. Instantly, I am washed clean of dust and dirt. Fresh and free. I roll onto my back, gazing up at the clouds scudding across the deep blue sky. I move my hands in small, delicate waves, just enough to keep afloat.

Keep afloat, don't drown. Must keep afloat, Adrienne.

From the water's edge, Bambou calls to me. Smiling, he takes off the tie-dye trousers and shirt. Wearing only the leather necklace and bead bracelets, he glides toward me, the sun glinting from his tall, lean, sun-tanned body. I cannot stop staring at his long, stiff penis.

'What are you grinning about?' Bambou said, his eyes sparkling like my daydream lake.

'What? Oh, nothing.'

My heart beat wildly. The heat of a blush crept up my throat, and my cheeks burned with shame. I turned away, banishing those wicked thoughts, wondering whatever had made me conjure up images like that. Apart from my husband, I'd never seen a man naked, and had no idea if a man's dangly part could be as enormous as I'd imagined.

Is this what lust is?

I'd never felt such a thing with Emile and, as the roadside trees thickened into dense woods, I wondered, yet again, why I was sitting in this stranger's van, allowing him to take me wherever he wanted.

The Jimi Hendrix song *Foxy Lady* came on, and to calm my nerves once more, I hummed along to Bambou's singing. I gripped my handbag, bouncing about on my lap, the unspent grocery money jingling in my purse.

A thought struck me. I could ask Bambou to drop me off at one of those lovely lakeside cottages Emile had rented for our honeymoon. I'd use the grocery money to pay for an overnight stay, then tomorrow I'd enjoy a cool swim in the lake.

And after that, I'd go home to my husband.

~

But still I didn't ask anything of Bambou. Still I remained sitting in that Combi, the hills looming closer, larger, as the shadows lengthened over valleys and ridges.

In a few hours Emile would come home from work and wonder where I was, but he wouldn't worry yet. He'd assume I'd found a friend to chat with at the supermarket — as if I ever did that — or I'd got delayed doing some other errands. He'd be certain I'd come home eventually, even after the shops closed. Because where else would Emile's wife be, besides cooking his dinner? Then later, when no Adrienne and no dinner appeared, Emile would worry. He'd pace around the flat, frowning and running a smooth hand through his perfectly combed hair.

I should ask Bambou to stop at a telephone box, to let Emile know I wasn't coming home tonight, but that I'd be back tomorrow, after the lake.

But as Bambou sang to me again — that *Chicago* song, *Beginnings* — I banished those thoughts of Emile and home. After all, maybe it would be good for my husband to worry about me, a little.

Bambou turned off the main road. The van edged deeper into the thick woods, and my heart leapt into my throat. His face had seemed familiar, but now I realised I didn't know Bambou at all. He'd simply reminded me of a boy at school I had a crush on, before I met Emile.

I could fling open the door, roll to the ground, scramble upright and run away to safety. But would Bambou try to stop me? Run after me?

As we jolted along that rough dirt track, the sky darkening by the minute, my hand crept up to the door, fingers edging around the handle.

I took a deep breath, about to flick open the handle, as we reached the end of the track. A gate stood open, its rotting wood and rusted hinges creaking in the breeze.

A great flap of wings sent the blood racing through my veins, my whole body quaking as a raven took flight from a gatepost. I read the weathered sign that dangled from one corner: *Bienvenue à La Vallée du Bonheur.*

4
Adrienne

I'd sweated so much in those last panicky moments, that when Bambou parked beside a semi-circle of tents and wooden huts, I slid down from the seat.

A woman about ten years younger than me, with hair long enough to sit on, emerged from one of the tents which, now I looked closer, were simply canvas sheets strung between wooden posts.

'*Salut,* I'm Jasmin. Welcome to La Vallée du Bonheur.' She smiled as if I was a friend she'd been waiting on, rather than some random person Bambou had found — a lost dog on the roadside. 'Let's get you a drink, you must be thirsty?'

'Thank you. I'm Adrienne.' Still clutching my handbag, I let Jasmin take my other hand and lead me into the tent.

From a stained and chipped jug — nothing like my exquisite crystal jug — Jasmin filled two glasses with amber-coloured liquid. As Bambou and I gulped down the tangy lemony-ginger drink, I tried not to compare the cheap, plain glasses with the delicate leaf-patterned ones in my kitchen cupboards.

Jasmin touched her fingertips to my forearm. 'You look frazzled, Adrienne. Why not relax for a moment before Bambou shows you around?' She pointed to a jumble of ragged, floral-patterned cushions in one corner, where two cats and a baby slept.

I sank down onto the cushions beside the baby, and that same wistful reminiscence overwhelmed me as I recalled watching my own twins sleep, marvelling at the tiny miracles Emile and I had made.

I did relax then, with Bambou and Jasmin, who turned out to be not the least bit frightening. My angst back in the Combi had been irrational, and I'd overreacted. Just like in Carrefour.

The baby started crying and flailing its little fists. Jasmin picked up the infant and flopped out a milk-filled breast, and Bambou took my hand, pulling me upright.

'Let me show you around,' he said, his touch sending a shiver through me. I had to resist the urge to reach up and run my fingers through that sun-bleached hair, to kiss those inviting lips and to hold that beautiful body against mine.

I'd never felt like this about any man, not even in the beginning with Emile. I didn't understand what was happening to me, and it both terrified and thrilled me.

The warm afternoon breeze caressing my bare limbs, Bambou introduced me to them all, from the young children to the wrinkly old people. A group sat cross-legged in the shade of a tree, all wearing the same loose, floral-patterned clothing, or tie-dye, like Bambou's trousers. They greeted me with friendly smiles as they wove baskets, braided one another's hair, or darned clothes.

I smothered a giggle at the sight of men sewing and braiding hair, imagining my husband and my son — *any* man I knew — doing such jobs.

Bambou led me down to the riverbank, to another group who were painting scenes of the ducks gliding across the water, the birds soaring overhead, and the colourful wildflowers bent by the breeze. He waved at two men milking goats, and at others dressed in earth-coloured shifts weeding a vegetable patch and brushing soil from plucked carrots, potatoes and beans. How happy and carefree they looked, chatting and working beneath that halo of peace and calm.

Bambou smiled at a cluster of wild-haired children dashing about a hen house, collecting eggs, and another group of dirt-streaked youngsters, giggling and playing hide-and-seek.

Before today, I'd have died before letting my twins run around naked, or even barefoot, *or* get dirty. What would people have said, or thought of me, as a mother? Emile and his parents would have keeled over with heart attacks, but now I wondered about all that fuss over a bit of dirt. Besides, letting my children run naked would have cut down on my never-ending laundry.

'We built our sleeping huts from wattle and daub, scrap wood and whatever else we could salvage,' Bambou said, as we circled back to the cluster of dwellings, bordered by petunias, pansies, and murmuring bees. 'Though some of us prefer sleeping outdoors beneath the stars and the moon, even the rain. We welcome all of Mother Nature's moods.'

Bambou's Combi was a time machine in which he'd driven me back to the Middle Ages; to this place I'd not even imagined existed. Still clasping my hand, he took me into another tent.

'We make some of our food here, like bread and cheese ... we're almost self-sufficient vegetarians.'

'Give us a hand, Bambou?' a man with straggly grey hair called, from a group of men bent over a roll of twine, and he loped off, leaving me standing there alone and a little lost without my new friend.

As if she'd known, the long-haired Jasmin reappeared, the baby swaddled in a cloth strapped to her chest.

'I bet you feel like a shower?' she said, with her placid smile, as I followed her to a cleared area behind one of the huts.

'Well, it *has* been a long and sweaty day,' I said, wondering whatever the bathroom would be like at this place.

~

There was no bathroom. Thankfully though, there were several hut-enclosed toilets.

'Composting toilets,' Jasmin said, whatever that meant.

I stood in the outdoor shower area, beneath water flowing from a hollowed-out bamboo pipe. My body tingled not only from the cool, fresh water, but with the thrill of standing in the open air with a breeze tickling my naked body, to the chorus of birdsong.

Far nicer than being closed up in a marbled bathroom with tiles that needed scrubbing, and drains that needed clogged hair removing. How wonderful, not to have to worry about all of that.

Jasmin returned, passing me a stained and threadbare towel. Nothing like the plump, fluffy towels in my linen cupboard, but I thanked her, and dabbed myself dry. She handed me a dress too, much like the one she was wearing — loose, ankle-length, with a sunflower pattern. It was faded and had obviously seen lots of wear, but looked clean, and I immediately loved it.

'This is to clean your teeth,' Jasmin said, handing me what looked like a twig. 'Works as well as a toothbrush. But I can't give you any underwear,' she said with a grin. 'We don't wear any at La Vallée du Bonheur.'

No underwear!

I left the shower area, revelling in the freedom of no knickers, slip or bra, though I couldn't help letting out a brief, self-conscious giggle. I walked freely in the floral dress, so much more comfortable than the tight frock I'd worn to Carrefour after lunch.

Only after lunch? It seems like years ago.

I pictured my vast bedroom wardrobe, and all those fancy dresses I kept for Emile's important medical events.

'Go and buy yourself something new,' Emile would say. 'A doctor's wife must look her best not only for special events, but every time she leaves her home.'

I recalled that last medical dinner, in a gastronomic Lyonnais restaurant, the kind of place I'd always felt like an imposter. I'd never been to any fancy places like that until I married Emile.

'Oh, so you wore *that* dress,' Emile had said, as we left the flat.

'You don't like it?'

'It's a lovely dress,' he said. 'But I thought you'd choose something more … more slimming.'

'You think I look fat?' I said, as we stepped into the lift.

'I didn't say that, Adrienne. Why do you always overreact?'

'Do you want me to go back and change?'

'No, we'll be late,' he said with a frown, checking his Rolex as the lift reached the lobby. 'But in future, perhaps think more carefully about your appearance when we're with my colleagues.'

I now realised how endless that had become, his constant chiselling away at me, letting me know how I'd failed to live up to his wifely expectations.

I cringed at the thought of those itchy crinolines I'd suffered early in our marriage — horsehair, taffeta and net — to ensure my skirt was as full as that of the other doctors' wives. How important that had been, but how ridiculous and outdated those petticoats now seemed.

My mind set on getting rid of things, I balled up my clingy frock, along with my slip, knickers, and the bra that cut into my flesh, and flung them into a bin. With a satisfied sigh, I also threw in my high-heeled, toe-crushing shoes, and walked off like a prisoner freed from her shackles.

I wondered what Emile would say if I dressed this way when I returned home. He'd point out that my breasts hung too low to go bra-less. 'And what if the wind catches that frock, and people see your private parts?'

Before today, I'd have fainted with embarrassment at the thought of exposing my private parts to the world, but now I let out a great belly laugh. And I had an urge to prance around with my dress hiked up to my waist.

5
Adrienne

'This can be your bed,' Jasmin said, pointing to one of four floor-mattresses inside one of the huts. A spider's web glistened in the dim flicker of her candlelight, and I masked my shudder as the spider scurried off into a dark corner.

'These straw mattresses are comfortable,' she said, 'but naturally, you can sleep where you want ... where your heart desires.' Jasmin nodded at my handbag, which I couldn't let go of. 'Dump your bag in a corner, nobody has *possessions* here, and join us around the fire when you're ready.'

'Thank you,' I said, gazing around the hut decorated with paintings — likely from those riverside artists — and embroideries of all levels of skill.

Without knowing why, I tugged off my wedding ring, and slid it into the inside pocket of my ridiculous out-of-place handbag. I flung the bag into a corner, went outside and sat, cross-legged around the small fire.

As the golden dusk sky filled with stars that sparkled like thousands of candle tips, people strummed guitars, or played flutes, and other musical instruments I couldn't identify. Some swayed to the music, others sang or hummed. Nowhere in the city had I witnessed such a brilliant sunset of yellow, orange and scarlet swirls across the westward hills.

'Anyone keen to join me at the Isle of Wight music festival?' an older, grey-haired man asked. 'Joe Cocker, the Moody Blues, and Jefferson Airplane played there last year.'

'Oh yeah, I heard it's going to be bigger than Woodstock,' Bambou said.

They'd televised that crazy music festival in America last summer. Secretly, I'd thought those crowds of unwashed, half-naked people singing and laughing looked like great fun, but Emile had frowned, mumbling about dirty, sex-crazed, drug-addled layabouts.

'I'd love to go!' a red-haired woman said, handing skewers threaded with courgettes, aubergines and carrots to a huddle of children, who roasted them over the flames.

No delicate oven dishes here, or fancy upward-opening glass oven doors, like the one I'd been ecstatic over in my new kitchen. And no wife hurriedly brushing her hair and daubing on lipstick as her husband walked through the door. As I glanced around at each contented face, I almost laughed at the silliness of all that.

Everyone smiled as a little girl dropped her skewer into the flames, and the red-haired woman — her mother I assumed — kissed her brow and passed her another one.

Clumsy Adrienne. That girl drops everything!

Grandmère's sharp voice threatened to spoil this moment, but as Bambou folded his long legs into a sitting position beside me, it faded.

'I made you a welcome gift,' he said, threading a daisy-chain wreath on my head. His gaze was almost a physical pressure, and my pulse quickened, a flush warming my insides. I could hardly believe a person I'd only met only that day exhilarated me so. Never had I appreciated a gift so much; simple — free, even! — but more precious than the fancy jewellery Emile had bought me.

Several people were smoking thin roll ups, others puffed on what I suspected was marijuana. I'd never tried it, but Emile had told me that's what it was, one day when we were strolling through La Croix-Rousse, the hippie part of Lyon.

I'd heard it relaxed you and made you laugh and not worry about anything. Over the years, and especially this last year — with the twins gone to boarding school — I'd have loved to relax and not worry about anything. Not that I'd had any idea where to get marijuana.

Bambou puffed on the joint, and offered it to me. I tried not to cough too much as I took several puffs. Almost immediately, as I exhaled a smoke stream, my mind was at peace, and I smiled. Soon I was smiling so much my face hurt.

'Have you thought of your new La Vallée du Bonheur name?' Bambou asked, and his voice made my heart beat softer, faster. That familiar tight feeling across my brow, like the start of an anxious episode, vanished.

'Choose one for yourself,' the grey-haired man said, 'rather than some traditional name your parents decided to lump you with for life.'

A thrilling pulse shot through my body. Nobody had ever let me decide anything as important as a name. The twins had been given names from Emile's family — Antoine and Martine — to be carried on down the generations.

'Yes, we'd all love to know your La Vallée du Bonheur name,' Jasmin said, as two men lugged out large pots, which they placed on trestles over the fire.

'Well, I *do* love the Atlantic Ocean, so what about Océane?' I said, looking around the circle of people, waiting for someone to say, 'No that's a silly name.' But nobody did, and they all smiled and clapped, and raised cups of the refreshing apple-celery-and-ginger-flavoured brew.

'Océane's a beautiful name,' the red-haired woman said. 'With your lovely green eyes — and those beige flecks, like the seabed sand — it's your perfect name.' She addressed the fireside circle: 'Welcome to La Vallée du Bonheur, Océane.'

'How do you like it here so far, Océane?' a man with a long, thick beard asked as I devoured my bowl of black beans stewed in a delicious tomato, garlic, onion and herb sauce. 'I'm Olive, by the way ... because I love olives.' He let out a cackle. 'And because olive trees are old and wise.'

'*Salut*, Olive,' I said. 'I love it, and everyone's made me feel so welcome.' As the light darkened to a deep violet, I looked around at this friendly group of people living their lives outside at night, like bats, existing in a cluster of primitive huts, trees, fields and river isolating them from the rest of the world.

'People nowadays are choosing simple experiences over ownership,' Olive said. 'We value figuring out who we are, and what kind of life we want, rather than what we want to *own*.'

'We share everything,' Bambou said, taking the joint again. 'And we value, above all else — above our own individual needs — a strong community.'

'People from all walks of life are choosing to live together in peace,' Olive went on. 'Far away from governments who are sending them off to die in wars they don't believe in, or even *care* about. Look at the Vietnam fiasco — men forced to fight a war they didn't believe in, only to return home to a country that didn't want them!' He waved a bony arm. 'We're establishing our own counterculture to defy those governments telling us how to live, and die.'

'Instead of obediently accepting society's expectations, we're rejecting the gender roles of previous generations,' Jasmin said, as her baby suckled at her breast. 'Times are changing fast in France, and moral outrage is no longer such a potent force.' She burped the baby, and changed breasts. 'I don't know who, amongst the men here, is my baby's biological father. But it doesn't matter, since *all* the men of La Vallée du Bonheur are her father.'

'As all the women are her mother,' the red-haired woman said.

As strange as that sounded, it made sense to have a tribe of mothers, which was surely easier, and less lonely, than doing it on your own.

'And all the children are her siblings,' Jasmin said, stroking her baby's head.

'We reject that so-popular nuclear home,' Olive said, 'which, for many of us, were childhoods filled with heartbreak and suffering.'

Oh yes, I could tell you about childhood heartbreak and suffering.

'I got trapped into marriage and being a housewife,' said a woman about my age, a flower-wreath propped on her curly blonde hair. 'Crumbled under the pressure that says you aren't a real woman unless you settle down, service your husband in every way, and have his babies.'

'Nothing short of emotional blackmail, isn't that right, Fleur?' Jasmin said.

Fleur nodded. 'Yes, and thankfully we have more choices now, since birth control's been finally legalised again … after fifty years!'

'I adore my five little rascals,' the red-haired woman said with a smile, ruffling her daughter's tangled nest of hair. 'But I also love my daily pill that stops me having number six.'

I too was thankful for the contraceptive pill I'd been taking since it became legal just over two years ago. I'd coped so badly with the twins, that the thought of more children was simply terrifying.

'Once I realised marriage was this big delusion, I wanted no part of it,' Fleur said. 'I ran away from my husband, and found this wonderful new life, a long way from society's great emotional blackmail.'

'Basically, we just like breaking the rules,' Bambou said with a laugh, and that special tilt of his head. He lay a hand on my folded knee and his warmth, and the balmy fug of firelight and music, smoke and chatter, drew me in even more.

'Life's too short *not* to break a few rules,' Fleur said.

I drank it all in, and was reminded again of that Kibbutz television show. I'd called out to Emile to come and watch it with me.

'I don't know how you can listen to those weirdos' waffle,' he'd said. 'If it was up to me, I'd certify the lot of them insane.'

I'd decided my husband was probably right, and turned off the television. But that was before I knew about La Vallée du Bonheur, when I'd never thought deeply about all this important stuff. It had simply skirted the edges of my mind, but now I understood the sense in everything they were saying.

Besides, in that bewitching moment, as I looked at those shining faces, I didn't want to think about my husband or that television set — Emile's surprise Christmas present last year — in my plush, dust-free living room on the top floor of a swanky building.

The children gradually fell asleep, and parents carried them off to bed. People dwindled off to huts and I was alone with Bambou.

We sat there, staring into the fire. The sparks from those last embers glowed and flared. Sharp and shooting.

~

Our heads bent together like two wind-curved trees, Bambou and I watched the last sparks flicker and die. The moonlight shadows of hills and trees shifted on the smooth surface of the river, its quiet gurgle the only noise, besides the rustle of night creatures.

'What's your take on that slogan, *Sous les pavés, la plage?*' Bambou asked.

I'd heard of the slogan — *Under the cobblestones, the beach* — but had no idea what it meant.

The hoot of an owl and the flap of its great wings, startled me, as Bambou explained that they'd used the slogan in the student demonstrations of sixty-eight.

'We expressed the desire that beneath the city, hardened by stone, lies the freedom of the beach ... the sand in which the pavers were placed,' he said, and took my hand. 'Did you march?'

'Sadly, no,' I said, recalling Emile's horrified reaction when I'd suggested joining in those rowdy demonstrations, and be a part of these changing times.

Bambou spoke about the terrible famines in China not ten years ago, and how so many in Africa had died from starvation only a few years before.

'Terrible,' I said, too embarrassed to say I hadn't heard much about this. I hated to admit I knew nothing about world affairs; that I'd never bothered to learn about them, but Bambou seemed interested in every naïve word I uttered.

We chatted as easily as old friends. I'd never glanced at another man; never even daydreamed about someone else. Until today. And now I realised that I hadn't really known what Emile was like, even in the beginning. I was simply relieved he'd rescued me from the shipwreck of my childhood that had cast me onto jagged rocks. Oh yes, how easily I'd dived into Emile's rescue boat so that I could, finally, start my real life.

Married at eighteen, I was nineteen when the twins arrived. Since then, my life had been my home, my husband and my children. That is until my husband sent them away from me. At least the joint was quelling my anger at Emile over that — a red-hot poker burning the pit of my stomach.

After all I'd been through today, I should have been exhausted, but I'd have stayed up all night chatting to Bambou, not wanting to forego a second of this special moment. I couldn't recall ever being this aware of myself, of what was *inside* me.

Bambou edged closer, our limbs touching. We fell silent again, and as Bambou wrapped his long arms around me, I knew he desired me. It was intoxicating, and I — almost — forgot that what I was doing was terribly wrong. A crime, even. But I'd never felt so hungry for someone, and when his lips fell on mine, it was all I could do not to groan out loud.

The kiss was like nothing I'd ever known — tender and soft at first, then searching and urgent. For the first time in my life, my body and mind screamed at me to obey my instinct rather than the rules.

His kisses grew stronger until I thought I would die with longing. Bambou pressed his body against mine, his hand sliding the floral dress up to my thigh. I'd never felt this desire for Emile. Even on our honeymoon, our lovemaking had been a job on Emile's list that he had to tick off.

Bambou gently pushed me down onto the ground, his hands, his fingers exploring every part of me. I didn't hanker for a second, for my silky *chemise de nuit* or my coral-coloured satin bedsheets, nor did I care that dirt was smudging my body, or that my hair — that complicated hairdo that required nightly rollers not to resemble a frenzied bird's nest — was a grimy tangle.

He kissed my bare breasts and sucked my hard nipples.

'Oh ... yes ... please, don't stop.'

And when he asked, 'Océane, can I make love to you?' I nodded, surrendering to him completely. I fleetingly thought of my contraceptive pills, which I'd obviously not taken to Carrefour, but thankfully, Bambou slid on a condom and gently pushed into me. I wrapped my legs around his waist, pressing with my thighs, urgent, welcoming, his breath warm on my face.

Whether it was the marijuana coursing through my veins, or the loneliness that I understood, in that instant, had been my constant companion, this did not feel wrong.

And when my body exploded like a shooting star, time stopped still as Bambou's body shuddered on top of mine.

'Oh!' I gasped, as he flopped back onto the ground, knowing, for the first time, what all the hype in *Cosmopolitan* was about.

Bambou circled his strong arms around me and we drifted off to sleep beneath the glittering stars and the coin of moon dangling low, the sweet scent of wildflowers and dewy riverbank grass in my nostrils.

My blood was a warm glow through my body and I was a wanted person; desired, revered, and loved.

6
Adrienne

A shriek startled me awake at dawn. In that second between sleep and waking, I assumed I was in my wide, satin-sheeted bed, and the sound confused me. Then Bambou sat up beside me on the dusty ground, and I grabbed my dress to cover my nakedness.

The pearly-pink eastern sky lit up Mont Blanc's snowy crown and, as the rooster shrieked again, Bambou grinned at me and stood up. Still naked, he wandered over to the nearest tree and peed against it. I couldn't stop staring at those taut buttocks and that long, thick penis. I shivered, flushing with embarrassment as I recalled last night's delicious, lustful details.

I should've been quieter. Everyone must've heard us.

As people emerged from huts and tents, and began their tasks of collecting eggs, milking goats, plucking and chopping vegetables, washing clothes and children, they smiled and nodded at me as if nothing had happened. Nobody seemed to care what we'd got up to.

I imagined my neighbours' poisonous looks, the dark glares from other wives, if I'd done such a thing in my own neighbourhood. They'd be rallying to burn me at the stake, or have me jailed for the crime of adultery.

Yesterday, Fleur had said she'd teach me how to make bread, and as I joined her in the shade of a lime-flower tree, I ignored the wave of remorse sweeping through me — the guilt for not only avoiding going home to Emile, but for making love with another man.

'My poor husband must be thinking I've had an accident by now,' I said to Fleur as I kneaded the flour. 'And even if I'm not going home yet, perhaps I should at least phone to let him know I'm okay?'

I also wondered if Antoine and Martine *had* come home last night, and I was missing a rare weekend visit.

Don't be silly, Emile said the twins wouldn't be home this weekend, and he's always right.

Fleur laid a floury hand on my arm. 'If you feel you must call your husband, Bambou will drive you to a telephone booth.'

'I don't know what to do for the best,' I said, kneading and pounding the dough. 'My husband would never think I'd left him. I'd never do something as crazy as that. I mean, why would any wife leave *all of that*?'

Fleur shrugged, and didn't ask what '*all of that*' was.

'If I stay away much longer, he'll get concerned and go to the authorities, and what'll happen when they find me?' I said, copying Fleur shaping the dough into loaves. 'Do you think I'll be punished for running off from my husband, or fined, or perhaps even *jailed*?'

I imagined Emile reporting my disappearance.

My wife's gone mad. Insanity runs in her family, you see. She might be in danger. I insist on a search.

'For a start, I doubt the gendarmes would find you here.' Fleur smiled, as if indulging a child's silly notion. 'I'm not sure the authorities even know La Vallée du Bonheur exists. If your husband reports you missing, they'll probably send your details and a photo to all the police stations and Gendarmeries around France, but I doubt they'd actively search for you. And if it became obvious that you're alive and well, they definitely wouldn't search. Don't worry, Océane, many of us have run off from *situations*, but we're all safe at La Vallée du Bonheur,' she said, sliding the tray of loaves into the open-air oven.

I didn't know what *situations* Fleur might be referring to, but she was right — the gendarmes would never think to look for someone like me at La Vallée du Bonheur.

This wasn't Adrienne Chevalier's kind of place at all.

~

Several times throughout the rest of that month of June, Bambou drove me to the telephone booth in the nearby village of Sainte-Marie-du-Lac to call the twins' boarding school. Parents weren't permitted to speak directly to children, but in case Antoine and Martine heard from Emile, or from someone else, that I was no longer at home, I left messages to let them know I was all right. I could only hope the school passed them on before the twins left in July for the summer holidays.

I also mentioned that if my children wanted to see me over the holidays, to please write to the post office box where everyone at La Vallée du Bonheur received letters. I'd find a way to get to the twins wherever they were.

But I kept putting off that phone call to tell Emile I'd be home soon. Because 'soon' never came. And because Bambou and La Vallée du Bonheur became 'home'.

Besides, I couldn't face talking to my husband. He'd try and convince me to return home, and I wasn't ready for that because I still really had no idea why I'd left him, or our home. Though Emile wouldn't be worried about me, at least — surely he'd know, through the school, that I was all right.

Each sun-filled, serene day, I grew to love La Vallée du Bonheur a little more, despite the dull ache in my heart to see my children. But not as the silent obnoxious teenagers they'd become, but the little children who'd needed their maman — those years I'd been caught in such fierce protective love, tucking them into bed at night, reading a story, laughing at them galloping around me in the kitchen.

In Lyon, I'd lived close to the shops where I purchased our food. At La Vallée du Bonheur, I was at the heart of making that food — a very different life infused with raw, earthy, odours and sounds, and the scents of herbs and wildflowers.

I revelled in my simple, uncluttered existence, never pining for those things I'd thought so important — the decorative trinkets, fancy linen, ornate crockery, polished floors and gleaming marble bench tops.

Bambou shifted shudders of desire within me as we made love beneath the stars. In his arms, I was a whole and cherished person, even though I didn't know a thing about this man, or his past.

Some evenings Bambou didn't linger around the campfire with me, disappearing somewhere. On those nights, I slept on my straw mattress in the hut which, if I was honest, wasn't that comfortable. Occasionally, a flutter of panic swept through me as I recalled Jasmin saying she didn't know who the father of her baby was. Did that mean *all* the men here slept with *all* the women?

No, surely not. Bambou says he loves me.

By day, I flung grain at the chickens, collected their eggs and mucked out their coop. I plucked vegetables from the soil and milked the goats. I pounded herbs and spices to flavour delicious vegetarian dishes, and gathered fruit to simmer in great jam-making pots.

Amid those bright skies, one dark cloud hung low. Despite checking the post box several times, I didn't receive a single word from my children. In desperation, on the last school day before the summer holidays, I asked Bambou to drive me to the phone booth once again.

'May I have a quick word with my daughter, please?' I asked the receptionist.

'I'm sorry,' she said. 'You know the rules, Madame Chevalier, no telephone contact with students.'

'Please. I'll be quick, and it's very important!'

I caught her sigh down the line. 'Well, if you want the truth, the problem is not only the rules. Your husband, Dr Chevalier, has requested that the school not pass on your messages to Antoine and Martine.'

'*What*?' My heartbeat quickened. 'Why would Emile do that?'

'Apparently, in his capacity as a doctor, your husband believes his wife is no longer fit to see, or hear from, his children. I'm sorry, Madame Chevalier, but there's no point leaving all these messages.'

My shock was so deep I could no longer speak, or breathe. The blood drained to my feet and, in that tiny booth, I sank onto my haunches and sobbed, the receiver dangling in mid-air.

How could Emile do this? He must truly hate me.

'Hello? Madame Chevalier, are you still there?'

I pressed the receiver to my ear.

'I am quite fit to contact my children,' I said, aware of my shaky voice. 'And I don't know why my husband would do such a terrible thing.'

'Your husband *is* a renowned psychiatrist, Madame Chevalier. I don't know what else to say to you.'

I didn't know what else to say either and as I hung up the phone, a red-hot rage boiled inside me.

How dare Emile do this!

I had to speak to my husband right now. Shaking with anger, and bathed in sweat inside that tiny space, I dialled Emile's work number.

7
Adrienne

'*Bonjour*, Dr Chevalier speaking.'
'It's me ... Adrienne.'
'*Mon Dieu*, finally. Where are you? I've been worried *sick*.'

'Worried sick?' I said. 'I know the school told you I'm alive, since you ordered them not to let me speak to Antoine and Martine. *Merde!* Why, Emile?'

'Do I have to spell it out? Obviously, I did deduce that nothing untoward had happened to you, so I could only assume that my wife had run off from me.' Despite Emile's calm tone, he couldn't mask his annoyance, and his quick breath left me no time to interrupt. 'I simply don't understand how you could leave our wonderful home, and a husband who loves you and gives you everything. And how you imagine that I — or *anyone* — could view such behaviour as anything other than that of a madwoman?'

'You *do* provide well for me ... for us,' I said. 'But all those objects aren't important. Love is what's important and I never really *felt* your love, Emile. And those nicknames only made me feel worthless. I never found them funny and when you insisted they *were*, I felt like I was losing my mind.'

'What do you mean, you never *felt* my love?' Emile's voice rose a notch. 'Did you expect me to run around kissing and complimenting you all day, and buying you even *more* things? Unlike you, Adrienne, I am a responsible parent, working hard to give my family everything. And you should be ashamed that you abandoned your husband and children on some crazy whim.'

'I did *not* abandon our children,' I said, forcing myself not to shout. 'Because you sent them away from me, to that snobby boarding school.'

'You can't deny the twins are better off in an intellectual and stimulating environment, rather than at home with *you*.'

I sighed. As usual, there was no point arguing with Emile. Nothing I said would change his mind.

'Just tell me if the twins know I'm all right?' I said. 'I wouldn't want to worry them.'

'Oh, I doubt the twins are worried about a mother who abandoned her family. Anyway, I told you before, they'll be away all summer with friends, and won't return until school goes back in September.' He sighed, obviously reluctant to set my mind at ease. 'But yes, they are aware you're fine; that you simply left your loving husband and our beautiful home for no reason. And *that*, *ma petite chérie*, is precisely why I don't want you to see them. And you know what? They don't seem bothered by that. Our children are almost adults now, no longer the little beings you could manipulate and control.'

My body shook with rage, my hands curling into fists. Sweat beads rolled into my eyes.

'Control and manipulate? How can you, of all people, say that?'

'Anyway, where *are* you, Adrienne?'

'Somewhere safe. A peaceful place.'

'What the hell does that mean?' Emile said. 'Weren't you safe and peaceful in our home? And why *did* you leave?'

'I never planned to leave … there was this child in Carrefour who said … Oh never mind, I don't think that's why —'

'Please stop babbling,' Emile said. 'I can barely understand you.'

'I can't understand it all myself, but —'

'Well anyway, I imagine you're phoning me because you've come to your senses and you realise it's time to come home?' he said, ignoring everything I was trying to say. 'Where are you? I'll come and fetch you; I'll cancel my patients for the rest of the day.'

'I'm not ready to come home, Emile. I will, sometime, but I don't know when.'

'Not ready?' He sounded completely mystified. 'Have you forgotten you are my *wife*?' Emile's voice remained calm, though I sensed the boiling current beneath that calm exterior — that anger he always kept fettered, especially in public.

'Yes, your wife, but not your possession.'

'Possession? *Mon Dieu*, you really have lost your mind, Adrienne.'

Still trembling, I hung up without even a goodbye.

Waiting for Bambou to collect me from la place de la Fontaine, and gasping for a drink, I glanced across at the village bar, Chez Dédé.

'You don't want a drink from there,' Emile had said, on one of our holidays to Sainte-Marie-du-Lac. 'Those places are for the working classes.'

So I'd quickly used the toilet, avoiding eye contact with any of those working classes, and hurried back to my husband. But now I wished Emile could see me strolling confidently into the bar and ordering a Perrier-citron.

I sat at an outside table, beneath a striped parasol. The twins were all right. They knew I was alive. That was the main thing. Once school went back in September, I'd find a way to speak to them, and to erase the bleak picture their father had obviously painted of me.

8
Adrienne

Almost two months later, on a sweltering August morning, I was plucking basil, parsley and thyme when someone startled me from behind. I swivelled around to Bambou's cheeky smile.

'I'm heading to Sainte-Marie-du-Lac to collect some medicines from my herbal ladies, Clotilde and Bev. I thought you might fancy a picnic, and a swim in lac du Héron?'

Clotilde, the witch!

'Oh yes, I'd love that,' I said, and packed walnut and olive bread, cheese, plums, and plump dark tomatoes into a basket. 'But I don't have a swimming costume.'

Bambou grinned as he flung the basket into the Combi. 'Don't wear one then.'

'It might be okay to prance around La Vallée du Bonheur half-naked, but not in the *real* world,' I said with a laugh, as Jasmin pressed a baggy old swimming costume into my hands.

'Well, it should be,' Bambou said. 'If we went skinny dipping, others might do the same, like at Woodstock.'

'You'll get us arrested, you bad boy,' I said, imagining Emile's disgusted reaction if I'd suggested something as bold as swimming naked.

Lac du Héron had always been our special place — Emile's and mine — and now I was going there with another man. But as I clambered into the passenger seat and the Combi hawked to life, I recalled that last hateful phone conversation with Emile, and not the slightest wave of guilt rippled through me.

Bambou parked in front of a dilapidated lakeside house with a jungly mess of a garden, and I tumbled out of the van, inhaling soft whiffs of rosemary, thyme and lavender. Despite the gentle breeze filling the sky with scudding clouds and tinkling the coloured chimes hanging from Clotilde's porch, the air remained hot and thick. As we approached, I spotted a well-tended and flourishing herb patch amongst the wild greenery.

'Bambou, *mon cher!*' A blonde-haired woman around sixty years old boomed as she swept outside, a purple caftan billowing about her large body. 'And this must be your friend, Océane?' She kissed us both on each cheek, heavy eyeliner vanishing into wrinkles as she beamed.

'It's lovely to meet you, Clotilde,' I said.

'Océane, the perfect name for those pretty eyes,' she said.

'Océane's my La Vallée du Bonheur name. I was christened Adrienne,' I blurted out, and immediately regretted it.

'Bev will be sorry she missed your visit,' Clotilde said to Bambou. 'She had to rush back to Belgium to tend a sick relative.' She handed him a basket filled with vials, jars, and bottles of various liquids and creams. '*Voilà*, I've prepared everything you asked for. I know you're keen to rush off and cool down in the lake.'

We thanked Clotilde, bid her *au revoir*, skipped back to the van, and swapped the medicine basket for the picnic basket and towels.

As we walked along the lake-front path toward the bathing area, the breeze dropped and the air became even heavier, as if suddenly forced to bear some great weight.

We passed a neat wooden sign painted with little flowers and herons. Unlike the weathered La Vallée du Bonheur sign that hung from one nail only, it was fixed by all four corners, and fashioned in the shape of an arrow pointing toward a lovely old stone building, set high on the grassy knoll.

'L'Auberge de Léa,' I read. 'It's obviously been renovated. Last time I saw this place, it was all tumble-down and neglected. And rumoured to be haunted.'

I pictured us on holiday here, all those years ago, Emile and I sitting together in the shade, admiring the shimmering blue lake, and Mont Blanc's snowy helmet in the distance. We were enjoying a meal of lake-fresh fish with a glass of cool white wine — food that someone else had prepared. A meal that my husband could not describe as 'another of Adrienne's failures'.

Since that disastrous phone call, I'd had no contact with Emile, and sadly no news of the twins either. But each sun-filled, tranquil day, I relished not feeling like a failure, a frump, or a humourless fool. And I sensed that from now on I would think of everything that happened in my life as either *Before the Supermarket* or *After the Supermarket*.

The cries of birds winging toward the woods forced my gaze upward. Squinting against the glare, I spied a small plane in the distance amidst the clouds.

'That plane's flying a bit low, isn't it?' I said, as we flung the basket and towels onto the grass. 'It doesn't *sound* right either.'

'Stop worrying,' Bambou said with a laugh, flicking blond hair strands from his face and grasping my hand. 'Last one in the lake buys us a beer at Chez Dédé's bar,' he cried.

Eager as I was to rush into the cool water, I couldn't shake off my unease, or shift my gaze, from that little aircraft.

9
Blanche

That humid Saturday morning, Blanche Larue grimaced with the pain in her knee as she straightened from watering her front-porch petunias and pansies.

'Curse this damn arthritis.'

She glanced across at her neighbour, Clotilde's home, and the young couple dressed in those grimy-looking, unironed garments, hurrying toward a rusted red Combi van.

Blanche had seen this Combi, painted with flowers, rainbows and peace signs parked outside her neighbour's home several times. Clotilde had told her the fellow's name was Bambou (what kind of mother christens her infant with such a ridiculous name?) who purchased her and Bev's medicinal potions. He lived at that camp, La Vallée du Bonheur. Rumour had it the place was filled with misfits who'd rejected society and went around naked, smoking drugs and indulging in all-night orgies. They lived in primitive huts, hardly ever washed and lived off bean stews. Not that Blanche, or anyone she knew, had ever actually been to La Vallée du Bonheur. Apparently, even the gendarmes kept their distance.

Blanche caught only the briefest glimpse of the woman's face as the couple skittered off along the lake-front path toward the swimming area, and thought nothing more of them as her friend, Louise Bellefontaine, stepped up into the porch shade.

'Oh, I didn't see you coming,' Blanche said, as a noise forced her to look up at the cloudy sky. A palm shading her brow, Blanche pointed to a small plane. 'It's flying low, and making a strange noise, don't you think?'

'It's likely only just taken off,' Louise said, with a flick of a manicured hand, as Blanche followed the path of the aircraft toward lac du Héron.

'But isn't that smoke trailing from the tail?' Blanche said.

'Hard to tell, with all that cloud,' Louise said, squinting against the glare.

Blanche stared at the plane, more like an over-sized bird really, coming closer to the lake. And as it crossed a blue patch of sky, she could no longer see smoke. She must've imagined it.

'I've brought your eggs, since you said that pesky arthritis had flared up,' Louise said, thrusting a basket at Blanche.

'Thanks, but I'd have popped over to the inn after my housework.' Blanche took the basket from Louise and flapped a hand across her face, which did nothing to cool her down. 'But now you're here, how about a cup of tea? My knee could do with a rest. *Mon Dieu*, this arthritis makes me feel like a woman of eighty-five rather than sixty-five.'

'Shouldn't you be having a *long* rest, rather than making things worse with housework?' Louise said. 'Look how red and swollen that knee is.'

Blanche brushed off her friend. 'It'll settle down. Besides, I need to keep on top of things. You know how Roger likes to come home to everything sparkling,' she said with an indulgent smile.

Louise snorted. 'You should see the state of the auberge some days, before Léa decides to clean up.' She glanced up at the plane again. '*Mon Dieu*, you're right, that *is* smoke coming from the tail.'

Blanche clutched the basket to her chest and stared back at the plane, almost right over the lake. 'Maybe a bit of smoke is normal, and nothing to worry about?'

A sputtering, coughing sound made her jump. More coughing and rumbly sounds, like distressed hiccups. A strange *ddd, ddd* noise.

Then, no noise at all.

'That is *not* normal,' Louise said. 'Sounds like the engine has failed!'

Ddd, ddd, ddd.

'The pilot must be trying to restart the engine,' Louise said.

Then the plane *did* come back to life. Those terrifying engine noises disappeared, and Blanche exhaled the breath she didn't realise she'd been holding.

'*Dieu merci*,' Louise said, and both of them made the sign of the cross.

Relieved, Blanche shifted her gaze down to the lake, crowded with people splashing about in the cool, clear water, enjoying one of the last summer weekends.

On the shore, ducks quacked, long-beaked herons pecked at reeds and dogs barked. Children played and shrieked, and couples lay entwined on blankets, soaking up the sun.

'Thankfully, it does seem to be flying normally now,' Blanche said, 'but still, I'd hate to think that one of my family, or a friend, was up there. Don't you always think that, when you see trouble, or an accident, or hear a siren? Don't you run through your mind where your loved ones are, and then feel relieved when you know they couldn't possibly be involved in whatever awful thing might happen?'

'Yes, I was thinking precisely that,' Louise said. 'Where's Anna?'

'Oh, she's fine ... left with my shopping list just before you arrived. My daughter's been kind enough to get my groceries since this knee's been playing up. And as for Roger, I waved him off this morning for his golf game.'

Blanche thought of her husband driving off to his silly golf game, like every Saturday, his grin wide as a clown's. But it was golf the *entire* weekend this time, which was unusual. And when Blanche had asked Roger where he was going for the whole weekend, he'd simply smiled and waved away her questions.

'Thankfully, my whole family is at the auberge,' Louise said.

'Now I think about it, the plane looks like the four-seater that pilot acquaintance of Roger owns,' Blanche said. 'Calls it his *petit oiseau,* and always boasting to Roger about flying his "little bird". Roger's been on several joy flights with the fellow, whose name I can't recall, but you know the one who swoops over Sainte-Marie on weekends, as if he were going to dive his plane right into the lake?'

'*Ah oui,* shows off like a spoilt child. Lives in Romans.' Louise nodded at the opposite lake shore, toward the village of Romans-sur-Lac. 'Inherited a fortune from his father, and look what the silly man does with the money!' She gestured up at the plane.

'That's men for you,' Blanche said, shaking her head.

'*Mon Dieu*, that smoke is back,' Louise cried. 'Thicker!'

Amidst the cloud, it was still difficult to see the plane, but the engine was, once more, making those frightening puffing, coughing, sputtering noises.

Ddd, ddd, ddd.

Blanche's spine prickled, and she grabbed her friend's forearm.

'Well, if it *does* belong to the fellow Roger knows,' she said, 'he might be a know-it-all, but apparently the man's an experienced pilot.'

Seemingly oblivious to what was happening overhead, children still played in the lake and on the shore. The adults, though, like Blanche and Louise, had turned their gazes upward, heads darting about as they tried to glimpse the plane between the cloud patches. They pointed, clapped palms over mouths, as the aircraft wavered from left to right, black smoke roiling into the sky.

In the next instant, the plane, once again, made not a single sound. And that extended silence was more eerie and terrifying than those failing engine noises.

A chill swept through Blanche. She held her breath, still clasping her friend's forearm, trying to banish the thought that her husband's pilot friend *did* own that distressed plane; ignoring the niggling whisper telling her that Roger had, once again, lied about playing golf.

~

'Planes can glide for a while, can't they?' Blanche said.

Her friend nodded. 'And if the engine *does* fail, the pilot will search for a safe place to land, which is what he seems to be doing.'

'A *safe place?*' Blanche waved an arm toward the throng of lake-goers all staring up at the distressed plane. 'It's right over a crowded lake. There's only people and water, and the woods … and power lines!'

'I'm sure the pilot will find *somewhere*,' Louise said, as Blanche caught snatches of panicked conversation from the lac du Héron crowd.

'*Dieu* help us.'

'It's going down!'

'No, it's all right, the pilot's searching for a place to land.'

'Don't panic.'

… about to crash!'

'He's going to land it.'

The plane continued gliding down, gentle and slow, leaning from one side to the other, and levelling out again.

'Oh no!' Blanche gasped as black smoke, thicker, puffed from its tail, and the plane wavered again, above the crowd who shrieked and shouted and ran in all directions, dragging behind them children, belongings and dogs.

'*Raar, raar,*' cried a hedge of herons, soaring up and away from the shoreline. From the swamps, ducks quacked a mad chorus, and birds shrieked from the treetops.

'Look, he's found a safe place to land,' Louise cried, as the aircraft glided down toward the opposite shore, to a grassy patch between the lake and the woods, away from the crowd. 'It's going to be all right.'

'Yes, you're right, it's almost landed safely,' Blanche said. She and Louise crossed themselves again, and joined in the one great collective sigh of relief that rose from the lakeside crowd.

Then the wings dipped one way, and the other, the tail trailing a thicker stream of black, acrid smoke. For a second, Blanche was sure it was about to plunge into the water, but the pilot must have made a last, supreme effort, as the small aircraft rose again, barely clearing the woods beyond.

But then it floundered, and without warning, flipped onto one side. In mid-cartwheel, the plane slid sideways, and plummeted, like an unwieldy bird, into the earth.

10
Blanche

In those first moments, Blanche was numb, unable to speak or breathe. She couldn't know for sure that Roger had been in that plane, but nor could she shrug off that deep feeling of doom. She clasped Louise's arm as they stared across lac du Héron at the surging black and grey smoke, and the flames mushrooming from the wreck.

The deafening scream of sirens snapped Blanche from her stupor as the *pompiers* rushed to the fiery crash site. The gendarme vehicles came too, from the village of Romans, since Sainte-Marie was too small to have its own Gendarmerie.

Once the smoke and flames cleared a bit, Blanche saw the crowd that had gathered, some people grabbing things from the ground.

'What are they picking up?' Blanche hissed. 'Nobody — nothing! — could possibly have survived.'

'Passengers' belongings, I imagine.' Louise shook her head. 'They're looters ... simply disgraceful.'

A gendarme wielding a megaphone marched around, his voice pealing across the lake, loud and clear, even over the firefighters' shouts and the water rushing from thick hoses. 'Please do not touch anything. Keep away from the scene. Return to your homes.'

Many people did wander off, but others ignored the gendarme and kept searching for objects ejected from the plane before it exploded.

'Speaking of "home", I should get back to the inn,' Louise said. 'They might be in shock. Will you be all right on your own, Blanche? You look quite pale.'

'I'll be fine. It's a terrible tragedy but, thankfully, we didn't know any of the victims, did we?' Blanche was surprised at the shake in her voice, and how she had to clutch the door frame to hold herself upright.

As Louise hurried back to her daughter-in-law's auberge, Blanche's knee throbbed, and she longed to rest on her sofa with a cup of tea. A calming brew would surely banish these gloomy thoughts from her mind.

~

Several hours later, Blanche had not moved from the sofa, her tea sitting cold and untouched on the table. She didn't realise she'd been staring at nothing for so long until an urgent knock on her front door startled her.

Whoever could that be? Oh yes, it must be Anna with my groceries.

But Anna never knocked. Blanche's daughter simply waltzed in, as if she still lived here. Blanche groaned as she heaved herself upright, limped down the hallway, and opened the door.

Two blue-uniformed gendarmes stood on her doorstep. She peered outside, around them, at the crash site. The *pompiers* had extinguished the fire, but there was still a lot of commotion around the smoking ruin.

Blanche didn't know the short gendarme, but she did recognise the tall, grumpy-looking one with the gnarly eyebrows and a chunk of ear missing — Major Yves Rocamadour, Léa Bellefontaine's man friend.

Major Rocamadour removed his kepi and ran a hand through his dark, swept-back hair. 'May we come inside, Madame Larue?'

'Why, what's wrong?' Despite the heat, Blanche's body froze.

'It's about the plane ... er, incident,' the major said. 'You surely saw it?'

'How could I *not*?' Blanche crossed her arms over her housework pinafore and tried to rub away the goose bumps. 'The crash must be the talk of the village. My friend, Louise —'

'Madame —' the short gendarme interrupted.

'You surely know Louise Bellefontaine?' Blanche addressed the short gendarme since Yves Rocamadour obviously knew his own girlfriend's mother-in-law. 'Everyone in Sainte-Marie knows Louise. Her husband was our mayor before he passed. Anyway, Louise brought me some eggs. Normally I go to the auberge myself, but since this ...' She gestured at her swollen knee. 'How cruel it is to age. Little changes that slip by unnoticed then, suddenly, *ploof*.' She waved her arms.

'Madame Lar —'

'Louise and I were standing in the porch shade when we noticed the plane was in trouble —'

'Madame, can we all go inside and sit down?' Yves Rocamadour said.

But Blanche couldn't stop the words pouring out of her, not daring to take the smallest breath. No, she didn't want to hear what these gendarmes had come to say. It was never good news when they knocked on your door, and she feared the bad news that would surely come out of their mouths if she gave them a chance.

What bad news, Blanche couldn't imagine. Nobody from her family could have been in that doomed plane, could they? As she'd done earlier, with Louise, Blanche once again thought about where her loved ones were. She'd spoken to her daughter again *after* the crash, when Anna said she'd be over late afternoon with the shopping. And Roger had *driven* away this morning. Besides, whoever takes a plane to a golf game?

But why else would these gendarmes be here, mentioning the crash? Blanche's chest tightened, that crushing sensation of doom heavier.

'Can we come inside please, Madame Larue?' They came in anyway and she stood aside.

'*Dieu merci* the plane crashed where there were no people,' Blanche went on.

The gendarmes stood in the living room, awkwardly. 'Madame Larue, we —'

'Sit down.' She pointed to the sofa, where they perched, glancing warily at each other.

'Madame Larue, you should sit down too,' the major said, more forcefully, nodding at an armchair. Blanche limped to the chair but stayed standing. 'We're sorry to report that your husband, Monsieur Roger Larue, was one of the passengers on that plane.'

She'd known it was coming, but still Blanche's heart shuddered to a stop, then beat frantically. A palm clamped to her chest, she collapsed into the armchair.

'Roger? No, that can't be right. M-my husband is playing golf.' She couldn't stop shaking her head, like one of those silly fair clowns. 'You must have confused Roger with someone else.'

'I'm afraid there's no mistake, Madame,' the short gendarme said. 'Your husband was definitely on that plane.'

'Apparently, he hired the aircraft for a weekend trip to Lake Maggiore ... that's in Italy,' Shorty went on. 'The pilot is from a well-known family from Romans —'

'Just because Roger's friend owned the plane, that doesn't mean my husband was on it.' This man was irritating Blanche. 'And I *do* know where Lake Maggiore is, but my husband's got no business in Italy.'

The short gendarme cleared his throat. 'The other passenger was your husband's secretary, Brigitte Dufresne.'

'I know who that tramp is,' Blanche barked, immediately regretting her outburst. But she crossed herself, since she'd spoken ill of the dead.

'We're so sorry, Madame Larue,' Yves Rocamadour said. 'Can I make you a cup of tea, or coffee? Or something stronger? Perhaps we could phone your daughter?'

Blanche shook her head, and grabbed her teacup, but she didn't drink the cold tea, just gripped the handle. 'Anna will be here soon … she's bringing my groceries.' Her voice came out in a whisper.

'We'll stay until your daughter arrives,' Shorty said.

Blanche didn't want these gendarmes staring at her. She wanted to be alone, to try and grasp all of this. 'No, it's all right, please go.'

As they clomped out of her house — the home that would never be the same — Blanche trembled so much she had to put down the teacup.

How would she break the news to Anna that her beloved papa was gone? The father whose charming, affectionate veneer his daughter and the outside world saw, rather than the real Roger, who only Blanche knew?

11
Blanche

So, Roger is gone. Gone where? To Hell?
Knowing she shouldn't even contemplate such a terrible fate, Blanche made the sign of the cross. She clasped her teacup again and sat back on the sofa. Blanche was now a widow, alone for the rest of her days. And while Roger had been deeply flawed, at least he'd been a husband of sorts. A husband that, up till now, had avoided Blanche enduring spinsterhood, and the village pity that went with it.

Such a shame she never snagged a husband.

Her tea still undrunk, Blanche conjured up a picture of Roger and the tramp, Brigitte in that small aircraft.

Roger would be clutching his secretary's hand, thinking how lucky he was to have Brigitte. And even luckier to have a gullible wife who believed he'd taken up Saturday golf with his colleagues from the bank. To sustain this alibi, he'd had to actually purchase golf clubs. But the idiot Blanche wouldn't mind him taking a few more of her gold coins. After all, she'd never complained when he dipped his filthy paw into her inheritance.

Of course, I'd minded, Roger, but you knew I wouldn't … couldn't … say anything, didn't you?

Luckily for Roger, Blanche was terrible with money, so she'd always trusted him with their finances. Just as she trusted Roger to come home in the evening, like he'd done for the past few months of Saturdays, most likely reluctantly leaving Brigitte's warm bed and body, and promising his lover he'd be back as soon as he could.

Only this Saturday he'd have told his captivating young mistress he didn't have to go home to boring Blanche. No, because they were going on a lover's weekend jaunt to Italy!

I'll tell Blanche my car broke down, and I can't get home till Monday morning, when I can call a mechanic, she imagined Roger saying, then phoning to tell Blanche he'd stay with a friend from the bank who lived near the golf course.

Oh Roger, I've heard that *story before.*

Roger would be bursting with excitement, for the two delicious nights in Italy with Brigitte, not caring a fig how much it was costing. The aircraft jaunt, the fancy Lake Maggiore hotel and the expensive restaurants would be worth it.

It was all worth it, this money game he'd been playing with Blanche since the day they married. As a member of the vast but impoverished Larue clan, Roger hadn't had a choice, if he wanted to live in the quaint lakeside home Blanche had inherited from her papa. And Roger would have to continue playing the marriage game if he wanted to keep dipping into the gold coins Blanche's father had bequeathed her.

Unlike most husbands, who proudly insisted on being the breadwinner, Roger had never minded selling Blanche's father's Napoléons.

A horrifying thought struck Blanche, and she clamped a hand over her racing heart.

My Napoléons! However else could Roger pay for the weekend?

No, she was being ridiculous. She might have allowed Roger to purchase a few things with her gold, but surely he'd never insult her by using them to pay for a lover's weekend?

~

Blanche's father had never trusted cash.

'Gold is safer,' Michel Vidal had told Blanche, when she was a girl. 'Won't lose value and won't burn in a fire. And never trust banks. Keep your gold close to your heart.'

Over the years, Michel Vidal had added his own coins to the stash he'd inherited from his father, squirreling them away in the brown leather pouch that bore his initials, MV.

When Blanche inherited the gold, it had seemed pointless selling it all and opening a bank account. Besides, women weren't allowed their own bank account back then, and the Napoléons had been safe enough in their hiding spot right through the Nazi Occupation, when the hateful German soldiers were billeted in this house and had requisitioned almost everything from Blanche's parents. That had made her father's leather pouch even more precious, reminding her that, on occasions, good wins over evil.

Blanche had kept the pouch hidden in the same nook as her father, that only she, Roger and Anna were aware of, and anxious to reassure herself it was still there, she leapt upright. Almost crumpling with the pain in her knee, she knocked her teacup off the table.

'Merde, merde et merde!' Blanche was surprised to hear herself cursing as the tea splashed across the wooden parquetry she'd washed only this morning. Now she'd have to mop up the tea *and* scrub the floorboards before Roger came home.

But no! She wouldn't have to clean *anything* now. The entire house could get as messy and dirty as she chose, and a small smile creased Blanche's lips as she limped into the bedroom.

Groaning, she bent down and pulled up the loose floorboard, set it aside and dipped her hand into the crevice, feeling around for the soft leather.

Empty, and that smile vanished as quickly as it had come.

She pushed her hand in deeper, fingers flailing around but still finding nothing.

Thoughts swirled through Blanche's mind. Had she fetched the pouch earlier, to give Anna some coins to sell, to pay for her groceries?

Yes, that's it. I left it lying around and forgot to put it away.

Blanche limped from room to room, searching for the little brown bag, crying out as pain shot through her knee. She tossed aside sofa cushions, and the folded blanket and shawl she kept handy for cold winter nights. She reefed open drawers and cupboards, upending everything into jumbled piles.

The pain in her knee was agonising. Her once-neat home resembled a bomb site. Tears coursed down Blanche's cheeks. Her heart beat too fast and her chest burned. She couldn't catch her breath.

Am I having a heart attack?

Blanche didn't have time for a heart attack, so on she hobbled, clutching her chest as she checked under beds, beneath mattresses, in the fridge. Even in the toilet.

On she searched for the gold coins Blanche was certain she'd never find; her beloved father's pouch that she knew, deep inside her aching, breaking heart, was forever lost.

It was bad enough that Roger had paid for his lust-filled weekend with her gold, but why had he taken *all* of it?

~

'It's only me, *chérie*.' From where Blanche lay, slumped on the living-room floor, she heard Louise's voice, then her heels clicking across the wooden floor.

Amidst the wreckage of what had, a few hours earlier, surely been the neatest home in all of Sainte-Marie-du-Lac, Blanche sobbed. And even when her friend knelt down and wrapped her arms around her, Blanche couldn't stem her tears.

'*Ma pauvre.*' Louise hugged Blanche and patted her back. 'I heard the terrible news about Roger. I'm so sorry. Come on, let's get you up onto the sofa, I'll find some painkillers for that knee.'

'I'm better on the ground,' Blanche sobbed. 'It's less painful if I don't move.'

Releasing herself from Blanche's grip, Louise strode into the bathroom and rattled around, making *tut-tut* noises, probably at the mess of medicines, hairbrushes and towels Blanche had strewn across the tiles.

Louise reappeared with an aspirin and a glass of water, kneeled beside Blanche, and held up her head. 'Take this, you'll feel better.'

Afterwards, as Louise struggled to help Blanche onto the sofa, propping a pillow beneath her knee, she asked the question Blanche been dreading.

'Whatever was Roger doing in that plane?'

'Well, Roger's friend did own that aircraft, but who knows why my husband was inside it?' Blanche crossed herself for her lie. 'He told me he was going on a golfing weekend.'

Blanche wished she could tell Louise the truth because isn't that was good friends are for, to share your bitter secrets?

But the embarrassment and shame of her farce of a marriage were too great. Though she'd always been surprised that Louise, with her instinct for these sorts of things, had never guessed. In all the years they'd been friends, Louise had never hinted she knew the real Roger. Or that Blanche had only stayed in their marriage because the thought of being a divorced woman was unbearable. Impossible even, since they were Catholics.

'I do understand you are in shock,' Louise said, her gaze roaming across the mess, 'but whatever happened? Blanche Larue is the tidiest person I know.'

'I have no idea what happened … it seems I have no idea about anything,' Blanche said. 'I was looking for my Napoléons … couldn't find them … must've misplaced the pouch.' She shrugged. 'Never mind, they'll eventually turn up.'

'But it's so unlike you to turn your home completely upside down, like this,' Louise said.

'Blanche?' A booming voice rang out from the doorway and Blanche's neighbour, Clotilde swept into the living room.

'What do *you* want, Madame Bonnefille?' Louise said, her voice sharp as broken glass. 'I am quite capable of caring for Blanche myself.'

Ignoring Louise, as always, Clotilde set her basket down, and plonked her hefty frame onto the sofa beside Blanche.

'I'm so sorry, *chérie*, I've just heard. I was coming over anyway, with your arthritis balm, so I've brought a special herbal mixture too, that will help the shock and grief.'

Clotilde plucked a vial of dark-coloured liquid from her basket and waved it at Louise. 'Make yourself useful, Loulou, and bring me a glass of water to mix this up for Blanche.'

'We do not require any of your charlatan potions,' Louise said. Even though nobody, besides Clotilde, referred to Louise Bellefontaine as 'Loulou', she did fetch the glass of water.

'Whatever is that?' Louise wrinkled her nose as Clotilde poured the liquid into the water.

'Eye of newt and tongue of dodo,' Clotilde said, winking at Blanche as she drank the potion. Louise scowled at *la sorcière* as Clotilde massaged the rose-coloured balm into her knee.

'The swelling and pain will soon pass,' Clotilde said. 'The grief will take longer, but I'll be back tomorrow to check on you, so rest up now, you hear me?'

'It already feels better. *Merci beaucoup*,' Blanche said as Clotilde clomped out of the house, her basket swinging from a chunky arm. She didn't stare, or comment on the chaos, but Blanche knew that her observant neighbour would have noticed.

'And good riddance to that one,' Louise said, when Clotilde shut the door behind her. 'So intrusive, isn't she? So certain of her welcome, and so entirely lacking in self-consciousness.'

'You might not trust Clotilde or her medicines,' Blanche said, 'but the doctor's done nothing to ease this knee pain, and her new cream really is helping. And I do feel calmer after that drink.'

'*Humph*,' Louise said, refolding the blanket and shawl, and placing them back on the sofa.

'I suppose I'll be a real member of your widows' circle now,' Blanche said. 'Rather than the imposter I've been all this time.'

'Don't be silly. You know my widows' circle is for all women, not only widows,' Louise said, plumping up cushions, and picking up the kitchen chairs Blanche had overturned in her rampage. 'Anyway, I don't like to leave you alone here, after the shocking news, and amidst this terrible disorder. Let me take you to the auberge for a while.'

'Thank you, but no,' Blanche said, an inexplicable tightness contracting her chest at the thought of leaving her home. 'Anna will be here soon with my groceries. She was supposed to come hours ago so I don't know where she is.' She fell silent. 'Oh, *mon Dieu!* Maybe …? Do you think Anna already knows about Roger? I should be with her and my granddaughters.'

'So let me drive you up to Anna's,' Louise said. 'Then we can check on them, and I'll help you bring back your groceries.'

Blanche nodded, groaning as she stood upright. She shuffled down the hallway, but as she went to open the door, her heart beat faster, out of control. It was all too much. It must be the shock. Or another heart attack. Or the same attack, but worsening? And this time it might be fatal.

Her hand stilled on the door handle. 'No, I can't go out … I can't.'

'Yes, you can.' Louise reached around Blanche, and opened the door. 'Now let's go.' She gave her friend a gentle nudge, but Blanche's feet were glued to the floorboards.

'No, no! Just the thought of being out there makes me breathless, like I might suffocate.'

'I know you've had the most awful shock, but this is being silly,' Louise said. 'Come along, you need to be with your daughter now.'

'No, I can't. I don't know why. I'll feel better tomorrow. I'm sure Anna will be here soon. I'll lie on the sofa and wait for her.'

Louise finally gave in, telling Blanche she'd check on Anna herself, and the groceries.

As Blanche sank back down onto her sofa, concentrating on breathing deeply — she'd heard deep breathing helped every ailment — she couldn't imagine ever being able to leave her home again.

But she'd have to force herself to go out for the funeral. *Mon Dieu*, Roger's burial. She might even have to organise that too, if Anna wouldn't.

How do you organise a funeral?

How does a wife do anything once she's no longer a wife? Once she's left on her own?

It was like half of her had been amputated. And, without that other half, Blanche would never be able to function.

12
Adrienne

Since the people of La Vallée du Bonheur had little interest in the outside world, I was surprised when Bambou and I got back to see one tent crowded with people huddled around a radio. They'd obviously been preserving food for winter, as the long table was lined with upside down jars of cooked fruit and vegetables.

'... aircraft went down ... popular lac du Héron,' the newsreader was saying.

'You two must've seen it happen?' Jasmin said, cradling the baby to her breast.

'Even from here we could see the plane was in trouble,' Olive said. 'Then we heard the explosion.'

'There wasn't a thing we could do to help,' I said, hands trembling as I sipped the calming brew someone had handed me.

'The gendarmes didn't want people there anyway,' Bambou said, circling his free arm around my waist, holding my shivery body close.

And later, as we sat around the campfire, Bambou and I sharing a joint to calm our nerves, we learned from another radio report that three people had perished — the pilot, a man in his sixties and a woman in her twenties.'

'Only in her twenties,' I said. 'So young!'

'Tragically, life can be so short,' Bambou said, exhaling a stream of pungent smoke into the purple dusk air.

Yes, seeing that plane go down had made that glaringly obvious to me. And as I relived those terrible crash images, my own life reeled through my mind.

I couldn't pinpoint the moment my feelings about my life had changed, but now I saw there'd definitely been a shift. Long *Before the Supermarket*, the first crack had appeared beneath my feet. But I'd been too consumed by everyday tasks to notice that silent fault line. I hadn't seen each tiny fissure widen, and become a gaping earthquake hole into which I'd tumbled, waiting in that Carrefour queue.

Falling, falling, falling.

Until, *After the Supermarket*, I landed at La Vallée du Bonheur, where Adrienne Chevalier no longer existed. She'd been reborn as Océane, a new person living a nice, peaceful life.

Nobody at La Vallée du Bonheur ever questioned me about my past, or how, or why, I'd ended up here. It was as though a person's reasons for coming here weren't important. Your past no longer mattered, or even existed.

I still wasn't certain I'd ever truly loved Emile, though it was now clear in my mind that I no longer loved my old life with him, and I couldn't bear the thought of returning to it. But why I had abandoned my husband to escape that life was still a mystery to me.

I imagined this new and wonderful life would go on forever, until a week later, when I strolled into Bambou's hut one morning. What I saw made me gasp, and clutch the doorway to hold myself upright.

~

An icy wave froze my body. I wanted to look away, but couldn't stop staring down at the naked, entwined bodies of Bambou, Fleur and Jasmin.

Fleur lay on her back, legs spread, Bambou's hand nestled between her thighs, his stiff penis standing up like some great bobbing statue. He was sucking on Jasmin's nipple, like her baby did, a trickle of milk drooling from the side of his mouth, which I found sickening.

The three of them looked up and smiled, not even stopping what they were doing. Not the least bit bothered, or guilty.

'Come and join us, Océane,' Jasmin said.

'Three is fun, but four is even better,' Fleur said, with a giggle still lying there, legs spread.

Bambou must have noticed I was upset, as he withdrew his hand from Fleur's russet-coloured bush, and released Jasmin's nipple.

'Whatever's wrong, my sweet Océane?' He frowned and seemed genuinely concerned.

'What's *wrong?*' I said. 'You're joking, surely?'

'Oh, you mean *this?*' He laughed. 'I thought you knew? None of us at La Vallée du Bonheur swear fidelity to one person.'

'We're not shackled to anyone in particular,' Fleur said, sitting up and — thankfully! — crossing her legs. 'We can do whatever we want, with whoever is willing.'

'So why not join us?' Jasmin said, as she pushed a dense, milk-filled breast at Bambou's lips. 'I promise you'll enjoy it ... enjoy us.'

I glared at Bambou. 'You said you loved me.'

'I do, Océane. I love everyone at La Vallée du Bonheur.'

'We all love one another,' Fleur said.

'Oh, well!' I didn't know what else to say. All I knew was that I had no idea people did things like this; never knew this kind of thing existed. I spun around and ran from the hut.

Down at the river, I sank onto the grassy bank in the shade of a willow tree, shaking my head to try and rid that shocking scene from my mind. I kept expecting Bambou to come running after me, full of regret and shame.

It was all a big mistake. Please forgive me. I love only you, Océane.'

But he didn't. Nobody came and rescued me from my misery, and I sat there, sobbing, the ache of Bambou's betrayal a lead ball crushing my chest. I'd imagined I was a free spirit like everyone else at La Vallée du Bonheur, but I wasn't, since this had cut me to shreds.

I'd thought sex meant love, but it didn't. All it meant was that you liked the sex with that particular person. I'd given Bambou my heart and soul, even refused to return to my husband because of him. But to Bambou, I was simply another person for pleasure, a vessel with which to fill his seed. Well, into a rubber at least.

I thought now, of those nights he'd disappeared. Taking pleasure with another woman — or women — no doubt.

Could Bambou be the father of Jasmin's baby, and of other La Vallée du Bonheur children?

Through my tears, I saw the river water rippling in a blurry rush over rocks and ferns, as swiftly as the sadness flowing through me. It was clear that Bambou didn't love me as I knew love. I should've predicted this might happen, and I slapped my thigh, cursing myself for being so naïve.

Suddenly, I was as lost and alone as *Before the Supermarket*. Had this all been a silly mistake? Should I hang my head in shame and crawl home to Emile? Brush my hair that, over the summer, had grown into a tangled mess? I'd thought there was something liberating about that, like discarding my underwear and frumpy, rich-wife clothes, but now I wasn't sure. It was, perhaps, just part of this far-fetched fantasy. This cruel illusion.

Madness runs in families you know, Adrienne. You know your mother …

Like every time I strayed from Emile's well-defined rules of behaviour, his familiar words echoed through my mind.

After the Supermarket had begun the first week of June, and it was now the end of August. I'd been away from my home and my husband for almost three months.

Maybe it was time to end this crazy getaway, but how to explain everything to Emile? He'd certainly guess I'd committed the sin of adultery, and he'd never forgive that.

A grasshopper stirred, tickling my ankles, and I dragged myself upright and trudged back to the hut.

From that hideous handbag I'd arrived with, I took my wedding ring, handkerchief, bus pass, identity card and the purse still jingling with the Carrefour money. Not bothering to take the lipstick or face powder, I flung the expensive bag onto the straw mattress. What a waste of so much money on a *handbag* when one and a half million African people had died of starvation!

I stuffed everything, along with the other dress Jasmin had given me — with the faded pink paisley pattern — into the fabric shoulder bag Olive had sewed for me. From beside my mattress, I picked up Bambou's long-dead daisy-chain wreath, and without a backward glance, I fled La Vallée du Bonheur.

Plodding along the bumpy track, through shimmering waves of heat hovering above yellowed fields, I crushed the dried daisy petals, one by one, letting them fall to the pot-holed dirt.

13

Blanche

As the pallbearers lowered Roger's coffin into the ground, Blanche raised a palm to shade her face from the overbright sun. Though she did feel better outside in the graveyard, rather than trapped inside Saint Julien's church. Despite the oppressive cemetery heat, she could at least breathe in the open air, though she still kept a grip on her daughter's arm.

It was a week since the plane crash, and already a week of September gone, but the air clung onto that heavy summer heat, with not the faintest whisper of autumn.

Back inside the church, amidst her husband's vast family, Blanche had felt like an injured, caged animal as she endured Père Châtaigne's long-winded ode — all lies and falsities — to Roger. She felt dead inside, as if it were she rather than Roger nailed inside the coffin perched on the altar.

The entire Larue clan suffocated her, so that by the end of the priest's laborious sermon, Blanche was gasping for breath. She had to stop herself screaming in a wild panic, stumbling from the pew, and racing outside to gulp in the fresh air.

Thankfully, the villagers assumed her agitation was still the grief over losing her beloved husband. Mercifully, Blanche did not have to explain that since Roger's death, she still could not leave her home.

Apart from today, when she'd had to fight that rock pressing down on her chest, and force herself outside for his funeral. Thankfully, Clotilde's potion had taken the edge off her feathery heartbeat and the thready pulse she could almost see throbbing in her wrist.

'It's quite normal to feel this way in such circumstances,' Clotilde kept telling her, when she popped in each morning with Blanche's arthritis cream, and draughts for this new panicky thing that had struck her down. Agoraphobia, Clotilde called it.

'You should see the proper doctor, rather than that *charlatan*,' Louise insisted, but thanks to Clotilde, Blanche's arthritic knee was far less red and swollen, and she no longer limped.

Thankfully, Anna had organised her father's funeral. Blanche couldn't have coped with all that paperwork, the phone calls and whatever other administrative things you had to go out and do when your husband died. The first in a long line of tasks she'd now have to do on her own.

But she couldn't keep asking her daughter to fetch her groceries and change her library books. Anna had her own life. Nor could Blanche keep relying on Louise to bring over vegetables from the auberge garden, even though Louise Bellefontaine basked in feeling useful, commanding every situation, and bossing Blanche around.

And soon, she'd need a haircut. How would she stay cooped up inside that tiny salon? She'd feel locked in, like in the church, unable to breathe, and with no way of escape. And Saint Julien's church was enormous, compared with the hairdressing salon.

Blanche could never admit to her friends and family that home was the only place she felt safe and at ease. They'd think her ridiculous, weak or crazy. They'd whisper about her, and she couldn't bear that.

Blanche still hadn't admitted to Anna that her father had stolen the gold coins, or that the Napoléons were even gone. Anna had loved her papa — the fun, light-hearted parent, as opposed to her mother's mundane, housewifely dullness. She could not destroy her daughter's illusions.

Naturally, Blanche missed no longer having the coins to sell for her day-to-day expenses — who knew how long she'd have to wait after Roger's death to access his bank account? — but she grieved even more the actual pouch that bore her dear father's initials, MV.

Whatever had become of it? Destroyed when the plane exploded, the melted coins fused into a mass of gold lying around somewhere? Or ejected along with those other cabin items, that some looter had picked up and not handed in to the Gendarmerie?

A knife-like pain shot through Blanche's chest as she cast a glance at her parents' plot, imagining her father sitting up in his grave, and jabbing a finger at her. 'I trusted you to look after my Napoléons, Blanche, and you let that worthless leech, Roger take the lot of them.'

She looked back at the arc of black-clad mourners on the rim of Roger's resting place, and down to the underground coffins stacked up on each side of the vast Larue family plot like some macabre holiday-camp bunk beds.

Despite the warmth, Blanche shivered. So many of Roger's kin buried in that plot, but hordes of the Larue family still living, here in Sainte-Marie-du-Lac. Even the hundred-year-old great grandparents, whose eightieth wedding anniversary they'd celebrated in a huge village party this summer, were parked in the chairs the family lugged to every event, identical crocheted blankets covering their knees, whatever the season.

Marrying into such an enormous clan, Blanche had always felt like a loose and insignificant thread within the tight Larue knot. They must all feel comforted by each other now, after losing one of their own — Roger — before his time.

'And only in his early sixties,' Blanche heard one of them whisper.

A family rich in number, but poor in cash. Which was why Roger had always been content to live the good life on Blanche's gold coins. She made the sign of the cross and reminded herself once again not to think badly of the dead.

She shifted her focus to the withered flowers that people had planted last spring: purple and yellow pansies, tulips, hyacinths and daffodils. The blooms were all dead now, but still they gave off some nostalgic sense of caring and beauty.

Dieu merci it was finally over. They were covering Roger's coffin with soil, and now all she had to do was endure the wake at L'Auberge de Léa. No way could Blanche avoid the gastronomical feast Louise would surely have prepared in Roger's honour. But honestly, she'd have preferred to go straight home and sink into her sofa with a cup of tea and a couple of *petit-beurre* biscuits.

As the crowd filed from the graveyard, Blanche's gaze strayed to another grave — that of Suzanne Rossignol who'd lived with her husband Jules and their simpleton son, Victor, in the ancient house that Louise's daughter-in-law, Léa Bellefontaine had transformed into the thriving L'Auberge de Léa.

Every Sainte-Marie villager had heard the rumour surrounding Suzanne, and Jules, who'd fought bravely in the trenches, though nobody knew the true version of the tragedy. And since the only Rossignol still alive was

Victor — starved of oxygen at birth — the real story was lost forever.

~

Nursing a cool drink, Blanche sat beneath the pergola of L'Auberge de Léa, in the shade of plaited vine tendrils.

'How are you bearing up, Madame Larue?' Major Yves Rocamadour asked. With Victor Rossignol's help, the gendarme who'd come with the bad news about Roger, was stretching a canvas sheet from the pergola to an oak tree, to provide more shade for the crowd.

'Me? Oh, I'm all right, thank you,' Blanche said, and the major gave her his sort-of smile. With that bit of ear missing, and coming across all gruff, it was obvious that Yves Rocamadour had been in his share of scuffles. But, as she'd watched him earlier, playing hide-and-seek and laughing with the children, Blanche sensed a big softie was hiding inside that rough, scowling exterior.

Blanche had told the major she felt all right, but suddenly she didn't. All those hot bodies hemmed her in, she choked on the Gauloises' smoke, and sweat beaded her brow. The now familiar panic constricted her throat.

Gripping her drink, Blanche stumbled away, and skittered down the grassy knoll toward lac du Héron. Beneath the dark lapis sky, the yellowed fields and faded-green trees gave off that end-of-summer melancholy as if desperately clinging on to summer's dying luxuriousness. Away from the stifling crowd, Blanche breathed more easily.

Averting her gaze from the grim crash site on the opposite shore, she sat down on one of the recliners Léa Bellefontaine kept out for her inn guests. She smiled and waved at her granddaughters, Sonia and Elise, playing on the shoreline with Louise's granddaughter, Juliette, and her cousin, Linda Renard.

The auberge dogs, Belle and Beau, barked, tails wagging and tongues lolling, urging the girls to throw the ball into the lake yet again. As Blanche watched them dashing around after the dogs whose paws kicked up spray and drenched the girls' best party — or funeral — dresses, she smiled at their utter freedom and joy.

'My lemonade might be the best in Sainte-Marie,' Louise said, parking herself in another recliner and handing Blanche a glass of white wine, 'but you look like you need something with a bit more kick. Is it this pesky agoraphobia again?'

'I'm fine, don't worry,' Blanche said. And she did feel better, with her friend sitting beside her. She nodded at Léa standing beside the pergola, chatting with her sister, Dommy.

'I do envy those two, don't you?' Blanche said. 'Running their own businesses — Léa with her auberge and Dommy with her sewing — entirely independent of their husbands. Not that Dommy Renard even needs to have her own money; her husband must earn a decent living from his chemist shop.'

'So why can't you be independent, especially now Roger's gone?' Louise said. 'Even I'm self-supporting these days.'

'But your daughter-in-law owns this inn,' Blanche said, waving an arm toward the stone building. 'It's not *your* business.'

'That Léa actually owns the inn is of little concern to me,' Louise said. 'I love that *feeling* of independence, and I adore preparing food and seeing people enjoy eating it.'

'Maybe, but Léa and Dommy are young — Anna's generation,' Blanche said, giving Louise a rueful smile. 'Perhaps you and I were born thirty years too early.'

'That's ridiculous, we might both be well over sixty, but it's never too late,' Louise said. Never one to sit for long, or relax, Louise jumped to her feet. 'I must get back to the kitchen to check on my vol-au-vents.'

As if Dommy had known Blanche was thinking about her, the seamstress came and sat in the recliner Louise had vacated.

'How are you bearing up?' Dommy smiled and patted her forearm. 'I bet you're sick of people asking you that?'

Blanche shrugged. 'Oh, you know …'

'Well, about that,' Dommy said. 'I've been thinking you might welcome some distraction. It's probably too soon to ask you this, so don't feel you have to give me an answer today, but I've got really busy with sewing orders, and since you're an excellent seamstress, I thought you'd like to help me out. What would you say to becoming my business partner?'

'Me, a *business* partner?' Alternating hot and cold ripples swept through Blanche. 'Oh! I've never worked for a wage. Roger wouldn't have it. Men of his generation believed they looked weak if their wives went out to work. Besides, I was always content looking after our home and our daughter.'

'Women all over the world are earning their own living nowadays,' Dommy said. She nodded back toward the pergola, where Léa stood beside Yves Rocamadour, the gendarme's arm around her waist. 'My sister can choose whether she wants to be with a man, rather than being forced to stay with one for financial reasons.' Dommy smiled at her. 'This could be the start of *la nouvelle vie de Blanche*!'

Blanche thought about that protest she'd seen recently on television — the women's strike for equality, in America — and pictured her sewing machine sitting idle. She wouldn't even have to go out anywhere; she could do the sewing jobs at home.

My own real job!

Even if Blanche was too afraid to venture beyond her own front door, wasn't this her chance to stare confidently at herself in the mirror, rather than shy away from her reflection, as she'd done for as long as she could recall? She'd be able to straighten her shoulders and walk tall, even if it was only from one room to another in her own house.

'All right, Dommy, I'll give it a try.'

But the moment she'd blurted out the words, Blanche immediately regretted them.

What if I can't remember how to sew properly? And what if the customers complain?

14
Adrienne

I trudged along the bumpy track in the leather sandals Bambou had fashioned for me on my arrival at La Vallée du Bonheur. I swivelled around for one last look at the wonky wooden sign, but it was already out of my sight. I was truly gone from a place I'd felt so contented — besides the heartache of missing my children — I'd thought I might stay forever. I just hadn't banked on falling in love with Bambou, and I'd never imagined having to share him.

Still reeling from his betrayal — well, the misunderstanding if I was honest, since he'd never sworn fidelity — my heart heaving with sadness, confused thought fragments swirled through my mind.

I can never go back to La Vallée du Bonheur. So where to?

I reached the main road, and stood there, gazing around at that hot and silent countryside. No chirping and ticking crickets or grasshoppers. No birds winging across the sky. I had no idea what to do, and I felt so terribly alone. If only I had a friend.

I pictured myself plodding home to the flat, explaining those months at La Vallée du Bonheur to my husband, avoiding the Bambou parts. Several times, when other men had flirted with me, Emile had said, 'I'm not jealous or worried, Adrienne. You'd never even look at another man.' But he'd see straight through my lies. I'd often had the impression that Emile's smart and sneaky psychiatrist's brain could read every one of my thoughts.

I squinted at a road sign up ahead. The village of Sainte-Marie-du-Lac was only five kilometres away. After three months of physical labour, and subsisting on vegetables, beans and rice — not to mention active lovemaking! — a five-kilometre walk was nothing.

Was I was meant to return to the enchanted spot where Emile had proposed, and where we'd enjoyed our honeymoon? Perhaps going back to Sainte-Marie-du-Lac and lac du Héron would rekindle that spark of desire, and I'd truly want to return to my husband.

I would, somehow, forgive Emile for cutting me off from the twins, hoping he'd allow me to see them again. And I would, somehow, learn to enjoy being his wife, like at the beginning of our marriage.

Besides, there was nowhere else to go. No other choice.

I fumbled in my bag for my wedding ring and slid it back onto my finger. My heart filled with renewed hope, I quickened my pace, grappling in the nooks of my mind to recapture the memories of that magical time of seventeen years ago.

~

It was a Saturday night in the summer of 1953. My torturous, pointless school days were finally over, and *hallelujah* for that! Emile smiled and clasped my hand.

'How about I take my *chérie* to lac du Héron tomorrow?'

'*Oh là là*. Yes!' I grinned at my handsome boyfriend, only a few years older than me. A day at the lake was a welcome escape from the suffocating heat of Lyon, and a reprieve from the cramped and stifling flat I lived in — since Maman was gone — with a sullen father and a cold and distant grandmother.

As Emile drove toward Sainte-Marie-du-Lac, he kept glancing at me and smirking.

'What's so funny?' I asked, smiling at him.

He didn't answer, just looked cagier, and I guessed — hoped — he was going to propose. Emile might have been my first boyfriend, but we'd already been together for two years.

As we languished in the cool clear water, then shared our picnic on the grassy bank, I struggled to hide my nervous excitement. For only when Emile slid that gold band onto my finger could I finally banish those childhood years of misery. Only when I became Madame Emile Chevalier could my true existence begin.

'No reason to wait, *chérie*,' Emile said. 'After all, I'll soon be a doctor, and I'll need a pretty wife by my side for all those important medical events.'

After a brief engagement, I floated up the church aisle — Emile's beautiful princess in a white lacy frock — toward my future husband waiting for me at the altar.

'Shall we go to lac du Héron for our honeymoon?' I'd asked Emile.

'Where else, *chérie*? It's our special place.'

My new husband rented a quaint lakeside cottage, and beneath cloudless blue skies and deliciously warm sun, we swam and sunbathed, and made love beneath starry skies. Every moment was rosy and romantic, exactly the married life I'd dreamed of.

On our last afternoon, relaxing on the grass listening to the cry of herons, the lap-lap of the water, and the quack of ducks, Emile cupped my chin in his soft hand, and stared into my eyes.

'It's my responsibility to take care of you now. I'll be earning well, so you won't need to work, but you'll have the responsibility of rearing our children.' He kissed my brow. 'Will you be up to that; to being the mistress of our home, Adrienne?'

I sighed with relief. I had no skills for any job, except some awful factory position, so I'd vowed, then and there, to become the best housewife and mother. I was certain that if I could always look my best, and please my husband, I'd become a better, happy person.

Besides having no desire to find a job, I certainly didn't end up needing one as I came home from our honeymoon pregnant. The seed Emile pumped into me daily had created a new little person, half-me and half-Emile. Such an everyday thing, but I marvelled at the miracle of it. I was sad that my own mother would never be a grandmother, but at least my pregnancy had pleased Emile's mother.

'Don't waste time starting a family, Adrienne,' she'd said, when we announced the engagement, 'or your eggs will shrivel into tiny, useless things. Get in while you're young and fertile.'

The following summer, Emile and I returned to lac du Héron for our first family holiday, with not only one miracle person, but two! Three-month-old twins. What more could any couple want? A boy, Antoine, to carry on Emile's family name and a girl, Martine, for me to do fun, girly things with. I was already planning what my daughter and I would do together when she grew up.

Emile would often give me a few moments of freedom to enjoy a quick swim as he wheeled the pram along the lake-side path. Passersby would peek into the pram and exclaim over how lovely the twins were.

'Beautiful babies!'

'Those little rose-bud lips.'

From the water's edge — I didn't dare drift far from them — I burst with pride and joy.

'Your husband is a real gem,' one woman called out to me. 'Taking care of your little ones to give you time to yourself. I hope you realise how lucky you are?'

'Oh, I do,' I said. 'I really do.'

15
Adrienne

Now that I had a destination, and a purpose — phoning Emile to take me home, and hopefully seeing my children again — even the grumble of thunder and the grey clouds clustering over the hills couldn't dampen my spirits.

A cool wind whipped my dress about my legs. I rubbed my goose-bumped arms, the first bulbous raindrop splattering my face as I reached the *centre-ville* of Sainte-Marie-du-Lac.

These late-summer thunderstorms were common, crawling in from the western hills and in that short, showery coolness you could see summer shifting toward autumn.

The rain fell harder, hurling squalls that hissed on the hot cobblestones. Wet and bedraggled, I hurried into the telephone booth. But my relief at finding shelter quickly turned to dismay as I saw the wrenched-out, damaged telephone cord.

Damn, I'd have to find another booth. Perhaps there was one down at the lake, given all the people who flocked there in the summer. Thunder cracked, lightning forks zig-zagged across the dark sky, and as I took shelter beneath the eaves Chez Dédé's bar, I wondered whether the storm was some kind of omen. Was this another bad decision in the collection I'd made since *After the Supermarket?*

But, like all late-summer storms, the rain abruptly stopped, and I headed toward lac du Héron, sweeping wet hair strands from my brow and feeling confident again. The leather sandals were soggy and uncomfortable, but I aimed for long strides, so anybody watching would think I was someone who knew exactly where she was going. I threw nervous twitches over my shoulders, but there wasn't a soul around.

I'd walked this route down to the lake many times, with Emile as my boyfriend, fiancé, then husband. I expected it would feel strange on my own, but it didn't. I was light and free, strolling through that electric-green countryside, the rain-fresh air streaming with possibilities.

Mist veiled the eastward view across the Alps and Mont Blanc, and if you hadn't witnessed it, you'd never guess that you could see right along that jagged chain of snowy mountains almost to Italy.

As lac du Héron came into view, I gasped, staring in dismay at the plane crash site. I'd assumed that dark crater, littered with twisted, jagged metal, wire and other wreckage, would have vanished, and I'd see only woods beyond the pretty lake. How silly, of course it wouldn't be cleared away in only a week!

It wasn't only the crash site that shocked me. In my mind's eye, I'd pictured people shrieking and splashing about in the water, and small boats going every which way, but there wasn't a single person. No sounds of ducks, herons or other waterbirds either. Just grey silence amidst that grim aura of desertion and destruction.

A stain of panic spread across my chest. Somehow, I'd ended up at the wrong lake. But no, this was definitely lac du Héron, though I'd only ever seen it turquoise, with golden sun-warmed ripples and throngs of joyful people.

On I trudged, my gaze flitting between charcoal-coloured sky and silvery-grey water, my heart beating faster as I searched for reminders of the magical spot where Emile had asked me to be his wife — desperate for those memories that would fill me with desire to return to my husband.

But however much I searched, the lac du Héron of my memories was no longer here. The place that had always held a special spot in my heart was gone. And I sensed there was no going back. Now there was only going forward.

~

Dejected, I had no clue what to do next, and even if I'd still wanted to phone Emile — which I didn't — there was no phone booth in sight. I glanced back at the crash site, that macabre scene pulling me toward it.

After half an hour's walk around the lakeshore, I tentatively approached the ghastly mess. Rounding a thick tree trunk, not concentrating on where I walked, I tripped on an exposed cluster of roots. I stumbled forward, crying out, a clump of bushes thankfully cushioning my fall.

As I pushed myself upright, brushing off bits of greenery, I recalled the last time Emile and I had been walking together. I'd slid on a wet pavement and almost toppled over. Emile had gripped my arm to steady me, but held on too tightly.

Goodness, you're so clumsy, Rien. Why can't you behave with the same poise as other doctors' wives?

Dwelling on that moment, and all the other times Emile had made me feel clumsy or stupid, I almost didn't see the object nestled in the bush. I reached in, my fingers curling around a brown leather pouch, old-looking, from its thin, wrinkly feel, and the faded gold initials MV. It was heavy and jangled as I brought it toward me.

And when I opened the pouch, I almost fell over again, as I stared at the stash of gold coins.

Emile had told me that older people could be mistrustful of banks, so they purchased gold, or hung onto Napoléons they inherited from family members. But they hid them in their homes, not outside in a bush, exposed to all kinds of weather.

I looked around me, half-expecting someone to jump out and say, 'It's mine!' But there was nobody and, as I glanced up at the crash site, it occurred to me that perhaps these Napoléons had fallen from the doomed plane. There seemed no other explanation.

As I stood there, gripping that bag of gold, it also occurred to me that now I'd left La Vallée du Bonheur, where nobody needed possessions, those unspent Carrefour francs would quickly run out. I'd have to get a job, but I had no skills for a *real* job.

I realised that I'd fled both my home and La Vallée du Bonheur without thinking all this through properly.

Maybe finding this gold was my stroke of luck — both the reason and the means not to return to Emile — and I shouldn't feel guilty about keeping it, at least until I found a job. Besides, the radio reporter said the only two plane passengers, along with the pilot, had died, so if the pouch *had* fallen from the plane, its owner was deceased.

As I shoved the leather pouch into my shoulder bag, I thought about selling all the gold, and opening a bank account. At La Vallée du Bonheur, I'd been safely out of reach of the gendarmes, and Emile, but here in the real world, even if I told people my name was 'Océane', I was still 'Adrienne Chevalier' on my identity card. If I opened a bank account, the gendarmes would soon locate me, and Emile would find a way of forcing them to tell him where I was, and I certainly didn't want him coming to Sainte-Marie-du-Lac.

Besides, even though women had been allowed their own bank accounts for several years, I didn't know how to open one.

'Leave our finances to me, *chérie*,' Emile would say. 'You know how bad you are with numbers.'

So, no bank account. Well, I'd simply sell some of the gold, to buy things like clothes and toiletries, and a real toothbrush. Oh, and underwear! Going around half-naked, with tangled hair, might be acceptable at La Vallée du Bonheur, but nowhere else.

The pouch dragging down my shoulder, I trudged back around the lake. Hungry, thirsty and tired, I headed for that nice-looking inn — L'Auberge de Léa — I'd spotted with Bambou, the day of the crash. I'd use the Carrefour money to stay there for a few nights until I worked out what to do next.

'*Raar, raar, raar.*'

The croak of herons startled me as I reached the auberge, and the birds took magnificent flight across the lake, on which the post-storm sun shone so brightly the glare hurt my eyes.

I knocked on the door. No answer. No sound from inside. I wandered around, admiring the vegetable patch — like the one at La Vallée du Bonheur — a chicken coop, some bleating goats in a pen, and a vacant barn. I strolled down one side of the house, toward an orchard filled with fruit trees, beside two pretty, white-washed cottages with pink and red geraniums spilling from window boxes.

There was nobody home at the cottages, and I walked around to the back of the inn, glancing into the woods behind. I reached the other side of the house, where a ladder was propped against the wall, beside a load of firewood neatly stacked beneath the eaves.

Crates of newspapers — for kindling no doubt — were piled up beside the ladder, and the bold headlines of one newspaper immediately drew my gaze.

DISPARITION D'UNE FEMME AU FOYER

My heart hammering, my quivering fingers plucked the newspaper from the pile.

16
Adrienne

One glance at the photograph, and I didn't have to read past the bold headline to know that this story of a missing Lyon housewife was about me. Dated Monday, 8 June 1970 — three days *After the Supermarket* — the newspaper trembled in my hand, and the words blurred.

> Madame Adrienne Chevalier, wife of eminent Lyonnais psychiatrist, Dr Emile Chevalier, was last seen on Friday 5 June, three days ago, at a Carrefour supermarket, waiting in the cash register queue with a full trolley.
>
> Upon arriving home, Dr Chevalier found a chicken (which the family cat had gnawed) defrosting in the kitchen, and a saucepan of congealed lemon sauce. But there was no sign of his wife, who seems to have vanished into thin air.
>
> Other shopping housewives and the cashier claimed Madame Chevalier was acting normally until she froze into a trance-like state and left her trolley — even frozen goods! — in the aisle and walked out of the supermarket. It was reported that some people tried to follow her to establish she was all right, but it was as if she was deaf, which her husband claims is not the case.

The further I read on, the more my hands shook.

> Dr Chevalier told the authorities his wife is 160 cm tall, with mud-coloured hair, although her children claim their mother is closer to 170 cm tall, with light brown hair. The family describes her eyes as the colour of seawater, or maybe stormwater, but they couldn't state whether she has any identifying marks.
>
> Acquaintances of the missing woman say she appeared to be a devoted wife and mother. Coupled with the fact that Madame Chevalier had everything a wife could possibly want, there appears to be no reason for her to leave her elegant home of her own accord. Thus, at this point, the authorities are fearing foul play.
>
> Anyone with any information about the missing woman …

Where had Emile found that photo? Probably taken on our engagement weekend at this very place. That slow, sneaky weight gain over the years of married life and mothering meant that I'd looked nothing like this for a long time. But ironically, after three months at La Vallée du Bonheur, I once again resembled the woman in the photo.

The article was written three months ago, and now neither my family, nor the authorities, were concerned I'd met with foul play.

From the crate of newspapers, stacked in daily order, I pulled out the copies from the following days, and flicked through them. I wasn't featured on any of the front pages. Even if I hadn't made the headlines, there would surely be ongoing stories about Madame Chevalier, and the search for me. But there wasn't a single other mention of my disappearance. My heart heavy as lead, I shovelled the newspapers back onto the pile.

*How unimportant I am, if they forgot about me that quickly.
No reason for her to leave her elegant home ... no reason.*

No reason that anybody else could see, but now I saw so many reasons for leaving.

~

I trudged back around to the front of L'Auberge de Léa, which still held the quiet stillness of nobody at home. Even more hungry and thirsty, and dismayed after reading the newspaper, I sank down beneath a vine-covered pergola onto a bench seat on which a cat was cleaning itself. It jumped down, miaowing and weaving through my ankles, as if asking me when its owner would be back to feed it.

'*Coucou* kitty, what's your name?'

I patted the cat, who miaowed again, purred and rubbed itself against my leg.

'I have ... had a cat like you, though Minou wasn't so friendly. More like nasty and aloof.' Yes, now I realised it, judgement and scorn were what I'd always seen in those staring yellow eyes.

Over the miaow sound, another cat miaowed from somewhere above me. I looked up through the steep boughs of the oak tree towering over the pergola.

'Miaow, miaow.' I squinted up through branches and thick leaves, but couldn't see any parts of a cat — no furry bits, pointy little ears or swishing tail. I looked back at the cat nudging my leg.

'Do you have a friend stuck up that tree?'

'Miaow,' went the cat on the ground.

'Miaow,' went the cat up the tree.

'Oh poor kitty, don't worry, I'll get you down,' I said.

Leaving my shoulder bag on the table, I hurried back to the firewood and newspaper pile, dragged the ladder around and propped it against the sturdy oak trunk. I shook it. No wobbles, so I climbed up the rungs.

'Miaow.'

'Miaow.'

'Don't fret, kitty, I'm coming.'

I reached the top of the ladder and parted the leaves, trying to see where the miaows were coming from. I glanced down — such a long way to the ground! — and took great care to keep my balance.

A bird fluttered and flapped its wings in a flash of blue. And, as it took flight, the bird let out a strange non-birdlike sound. A miaow sound.

I finally understood and giggled at that cheeky jay winging away, showing off its pinkish plumage. I'd seen these birds on television, mimicking the sounds of other animals, and even humans.

Feeling silly, but relieved for the non-existent trapped cat, I climbed back down the ladder. I'd almost reached the bottom when I heard distant sounds — children giggling and dogs barking.

They got louder, closer. I peered around the tree trunk. A group of people were heading straight for L'Auberge de Léa. The girls' satchels told me they were on their way home after school, and two older women –– one around my age, the other about the same age as Clotilde, the witch — must have been to fetch them. From the baguettes poking from a basket, they'd obviously been to the bakery too. Two dogs — one older, more sedate looking, the other an excited, oversized puppy — loped along beside them, tails wagging, noses to the ground.

I'd left my shoulder bag, with the gold pouch, on the table and even though I was certain it didn't belong to these people, I didn't want them knowing I'd held onto something that wasn't mine.

If I jumped the rest of the way to the ground — it wasn't that far — I might just have time to snatch my bag.

I took a breath and jumped. But as soon as I left the safety of the ladder rung, the ground looked much further away.

I screamed as I hit the hard ground, even before the pain in my ankle shot, like a lancet, through my foot, and up my leg.

'Merde!' I screeched. 'Ow, ow, ow!'

If I hadn't been lying in a bedraggled heap, I'd have fainted with the pain.

Clutching at my ankle, I couldn't stop the tears coming as that arc of women, children and dogs peered down at me.

17
Adrienne

Beneath those looming faces, I felt like an insect about to be squashed.

'I'm so-sorry, I wasn't tr-trespassing,' I sobbed, pointing at the tree. 'I was looking for a place to stay, a-and I thought there was a c-cat up there, b-but — '

'*Mon Dieu*, poor girl,' the older woman interrupted. 'I'm Louise Bellefontaine, and you mustn't worry. We're going to take care of you.' In her high heels and tailored dress, silver-threaded blonde hair stretched into a neat bun, she looked sympathetic, serious and efficient all at the same time.

'Yes, we'll help you,' said the one about my age, both of them helping me upright. 'I'm Léa Bellefontaine, Louise's daughter-in-law.'

And owner of L'Auberge de Léa, no doubt.

The older dog licked my injured foot, which felt strangely nice, as the puppy scampered around, barking and wagging its tail.

'Hush, Beau,' the older woman — Louise — said, but the puppy only yapped louder.

'Thank you, you're kind. Yes, I think I can stand on one foot.' I tried not to cry out with the pain, or swear again, in front of the young girls. 'I'm Océane.' I said it without thinking, as if Adrienne Chevalier truly had vanished *After the Supermarket*.

I wondered though, if they might recognise me from the newspaper photo, but surely that story was too long ago.

'I was hoping you'd have a room free for a few nights,' I said, and explained the bird imitating the cat's miaow. The little girls burst into giggles.

'Our jay is the best copycat. He mimics *everyone*,' one of them said. So alike they were, I thought the girls must be sisters, twins even. A dart pierced my heart — there, then quickly gone but leaving a lingering ache — as I wondered if, now back in their school routine after the excitement of summer, my own children were missing me.

'The jay copies my cat. She's called Noisette, and my name's Juliette Bellefontaine,' one of them said, 'and this is Linda. She's my cousin *and* my best friend. Our jay can also bark like the dogs — they're called Belle and Beau — and give orders like my grandmother, Mamie Louise, and do goat bleats and hen clucks.'

Despite the pain, I couldn't help smiling at Juliette's enthusiasm; at how, like most children, she blurted out everything without the slightest pause for breath.

'What a clever bird your jay is, Juliette. *Ouch*,' I whimpered, as Louise and Léa helped me across the cobbled courtyard and into a large and bright kitchen.

The spotless kitchen was obviously the cosy heart of the inn. Beneath the great wooden ceiling beams, pots and pans of all sizes hung from a wall rack, alongside rows of every possible cooking utensil, all of it gleaming. Old-fashioned fancy crockery was stacked in two wide sideboards, and a long wooden table took up the centre of the room. Set off on one side was what looked like a small pantry room, and on the wall was a telephone, which I hoped to use as soon as possible. Now I wasn't going back to Emile, I'd have to plead, once again, with the boarding school.

~

'That ankle is already swelling,' Louise said with a frown. 'Let's get you onto the sofa.' She turned to the girls. 'Juliette, Linda, bring some ice wrapped in a tea towel, please.'

'I'll brew some tea,' Léa said, as they settled me in the living room onto a comfortable sofa, gently easing my swollen ankle onto a cushion. 'You look like you could do with a warm drink, Océane.'

'Thank you, tea would be lovely,' I said, wedging the shoulder bag between my body and the sofa to avoid the gold coins jangling.

The sweet girls who had the same dark hair and green eyes as Léa, propped ice around my ankle like sandbags, making far more fuss than was necessary. Such small acts of kindness reminded me of my twins at this age: Martine bringing me a — cold — cup of tea when I'd had a migraine, most of it spilled into the saucer, and Antoine's proud, gap-toothed grin as he presented me with a ceramic vase he'd made at school for my birthday. I'd bought some flowers straightaway, so my little boy could see me using it.

I'd often wished my twins looked like me, but both of them were younger versions of Emile. Never seeing the slightest bit of myself in them had made me a little sad, as if I'd not actually had anything to do with conceiving the twins and carrying them for eight torturous months. Not to mention the horrendous effort of birthing them. No, Emile was the real star in the twins' existence.

'Should I get Tatie Clotilde, Maman?' Juliette asked Léa. 'To fix Océane's ankle with a magic balm.'

Tatie Clotilde? The witch is Juliette's aunt?

'You know I'll not tolerate that *sorcière* in this house,' Louise said, frowning at her granddaughter. 'And in case you're wondering, Océane, Clotilde Bonnefille is certainly *not* Juliette's aunt.'

'We might fetch Tatie Clotilde later,' Léa said, raising her eyebrows at her mother-in-law. 'But let's see if Océane's ankle recovers on its own.'

Merde! What if Clotilde comes here and recognises me?

I wasn't sure yet what I was going to tell these people, but I didn't want them thinking I was some flighty runaway wife who'd abandoned her family for a rough camp to smoke drugs and sleep with a hippie. I'd just have to avoid Clotilde until I could leave here, as soon as I could walk properly.

'Tatie Clotilde is our pretend aunt,' Juliette said, waving an arm toward Clotilde's home, a little way along the lakefront from the inn. 'She lets Linda and me play with Candice and Mimosa, who are her fluffy, white cats.'

'And Tatie Clotilde can read your palm and your cards,' Linda said.

'That's *tarot* cards,' Juliette said, 'in case you thought it was normal playing cards, which are nowhere near as interesting.'

'Juliette, Linda, *enough*,' Louise snapped. She glared at Léa, placing a steaming cup of tea on the coffee table beside me. 'I've said this a hundred times, Léa, I will never understand why you allow those girls to frequent that *witch's* house.'

'Don't listen to my mother-in-law,' Léa said, giving me a wink as I sipped the sugary tea, and washed down the aspirin she pressed into my hand. 'Clotilde Bonnefille is certainly no witch, charlatan or fake, or whatever other nasty names the small-minded villagers can conjure up. She only wants to help people.'

'*Humph,*' Louise said, tightening her already rigid shoulders, the high heels click-clacking off toward the kitchen.

Juliette and Linda sat cross-legged on one of several brightly coloured floor rugs, dangling an old sock at Beau, which the puppy kept batting and biting. I'd have loved a dog for company during the day with only the housework and a scornful cat for company. Antoine was allergic to dog hair though, so that idea had quickly been quashed.

'I wish I had a pretty name like Océane,' Linda said. 'Mine's so *boring.*'

'My mother named me after the Atlantic Ocean, where our family went for holidays,' I said. 'Maman loved the ocean.'

I'd been so young when they'd first carted Maman off to the asylum, that I had no idea about anything she might have loved, and I wondered why that lie had spilled so easily from me. Was I loath to tell these people that I hated my real name because I associated it with Emile's supposedly hilarious nicknames?

'Well, apart from falling from a ladder, spraining your ankle and getting soaked in a storm,' Louise said, as she marched back into the living room, 'you look exhausted and half-starved, like you've been living on lettuce leaves. Whatever happened to you, Océane? And how did you come to be here?'

I almost laughed. Nobody had ever called me 'half-starved', but what I'd have given, all these years, to be thin.

Fat potato-bum. Fat potato-bum.

An image of the vile little Pierre flashed through my mind's eye, the child bouncing about in the Carrefour trolley, squashing his mother's groceries. If I'd been thin back then, *After the Supermarket* might never have happened, and I'd still be trying to find Emile's nicknames funny, and dressing, cooking and cleaning to please him.

Perhaps then, seven-year-old Pierre's fat potato bum chant hadn't been such a disaster. A blessing, even?

'Where is your husband? Your home, your family?' Louise went on, fortunately not letting me get a word in, which gave me time to think up a story, and gather the courage to answer her. I was relieved though, that they obviously hadn't recognised me from the newspaper photo.

'What an exquisite clock,' I said, as a grandfather clock set in polished dark wood chimed the hour.

'The wood is *mahogany*, and the clock belonged to Victor's maman and papa,' Juliette said, as the puppy continued gnawing the sock. 'Suzanne and Jules Rossignol, who lived here during the Great War. We're doing a school project on the Great War, and how Victor's papa had to fight off the enemy Germans in awful trenches.'

She stroked the older dog, Belle, perched beside her like a sentry. 'Maman kept lots of the Rossignol's belongings at the auberge because we like them and so Victor feels at home.'

'Victor?' I asked.

'Suzanne and Jules' son,' Juliette said.

'He lives in one of the white cottages,' Linda said, waving an arm down toward the orchard.

'And Maman's friend Nelly, who works here, lives in the other cottage,' Juliette chimed in. 'But her daughter – – she's called Sophie — lives at boarding school in Lyon because she's a fast runner and will race in the Olympics one day, so you won't see her.'

The same boarding school as Antoine and Martine?

'You'll meet Nelly,' Linda said, as I choked back a sob, 'when she gets home from *kissing* her boyfriend, who breeds snails and sells them to Mamie Louise to cook in her restaurant.'

'I did see those lovely cottages when I was looking around to see if anyone was home,' I said, enjoying the thought of meeting the other occupants. As if I already belonged at this cosy place.

'When Maman turned the house into L'Auberge de Léa,' Juliette said, 'she felt sorry for Victor. Even though he's a grown-up man — over *fifty* — he's an orphan, and since the birth cord almost strangled him when he was being born, Victor can never get a proper job, so Maman gave him a handyman-gardener job.'

Louise waggled a finger at the girls. 'That's enough of your chatter. I do not imagine Océane is interested in every detail of our lives, or Victor's,' she chided, though I caught her indulgent smile. She turned her cool gaze to me. 'Now tell us about *yourself*, Océane.'

I swallowed the last of the tea, already flushed with guilt over the lie I was about to spout. Because, if I said I'd run away from my home and my husband, the obviously God-fearing Louise Bellefontaine would surely sit in judgement and scorn. Because no good wife does that.

Not even a bad wife abandons her husband.

18
Adrienne

'I'm a widow,' I said, unable to think of any other reason, on the spot, why I'd be wandering around the countryside on my own. 'My husband died three months ago … in June. A bad heart … a birth defect.'

'I'm so sorry, that's sad,' Léa said, patting my arm.

'I have no family and we never had children,' I went on. Even though the twins were no longer in my care, if these kind people knew I'd left my home, they'd assume I'd left my children too, and I sensed they wouldn't want that kind of mother under their roof. And right now, this roof was my only option. I took a shuddery breath and continued.

'I don't have much money, and I've been trying to find work since my husband passed, but the only skills I have are how to be an efficient wife. And when you're no longer a wife, that doesn't get you a job, does it?'

What a fool I'd been, rushing into marriage and children, and not training for any profession.

'But where is your home?' Louise asked, 'and how did you come to be in Sainte-Marie-du-Lac? I know you're not from here.'

I cast my gaze downward. 'My husband and I lived in a flat in Lyon, which I couldn't afford to keep without his wage.'

'But surely you'd have inherited the flat from your husband?' Louise said. 'Women *can* inherit property these days.'

'Oh, we were renting,' I blurted out. 'But I didn't want to stay there … too many happy memories.'

And how I wished those memories *had* been happy, instead of the bleak times I recalled since leaving.

'Poor soul,' Louise said, crossing herself. 'But don't you have any other family?'

I shook my head, not mentioning the father I hadn't seen since I married Emile, or the grandmother who could be dead by now, for all I knew. Or cared.

'I came to Sainte-Marie-du-Lac because my husband and I loved it here. It's where we got engaged and had our honeymoon.'

At least that part is true.

'How romantic,' Léa said.

'As I mentioned, I don't have much money,' I said, still not daring to move for fear of jingling the gold coins, or the pouch slipping out of my bag. These people likely knew nothing about its existence, but still I felt a twinge of guilt for keeping stolen property. 'But I could pay for a room for a few nights, if you have one free? Just until my ankle heals and I can find a job and somewhere to live.'

Even as I spoke, I wondered why I so suddenly and desperately wanted to stay at L'Auberge de Léa. I could easily sell some of the gold to pay for a hotel for *months*, by the look of all those coins. Besides, there was the risk of running into Clotilde.

But I hated the thought of being holed up in some lonely hotel room waiting for my ankle to heal before venturing out into the real world. And already I felt comfortable and safe, cocooned in the cosy atmosphere of this beautiful inn and its friendly people.

'You're most welcome to stay here as long as you need, until that ankle heals,' Louise said. 'No need for any payment.'

'Our busy summer season is almost over, but we have one free room,' Léa said, waving an arm toward the hallway. 'The guest rooms are here, on the ground floor, which will be easy with your bad ankle. A guest has booked the room in a few days, but by then you should be able to manage the stairs and you can move up to the attic.'

'The *attic*? That dusty old place full of cobwebs?' Louise scowled, yet again, at her daughter-in-law. 'Whatever are you thinking, Léa? The attic's not even renovated.'

'I haven't had time to fix up the attic for visitors,' Léa said. 'That's planned for this autumn, when we have fewer guests. But actually, it *is* clean, Louise. Yves and Victor got rid of the dust and cobwebs, to prepare it for renovating. And there's already a comfortable bed up there.'

'Yves is Major Rocamadour — Maman's *boyfriend*,' Juliette said, and the girls giggled again. 'He's old, and his eyebrows join in the middle, and a dog bit off part of his ear, but he's nice.'

'He brings *bonbons* for us,' Linda said.

'The attic sounds perfect,' I said, recalling the past three months of an uncomfortable straw mattress, or the dirty ground. 'But I insist on working for my keep, as soon as I can walk properly.'

'What about the lady in the attic, Maman?' Juliette said, as Beau chewed on a raggedy cloth, the older dog, Belle, gazing scornfully at the puppy.

'*Oui*,' Linda said, 'there's a lady ghost up there who whispers to us when we're playing.

'Hush now, girls, you'll frighten Océane with your talk of ghosts,' Louise said. 'Besides, haven't I forbidden you to play in the attic?'

'*Oh là là*, I *love* ghosts,' I said, winking at the girls. 'As long as they're friendly.'

'The attic lady is friendly,' Juliette said.

'Friendly but frightened,' Linda said.

'We have other ghosts too,' Juliette said.

Linda nodded. 'They make noises that echo right across the lake.'

'Stop this ridiculous talk of ghosts,' Louise chided, waving a manicured hand. 'Pay no attention to the girls' over-active imaginations, Océane.'

'And sometimes the Virgin Mary makes noises,' Linda went on. 'So she's like a ghost, but not really a ghost.'

I frowned. 'Virgin Mary?'

'The girls are referring to our marble lake-front statue,' Louise said. 'The reason our village was named Sainte-Marie-du-Lac. Legend has it that the echoes across the lake are Mary's warning cries, protecting villagers from the dangerous, swampy parts. Nothing to do with ghosts.'

'But my mother thinks that's a load of religious rubbish, don't you, Maman?' Juliette said.

Léa laughed as she placed a plate of cookies on the coffee table. 'We all know statues can't talk, or cry out, and those echoes across the lake could be anything — willow trees in the breeze, herons calling to each other, or any other noise.'

'Strawberry macarons, Mamie's yummiest biscuits!' Juliette cried, clapping her small hands in glee. 'And my favourites.'

'*Mmn,* delicious,' I said, munching on a sweet cookie and resisting the urge to grab the lot and cram them into my mouth. 'I think they're my favourites too.'

Thanks to the aspirin, my ankle was already less painful, and knowing I had a bed for the next few nights, I relaxed even more into that comfy sofa.

'How old are you girls?' I asked Juliette and Linda.

'We're nine and a half,' Juliette said.

'We both turned nine in March,' Linda added.

I yearned to tell them about Martine and Antoine at nine years old, when they'd been as sweet and polite. Those days when I'd just wanted to kiss and hug my lovely twins; those days before they became sulky and distant teenagers; those days before Emile sent them away from me.

I recalled one evening, hurrying into the living room for something and almost tripped over their prone bodies, stretched out before the television.

'Maman, watch out!' Martine cried. 'You almost fell on top of us.'

As always, Antoine remained wordless, staring at the screen.

Not that I'd wanted any thanks from them — after all, they *were* teenagers — just a touch of human affection; some acknowledgement that they didn't completely despise me.

Louise's brisk voice jolted me from my daydream. 'So, Océane, once you're rested, we'll get you into some clean clothes. That dress looks like it's seen better days, and those soggy sandals will fall apart any second.'

Despite Bambou's betrayal, I still adored the leather sandals he'd crafted for me, though they *were* on the brink of shredding. I loved the loose, flowy feel of my dress too, even if time and wear had faded the sunflower pattern. Though I imagined that the prim and aristocratic-looking Louise Bellefontaine would prefer the frumpy frocks I'd worn *Before the Supermarket*.

'Léa is about your size,' Louise said. 'She'll find you some things. My daughter-in-law has far more clothes than one person could *ever* wear.'

'My sister has her own seamstress business,' Léa said, rolling her eyes at Louise. 'Dommy tries out her patterns on me.'

'Tatie Dommy sews clothes for me and Linda too,' Juliette said, as I devoured more strawberry macarons. 'But my aunt never makes Mamie Louise's clothes because my grandmother has her own special *couturier*.'

The ankle pain almost a dim memory, I almost dozed off on that snug sofa, inhaling the fresh pine scent of the air, the background chatter of the girls and the puppy's yapping homely music in my ears. The cat, Noisette, curled up on my lap, and purred, the post-storm sun's rays snaking across the floorboards and highlighting the hues of the coloured rugs. Warm, fed and watered, I basked in the attention of these people as if they were my real, loving family.

'And tomorrow afternoon you're welcome to join us for my widows' circle,' Louise said.

'Widows' circle?' I asked.

'Nothing formal,' Louise said. 'Simply a women's group I organised when I, too, lost my beloved husband. He was our village mayor,' she said proudly.

'That sounds nice,' I said, but not sure I wanted to join any such group.

As if Louise could see right into my guilty mind, she said: 'My circle isn't only for widows, it's simply a comfortable sanctuary where women meet for company, and to chat about whatever they want.'

'Which is mostly gossiping about their husbands, dead or alive,' Léa added with a laugh.

'My daughter-in-law even attends on the odd occasion,' Louise said, throwing Léa another glare. 'Though *Dieu merci,* my son Bruno is very much alive.' She gazed heavenward and crossed herself again.

'Oh yes, my ex-husband's even far more alive since he left me for his young and skinny girlfriend,' Léa said with a grin.

'At the widows' circle, we concentrate on enjoying what we have,' Louise said, ignoring Léa's jibe at her son. 'And I hope you will too, Océane, after the tragedy that has brought you to us.' And I felt even more of a fraud as she clapped her hands together.

'Right! Océane, you relax until you're ready to go to your room,' Louise said, 'but since our auberge guests will soon return from their outing, we must prepare their dinner. Come along now, Léa.' With a snappy click of her fingers, she clopped off back to the kitchen.

Léa winked at me as she trotted after her mother-in-law.

'Be careful,' she said, 'or Louise will make you actually *join* her widows' circle, then you'll never get away from Sainte-Marie-du-Lac.'

19
Adrienne

As Juliette and Linda helped me up from the sofa, and along the hallway, I eyed the telephone in the kitchen. But with Léa and Louise bustling about, there was no chance to call the boarding school.

'*Voilà, la chambre orange*,' Juliette said, as I hobbled past a room with orange mosaic-patterned wallpaper and sunshine-yellow linen and bedside table lamps.

'This is *la chambre bleue*,' Linda said, of the powder-blue room with its marine-themed wallpaper and navy bedspread.

'And here's the family room,' Juliette said, proudly pointing out the next larger room, decorated in turquoise colours.

Simply but tastefully decorated, the guest rooms looked inviting, the beds — with thick duvets and plumped pillows — so comfortable.

'This is your room,' Juliette said, as we reached the end of the hallway. 'Maman and Mamie Louise, and I — and Linda when she stays over — sleep on the second floor. And when your ankle's better, we'll take you up to your attic room, which is on the third floor.'

'And there are no more floors after that,' Linda said, as the girls hurried away, the puppy at their heels.

I didn't immediately go into my room, prettily decorated in shades of violet, but stood on one foot, holding onto the doorframe and gazing around this space

I was to have all to myself. After sharing Emile's bedroom for so many years, then the communal living at La Vallée du Bonheur, a room of my own was such luxury.

I limped inside, and closed the door on the girls' cheerful chatter, the puppy's yelps, and the commanding voice of Louise Bellefontaine.

Someone — Léa probably — had left a pile of clothes and a fluffy purple towel on the bed. Thankfully, nobody had asked why I had no luggage; why I'd left my city flat with only a small shoulder bag. I wouldn't have had an answer for that.

I heaved my shoulder bag onto the bed, the gold coins jingling. I would have to find a place to stash MV's leather pouch, but firstly, I simply sat on the bed amidst that utter peace, and stared into space. Just looking, but not at anything in particular. Just thinking, but not about anything in particular — a luxury I'd never had living with Emile, and certainly not before, with Grandmère's dog-bark clanging through my mind.

What would happen to me now, here? Would I find the *real* Adrienne Chevalier? Because running off like I'd done made me realise how very little I knew about myself. And what of the fake me? Could I go on as the tragically widowed Océane?

My eyelids drooped, and I sank back onto the feather pillow.

~

Martine and Antoine are sixteen months old when Emile and I return to lac du Héron for our second family holiday.

I hope the twins are old enough to play together, but they don't, and I am continually stopping them from bashing each other over the head. The crying jangles my nerves, the exhaustion weighs me down, and I am desperate for the briefest respite.

Emile spends his time fishing and swimming, and I wonder how I am so naïve as to imagine he'll give me a rest from the demanding twins.

The lake is a magnet to Martine and Antoine, who constantly dash off into the water. I stand knee-deep, so they don't drown, and when my little ones shiver, I haul them onto the shore, and they fall over each other in a tangle of chunky limbs, howling so loudly that people stare. I gather them up, cradling a comforting arm around each one, crooning and wiping away tears.

'My little loves, Maman will take care of you. There, there, don't cry, don't fret.'

They are finally asleep for an afternoon nap and I ask Emile if he'll watch them, while I have a quick swim.

'Oh yes, off you go, chérie,' he says, beaming at me. 'You're doing a wonderful job, notre petite maman.'

I've only been gone ten minutes when I spot Emile waving frantically from the shore. Alarmed that something is wrong with the twins, I swim back, lurching breathless and shaky from the water.

'They both woke up at the same time,' Emile says. 'I don't know how you'd think I could deal with two at once?'

~

A noise — a bird's shriek outside perhaps — startled me awake, and I immediately recalled my thoughts before I must have nodded off.

If only I'd had a little help with the twins, occasionally. After all, they *were* my responsibility. My job.

'Nobody helped me with my children,' Emile's mother would say, as if insulted I might even ask.

Oh yes, that rosy bloom of motherhood soon wilted to a brown and limp stem as the daily, relentless grind went on and on.

I sat on the bed, staring around me. I hadn't found answers to any of my questions, but I was convinced that coming to Sainte-Marie-du-Lac, rather than returning to Emile, had been the right decision.

I smoothed my hair as best I could, and limped back down the hallway, and into the kitchen with its delicious smells. A woman about the same age as Léa and me threw me a friendly smile from where she was stirring a strong-smelling cheese sauce on the stove.

'*Salut*, you must be Océane? I'm Nelly. It's lovely to meet you.'

'*Bonjour*, Nelly. Can I help anyone?' I asked.

An aproned Louise waved an egg whisk at me. 'Don't worry, there'll be plenty to help with once that ankle is healed.'

'You rest up,' Léa said from the sink, elbow-deep in sudsy water and large pans.

I wanted to stay in this kitchen, if not to help, then to inhale the tantalising aroma of cheese and — was that rosemary? — spiralling toward the high wooden-beamed ceiling. It seemed forever since I'd eaten something other than bean stew, and my mouth watered, my stomach grumbling.

'Whatever you're cooking smells divine,' I said, sitting at the table to take the weight off my aching ankle.

'My special goat's cheese pasta with chicken and rosemary,' Louise said.

'Luckily everyone loves my mother-in-law's goat's cheese,' Léa said with a smirk, 'since she puts it in most of our meals.'

A short man in blue overalls, his hair greying at the temples, waddled into the kitchen, and set down a pail of milk.

'Your goat milk,' he said to Louise.

'*Bonjour*, Madame,' he said to me, 'I am Victor.'

Ah yes, Victor Rossignol, the handyman-gardener, and son of the previous house owners.

'*Merci*, Victor,' Louise said, as he disappeared as quickly as he'd arrived. 'I'll be able to start my next batch of cheese.'

I almost blurted out that I'd become an expert goat-milker at La Vallée du Bonheur, even spitting on my hands so they wouldn't chafe.

'Victor seems sweet,' I said.

'He's kind, and a hard worker,' Léa said, hanging a sparkling-clean basting pan on a hook, amidst the row of others. 'He's not comfortable in big groups, though, so you won't see him at mealtimes. He prefers to eat alone in his cottage, or with his farmer friend, Jacques Jonquille.'

'Why don't you mingle with our guests, Océane?' Louise said, pointing her wooden spoon at me. 'I've placed a stool under the pergola table to rest your ankle.'

There was no chance of using the telephone in private, so I limped outside, sat at the pergola table, and introduced myself to the auberge guests.

The sun sank behind the Monts du Lyonnais and, in the twilight, the lake shone a golden amber, a deep purple cloak shrouding the woods. The only blight on that flawless landscape was the plane crash crater on the opposite shore.

Back from their outing to the medieval *centre-ville* of Sainte-Marie, the guests had voted to take their *apéritif* outside, to enjoy the lake and mountain view.

The Sainte-Marie-du-Lac grapevine must work at lightning speed, as someone from the village had brought down a pair of crutches for me, which Juliette and Linda were trying to use. Linda was apparently sleeping over at the auberge, and I gathered that the girls — both only children — spent most of their time together.

I joined in their infectious giggles as they fell over the too-long crutches, and the puppy, in a tangled heap. A pheasant — Fifi, Juliette told me — stood beside them like some domesticated pet, chirping *'eep, eep'*. And, from an overhead oak branch came the cheeky jay's, *'eep, eep'* reply.

Linda held out the crutches to me. 'Your turn, Océane.'

'Maybe tomorrow,' I said, loath to embarrass myself in front of everyone. That newspaper article might be three months old, but still I didn't want to draw attention to myself.

Léa appeared from the kitchen bearing a tray of *hors-d'oeuvres,* Nelly following with a tray of mulberry-coloured drinks. The delicate glasses, clinking as she crossed the cobbles, reminded me of my leaf-patterned glasses — yet another expensive object I never missed, or even thought about.

'That drink looks delicious,' one of the guests, a Dutch woman, said.

'A Kir, from the Burgundy region,' Léa said. 'One part *crème de cassis* to nine parts white wine.'

'Santé!' the guests chanted, raising and clinking their glasses.

I'd never tasted a Kir, but it was so sweet and aromatic that I had to stop myself gulping it down.

'A toast to Léa and her beautiful inn,' said a man with a Belgian accent, as everyone plucked *amuse-bouches* from the tray.

'And to Madame Bellefontaine's excellent cuisine,' the Dutch woman said as she bit into the warm, crumbly pastry.

'Parcels of fig and peppered goat's cheese,' Léa explained, wiping her hands on the tea-towel tucked into her waistband. 'And these twisty filo pastry ones are stuffed with honey, walnuts and more of my mother-in-law's cheese.'

As Nelly and Léa returned to the kitchen to help Louise finish the main course, it struck me that despite not having husbands, they seemed happy and content with their auberge lives. They obviously had no need of a husband for happiness. Or money.

I swallowed the last of the delicious Kir, wondering why, for all these years, I'd been convinced I absolutely needed a husband to get through life. How ridiculous that notion was now. I should have simply kept a string of boyfriends, like Bambou and his girlfriends. Uncomplicated and unfettered.

'Did they discover what caused the terrible crash?' the Dutch woman asked, nodding toward the gaping crater.

'Engine failure, most likely,' the Belgian man said.

'We saw the plane go down,' Juliette said.

'There was lots of thick smelly smoke and a huge explosion and flames,' Linda said, as the girls gave up on the crutches, leaving them in a heap on the grass.

'Three people perished,' Juliette said, looking around the solemn circle of adults. 'One was Mamie Louise's friend's husband, Roger Larue.'

'He was Sonia and Elise Larue's grandfather,' Linda said. 'They're our best friends, and they said the funeral was *mournful*.'

'And now Mamie Louise's friend — her name's Blanche — won't leave her house, except she had to once, for her husband's funeral,' Juliette said, cuddling Beau, who licked her face.

'Tatie Clotilde says it's the shock causing her *acraphobia*,' Linda said.

'*Agora*phobia,' Juliette corrected her cousin. 'And Tatie Clotilde gives Madame Larue potions to help her recover from the grief and the agoraphobia, so she'll soon be able to leave her house.'

'Shock can have terrible effects,' the Dutch woman said.

'Mamie Louise told Madame Larue not to sit at home being sad and doing nothing,' Juliette said. 'That's the worst thing for grief.'

'So, she's going to be my maman's partner in her sewing business,' Linda said, adding proudly, 'Maman's the best seamstress in the whole of France.'

I couldn't recall the last time my twins had spoken of me with such pride, and my heart ached.

Juliette's words chimed through my mind.

Three people perished …. Mamie Louise's friend's husband …

Was there any chance that this MV pouch belonged to the husband of this woman, Blanche Larue?

I would likely never know and, as I savoured Louise's delicate pastries, I reminded myself that until I could find a job, I needed my own money.

As I gazed down at lac du Héron — a deep and mysterious purple beneath the moonlight — the Kir and the easy conversation relaxing me, I forced my mind away from the Napoléons stashed in my guest-room wardrobe.

20
Blanche

Over a week after her husband's death, and two days since the funeral, Blanche still couldn't stop dwelling on her sham of a marriage. She hauled a shoebox brimming with photos down from the top shelf of a cupboard, and pulled out several images of their life together.

Perched on her sofa, where she'd sat almost non-stop since Roger's demise, Blanche flicked through their wedding photos — the marriage that had obviously meant nothing to her husband. When had Roger stopped caring? Perhaps he'd never cared, right from when Père Châtaigne had united them within the sanctity of Saint Julien's church over thirty years ago.

All those years she'd bathed him in love and affection, yearning for his in return, but never getting the slightest shred. When Anna was born, Blanche bestowed all her love onto her child, telling herself their beautiful daughter would fill the aching void. Which worked for a while, until Anna grew up, married, and had her own children.

Blanche suspected that she'd simply been a convenient, moderately wealthy woman whom Roger could call his wife. Someone to meet village expectations, while he made not the slightest effort to honour his sacred vows. And doing exactly what he wanted with her gold coins! A red rage bloomed deep inside Blanche as she brooded, yet again, on her dead husband stealing her father's pouch of Napoléons.

But why had he needed all *the gold?*

Perhaps he'd decided to leave her for good, for that slut, Brigitte. If that was the case, then thank the Lord Roger had died before Blanche became pitied and mocked as the village cuckquean!

She took a sharp breath, and quickly crossed herself for that ungodly thought, concentrating on her more pressing dilemma: as well as no longer having the gold coins to sell, Blanche had not a single object remaining from her dear father.

Her thoughts kept flitting back to the burning question — what had become of the pouch? The worst thing was that she'd likely never know.

'*Coucou!*' Clotilde's booming voice from the front door — her neighbour never bothered knocking — interrupted Blanche's silent fury. Vowing she'd never again torture herself with these fake memories, she shoved the photos back into the shoebox.

'Ready to go, *chérie?*' Clotilde plonked her hefty basket onto the coffee table and withdrew a vial of orange-coloured liquid.

'But —' Blanche started.

'No buts. We've been over and over this.' Clotilde wagged a chunky, bejewelled finger at her. 'It's been more than a week since the crash, and — thanks to my balm — your arthritis has almost disappeared, so it's high time you left this house. And today is the perfect occasion to get out for some fun with your friends.'

'I'm not sure ...' Blanche started, as Clotilde waddled into the kitchen and put a saucepan of water on the stove to boil.

'You are quite capable of walking the short distance to the auberge,' Clotilde said. 'No need to panic, I'll stay beside you the whole way. Anyway, you've been telling me Louise has been badgering you to come to her widows' circle. And surely Anna is concerned that her mother refuses to leave her house?'

Blanche wrung her hands. 'Anna thinks it's still the grief, which might be true. I'll be better once Roger's death isn't so … isn't such a bleeding wound.' She clasped a palm over her heart. 'But since you insist, I'll give it a go, though if I can't breathe, I'm coming straight home. Agreed?'

'*Not* agreed.' Clotilde placed the saucepan on the table, withdrew a sachet of leaves from her basket, emptied some into the hot water and stirred the brew. 'And soon I'll be taking you on longer walks, up to the village.'

'*Oh là là*, we'll see about that.' That familiar dizziness swirled through Blanche's mind, her chest tightening at the thought of leaving her home.

'Besides,' Clotilde went on, adding the orange liquid to the stewing tea leaves, 'I highly doubt grief is causing this agoraphobia.'

'What is it, then?' Blanche asked, truly confused.

'You've been living outside reality, Blanche. You've known of your husband's gallivanting for a long time, but the truth was too hard to admit, right?'

Blanche knew of several village women who consulted Clotilde for advice on unruly husbands, in the utmost secrecy, since nobody wanted to be the source of village gossip. Clotilde counselled them, read their cards, concocted healing potions, and apparently helped many women. But Blanche had always been too embarrassed to reveal her husband's ugly side to her healer friend, though she wasn't too surprised Clotilde knew the truth about Roger.

Blanche could still hear Roger's sharp voice, like nails scraping down a blackboard, and her arms erupted in goose bumps. 'I'll run those witches out of this village,' he'd say, when he glimpsed Clotilde or Bev plucking herbs, or hurrying off laden with baskets of healing potions.

Blanche had itched to retort: 'How the narrow-minded can twist the truth into vicious rumour.' But she never did. She'd just obeyed her husband, because that's what wives do.

Now Blanche no longer had to consult Clotilde in secrecy for her ailments which, besides not feeling obliged to have a sparkling home, was another good thing about Roger's death.

'I didn't think people knew,' Blanche said. 'Not even our daughter knew what Roger was really like.'

Clotilde poured the stewed tea into a cup, her beaded bracelet jangling. 'I'm a psychic, remember? Now drink this, it's a little brew for mood disorders and it'll take the edge off the anxiety.'

Blanche swallowed the liquid in one gulp, grimacing at the strange taste.

'You'd feel much better if you stopped living this lie,' Clotilde went on. 'Because even though Roger is gone, you are *still* living a lie which, in my opinion, is partly responsible for this agoraphobia.'

Blanche sighed and put down the empty teacup.

'I suppose the panic *did* worsen when I found out the other passenger was Roger's secretary. I'd always known my husband wasn't playing golf at weekends, and that wasn't the first time he'd taken liberties with our marriage and our vows. Not the first time my husband had sinned against me, the church and *God himself!*' Blanche couldn't help shouting that last bit, but excused herself by making the sign of the cross.

'So why keep pretending now he's gone?' Clotilde gave Blanche's hand a gentle squeeze. 'If the truth was out in the open, you'd be free of his hold over you, *and* this panicky fear of leaving your home.'

Blanche pulled away, fisting her hand. 'I'm too ashamed, too embarrassed. And Anna would hate me for saying dreadful things about her father. She had, *has*, such a rose-tinted vision of her papa.' Blanche waved an arm. 'You know the handsome Roger came across as so charming, confident and friendly.'

'Overbearing and cocky were more what came to my mind,' Clotilde said with a smirk, eye-liner wings disappearing into wrinkles.

Blanche winced. 'Yes, he was that too. And, to be honest, it *is* a weight off my chest that you know the truth, but you'll keep it to yourself, won't you? You're the only person in Sainte-Marie I can fully trust.' Her breath turned into a sigh. 'I've always been tempted to confide in Louise — she's a good friend and fairly trustworthy – – but I feared she'd let it slip or, more likely, try to help me. Despite her good intentions, Louise Bellefontaine can be so bossy.'

'Free your mind and soul,' Clotilde said, 'and you'll free yourself of those imaginary chains shackling you to this house.'

'But what would people say? I couldn't bear them whispering about how I put up with such a philanderer,' Blanche said. 'They wouldn't understand that I didn't have a choice … that a flawed husband is better than no husband.'

'But you *will* have a job now,' Clotilde said. 'I heard you'd accepted Dommy Renard's proposal to go into her seamstress business.' She flicked a blonde hair strand from her face, a large jade-coloured ring glinting in the sunlight. 'Besides, who gives a gnat's arse what people think? Imagine if Bev and I listened to every village whisper, we'd be sobbing into our cauldron.'

She helped Blanche stand upright. 'Hold your head high, Blanche Larue!'

She licked her trademark scarlet lips as she tugged Blanche toward the front door. 'Now let's get you away from this dismal shrine to Roger Larue's *slave*.'

'I only agreed to help Dommy with the sewing because I won't have to leave the house,' Blanche said, trying to breathe through the chest tightness as she peered around the — open! — front door.

She thought she was going to be all right, but at the last minute she pulled away from Clotilde, skittered back inside and sank down into her safe sofa.

'No, I can't go out, Clotilde. Sorry, I can't do it.'

21
Adrienne

'I'm sorry, Madame Chevalier, we cannot deliver messages to your children. The school remains under strict orders from Dr Chevalier.'

I let out a painful sigh, my heart breaking all over again. It was my second morning at the auberge, the bustling kitchen finally empty, so I'd taken my chance to call the twins' school.

It was a different secretary from the one I'd spoken to before, but obviously, they all had the same orders.

'Please, madame,' I said. 'I'm *begging* you.'

Sweaty fingers gripping the handset, I took a deep breath and told the secretary that I wasn't stupid, flighty or mad — as my husband claimed — and tried to explain the reasons I'd left him.

When I finished, the deep silence down the line set my whole body quivering, and I was certain she'd still refuse me.

'Well, I *am* familiar with those ... those kinds of husbands,' she said, her voice whispery. 'Tell me what you want to stay to Martine and Antoine, and I'll give them your message myself.'

'Oh, really?' My words spilled out in a rush of relief as I recited the phone number and address of L'Auberge de Léa. 'The twins can write or call me here, but it's *very* important my husband doesn't find out where I am,' I said.

'I understand,' the secretary said. 'I'll make sure your children know not to share your whereabouts.'

'You're so kind, *mille mercis*,' I said. '*Au revoir.*'

I took the crutches from where I'd leaned them against the wall and hobbled outside. As I inhaled the fresh, herb-scented air, for the first time in ages, I smelled hope.

~

By that afternoon, I was confident with the crutches, tottering around the auberge grounds admiring the gardens, the orchard and the animals. I waved to Louise at the vegetable patch, and to Victor, plucking dark tomatoes, purple aubergines and giant zucchinis. Fifi the pheasant strutted by Victor's side like a loyal little dog.

I hobbled over to the oak tree with its cheeky jay and sank down onto the bench seat beneath the pergola to rest my aching ankle. I gazed across the lake, and up to the snow-wreathed Mont Blanc and the Alps.

'The grape harvest comes around once again,' Louise said. So deep in my thoughts, and in awe of the scenery, I'd not noticed her approach me. She placed her basket, brimming with beans, on the table and pointed toward the valley stretching before us, and the vineyards, where harvesters were snipping off grape bunches.

'When we were young, my late husband and I always joined in the harvest,' Louise said with a nostalgic smile. 'Such a convivial time with the entire village, and our little Bruno dashing about with the other children.' She sighed and shook her head. 'But these days it's mostly foreigners who come for the harvest, which provides income for our village, I suppose.'

'Sounds like fun,' I said.

'Sadly, those days are gone,' Louise said. 'I had to begin over, after my husband passed away. I wasn't yet sixty years old, and thought we had many more years together, but that wasn't to be. I still miss him.' She stared into the distance, at the ugly crash site.

'That emptiness prompted me to start the widows' circle. Then Léa opened her inn and needed my help, which also keeps me busy. I do enjoy cooking for the guests, not to mention for my restaurant, which is quite famous around these parts, even if I say so myself.'

'Where's the restaurant?' I asked.

'We transformed one of the old barns,' she said, pointing toward the orchard and the two white cottages. 'We open La Cuisine de Louise for midday meals, but only during autumn, winter, and spring. During the summer, there's too much work with the auberge guests.' Her gaze shifted back to me.

'What I'm saying, Océane, is that you too, as a young widow, must start a new life.'

'I already feel like a have a nice new life here,' I said, breathing off a wave of guilt, and changing the subject. 'Where does your son live now?'

'As Léa told you, she and Bruno are separated, and he resides up in the village with that Twiggy lookalike, Francine Duval.' Louise made a *tut-tut* noise, and crossed herself again. 'Naturally, I was disappointed when he left Léa and Juliette, for I *am* a practicing Catholic, you know.'

As if that isn't obvious.

'But Léa has a new boyfriend too,' I said, gazing back at the vineyard, where people were swishing away buckets filled with grape bunches, and tipping them out into baskets leaning against the vine posts at the end of the rows. 'She seems happy with Major Rocamadour.'

'*Eh oui*,' Louise said. 'Though I suspect Léa is keeping the major at arm's length. My daughter-in-law is enjoying her freedom, and I think she's simply thankful to Rocamadour — well we're *all* extremely thankful to him — for solving that terrible business with Juliette.'

I frowned. 'Terrible business?'

Louise pursed her lips, waving off my question with a shake of her head. She patted her chignon, though the breeze had failed to dislodge a single strand.

'But Rocamadour *is* persistent, and handy around here, assisting Victor with the heavy jobs. As much as I am against divorce, I must concede that everyone is happier now, with no more constant bickering that used to upset Juliette dreadfully. Though the breakdown wasn't entirely Bruno's fault, Léa often provoked him.'

As the willow trees gyrated in the breeze, cooler today, heralding the change of season, the very idea of a divorce from Emile seemed impossible. But alluring. I watched a hedge of herons gliding toward the dark woods, marvelling at their easy flight. Their complete freedom.

'After Bruno left, I remained living here,' Louise went on. 'It was easier to help run the auberge, and cook for the restaurant.' She smiled down at Juliette, attempting cartwheels on the grassy knoll with Linda. 'And to be close to my granddaughter, *mon petit macaron*.' Belle barked and galloped around them, the puppy licking the girls' faces as they collapsed onto the grass in giggling heaps.

If only I'd had a grandmother who called me 'my little macaron', rather than 'useless, clumsy girl.'

'Is Nelly separated from her husband too?' I asked, thinking of her snail-man boyfriend.

'*Mon Dieu non*, there was never a husband,' Louise said. 'Poor Nelly was the victim of a vicious attack by an unknown number of men. Sadly, a pregnancy ensued, and her parents banished her from their home. She found herself alone with a child, and limited finances.'

'How sad, I didn't know,' I said, a knife-like lance disarming me. Unlike poor Nelly, I had — as Emile constantly reminded me — everything a wife and mother could possibly need to raise her children, *and* be content.

Or so I'd thought. Now I knew that a husband who scorned, bad-mouthed and mocked his wife, wasn't so loving after all. And all those expensive objects were meaningless.

'We never mention the incident of course, it's too upsetting for Nelly,' Louise said. 'The girl is a diligent worker, and a marvellous friend.'

'But running the inn must still be a lot of work for the three of you?'

Louise nodded. 'As you've seen, the auberge is still almost full at this time of year. Guests come for the lake swimming and boating. They visit the medieval *centre-ville*, and stroll around the lake path to the Roman ruins at Romans-sur-Lac.' She waved an elegant hand at the opposite side of the lake. 'The number of guests will dwindle as autumn advances, with only scant bookings until next spring,' Louise went on. 'We do work hard during the high season and welcome the winter respite.'

'So you have only the income from La Cuisine de Louise over the cooler months?' I asked, curious at the notion of women earning their own living.

'Not only,' Louise said. 'As headmaster of the *Ecole Primaire Olympe de Gouges*, Bruno remains an excellent provider. After all, he *is* Juliette's father, and desires only the best for his daughter. We also sell my produce at the weekly market.'

'Is there any chance you'd have a job for me?' I asked. Sitting for too long hurt my ankle, so I stood up and moved around on the crutches. 'I love the auberge and I'd love to work here, or in your restaurant, or selling things at the market. I'd be happy to do *anything*.'

I held my breath, steeling myself for disappointment.

'Oh, I'm certain we can find something agreeable for you, Océane,' Louise said. 'Though we cannot afford to pay much. It would be as for Nelly — basic bed and board covered, and a little extra. And not before that ankle is healed.'

'Oh really? *Merci beaucoup!*' I couldn't mask my excitement.

My own job!

Louise looked up and smiled at a woman trudging along the lake-shore path toward us.

'How marvellous! Blanche has managed to leave her house.' She turned back to me. 'The shock and grief of losing her husband in the plane crash left my friend unable to venture beyond her own front door.'

It was obvious this friend was having trouble walking, clinging as she was, to the arm of a hefty blonde woman wearing a sea-green caftan that billowed in the breeze like sails. Clotilde! My breath caught in my throat.

I could hardly run off on crutches, so I remained beside Louise, head bowed, hoping desperately that Clotilde would have forgotten my face. After all, Bambou and I had only stayed five minutes, and she'd spoken mostly to him. Louise hurried the last steps toward Blanche.

'How proud of you, I am, *mon amie*. Did I not say that ridiculous *agoraphobia* was simply mind over matter?'

'It was touch and go,' Blanche said, her face flushed and smiling. 'But I made it.'

'I'll take care of Blanche now,' Louise snapped at Clotilde. 'You may be excused from your … your *duty*.'

Clotilde squinted at me, still hovering behind Louise, her frown telling me she *had* recognised me. She opened her mouth, surely about to blurt out that I was one of Bambou's many sexual conquests from La Vallée du

Bonheur, and I hoped she caught the tiny shake of my head.

'*Salut*! you must be Océane, the widowed girl who sprained her ankle?' she boomed. 'Yes, news travels fast around Sainte-Marie, so I imagine you already know I'm the village witch, and you're wondering where my hooked and warty nose, black pointy hat and broomstick are?' She let out a great belly cackle. 'Well, if you need any salve for that ankle, I'll be happy to whip up something.'

'Th-thank y-you,' I stuttered, the flush creeping up my throat and settling, hot and guilty, in my cheeks.

Why Clotilde had kept my secret was a mystery, but I exhaled a tight breath, my heartbeat slowing back to normal.

'I doubt we'll be needing your black magic. Océane's ankle is healing nicely,' Louise said as she took Blanche's arm. 'Now let's go inside; the widow circle ladies will be here soon.'

Clotilde winked at Louise. 'And you mustn't keep me from my coven gathering, Loulou.'

'*Humph*,' Louise said with a snort, glaring at Clotilde's ballooning caftan as she flounced back along the pathway.

'I'm so glad you've finally succeeded in getting out, Blanche,' Louise said, as I limped along behind the friends.

Blanche swivelled around to me, as if, in the clutches of her agoraphobia battle, she'd only just noticed I was there.

'Hello, Océane,' she said. 'Your face seems familiar. Haven't I seen you before somewhere?'

I couldn't imagine wherever Blanche might have seen me, unless — since she was Clotilde's neighbour — it was during that brief moment the day of the crash.

'Oh, I don't think so,' I said with a forced laugh. 'People say I have a common face.'

22

Adrienne

'What's that you're making?' Leaning on the crutches, I peered over Dommy's shoulder at her whirring sewing machine.

Léa had introduced me to her sister earlier, when everyone arrived for the widows' circle, and Dommy now sat with Blanche at the dining-room table, cut-out fabric and pinned patterns piled between the two seamstresses.

'Just a few clothes for the orphanage,' Dommy said.

'Those unfortunate children don't have much,' Blanche said.

'And it makes a nice change from the intricate wedding and christening gowns eh, Blanche?' Dommy said with a laugh.

'Everyone in Sainte-Marie, and from surrounding villages, comes to Dommy when they require garments for important occasions,' Louise said, as she fiddled with the dials on her radio, and the lyrics of Edith Piaf's *Non, je ne regrette rien* filled the room. 'And Blanche too, since she's about to become Dommy's *business* partner,' she added proudly, smiling at her friend.

'We don't only sew clothes for orphans,' Louise explained to me. 'We play cards too, and sometimes we have a drink and a bit of a dance and a singalong.'

I limped back to the sofa and slumped down between the two women Louise had introduced as Jeanne and Gisèle. Jeanne was crocheting a child's jumper, while

Gisèle was knitting small socks. Louise had told me these women were in their early sixties — similar ages to her and Blanche — and that they'd lost their husbands to 'drink and Gauloises'.

I took a pair of needles and a ball of pink wool from a basket, and began knitting a little bonnet. Noisette curled up on my lap as I hummed along to *Non, je ne regrette rien*, basking in the warmth of the turn-of-season amber sunlight bathing the room.

'I love how you and Léa have decorated the inn,' I said to Dommy. 'Such a cosy, lived-in feel. A *real* home, rather than a museum.'

Like my flat in Lyon, I almost blurted out, shaking my head at the incongruity of it all — the expensive sofa I kept covered to protect it from Minou's cat hair and teenage sweat and grime, the plastic runners to protect the parquetry floors from their great clomping shoes, those hours spent dusting fragile, never-used vases and bowls. A home, not to feel comfortable in, but to be viewed and admired; a home that Emile saw as a reflection of himself — grand, neat and expensive, which I now saw as stifling, cold and pretentious.

I inhaled the delicious scent of stewing lamb, mushrooms, onions, thyme and rosemary wafting from the kitchen, where Nelly was preparing the guests' evening meal, under Louise's instructions. Nelly was back from an outing with her snail man, but Léa was still out on a picnic with the gendarme.

I pictured them sitting together on a blanket in a quiet lake-side spot, away from the families and tourists who stayed near the auberge's grassy bank and swimming and boating spots. A stab of regret pierced my heart as I yearned to share a picnic with a man I actually enjoyed being with.

'Well, Louise,' Dommy said, 'as much as I love your circle meetings, I mightn't be able to come much over winter. I've got *so* many commissions. Thank goodness I'll soon have the highly talented Blanche helping me out.'

Blanche blushed and kept her gaze on the fabric she fed beneath the needle.

'Don't be silly, I'm not *that* good.'

'Why do women always demean themselves?' Louise said, shaking her head.

'Because that's how we're brought up,' I said. 'And if we don't belittle ourselves, our husbands do it for us.' For an awkward moment, silence fell across the room. Even the click of needles stopped.

'You're obviously an excellent seamstress, Blanche,' I said, changing the subject, and nodding at the pile of pinafore dresses she'd put together so quickly. 'I wish I was good at something.'

'I'm sure you have *some* talents, Océane,' Jeanne said

I shook my head. 'No, none. I used to think I was a good wife, but Emile kept saying …'

I clamped my lips, cursing my stupidity for letting slip my — very much alive! — husband's name. That newspaper article bore not only my photo, but his name. So far, nobody had connected me to the vanished wife of Dr Emile Chevalier, but if I kept opening my mouth, they soon would.

'I'm sure you were an *excellent* wife,' Louise said. 'It must have been difficult, living in constant fear of your husband's demise.'

'Louise told us how you became a widow, and ended up here,' Blanche said, against the click of knitting needles and crochet hooks, and the whirr of machines. The others nodded and smiled at me. 'We're all sorry for you, but I'm happy to have the chance to meet you, though your face really *does* look familiar.'

The guilty flush heated my cheeks again, like I was hopping over smouldering kindling that was about to erupt into flames.

Should I go now, before someone does *recognise me, and they discover the truth?*

But now I'd found this lovely auberge, and the promise of a job, I didn't want to leave. I was so enjoying the women's easy banter, sweet Linda and Juliette, and the animals. I admired Victor's quiet presence too, feeling wanted and useful as he went about his jobs without a fuss. I didn't even mind Louise's bossiness.

I adored this new, alien notion of belonging, and it was becoming harder and harder to keep lying to these friendly people, when all I yearned to do was spill everything and ask their advice.

But I couldn't risk it. The older ones — Louise, Blanche, Jeanne, and Gisèle — would surely tell me to swallow my pride, acknowledge that leaving my husband was selfish, and go back to him. They'd say that a wife never abandons her marriage; that even a bad marriage is better than no marriage at all.

'I'm not a widow,' Dommy said to me, as if she'd read my mind. 'Though I sometimes feel like one. My husband is the village pharmacist. Paul's job keeps him busy, then he goes off fishing most weekends ... he has one of those fishing shacks over across the lake. My daughter spends a lot of time here at the auberge, and while it's healthier for Linda to be playing outside rather than cooped up inside our flat above the chemist shop, it means I'm often alone with only my sewing for company. That's why I come to Louise's widows' circle ... for the company.'

In that moment, I finally understood loneliness. *Before the Supermarket*, I'd been lonely, but now I wasn't. Leaving behind my high-school friends when I married Emile, I'd concentrated so hard on trying to be the best wife and mother, there had never seemed time for many friends. Then later, with Emile so busy at work, and the twins becoming engrossed in their teenage lives, loneliness had become my companion.

'Oh, that looks delicious,' I said, as Nelly came in with a tray, and served out slices of cake.

'My Paris-Brest — almond-studded choux pastry with nutty praline crème mousseline,' Louise said. 'I made two; this one and another for the guests' dessert tonight.'

As Nelly poured the tea, I almost groaned in ecstasy as the mousseline melted on my tongue.

'How does it feel that you'll soon be an important *businesswoman*, Blanche?' Nelly said.

'Good, but strange.' Blanche cupped a palm over her heart. 'I've never worked before. Most husbands of my generation find it deeply shameful to admit their wife needs to work.'

Not only of your generation!

'A wife who takes a job outside her home is stealing a job from a man who needs it to support his family,' Emile would claim.

I was no longer sure that was true, but I did understand Blanche's dilemma. I'd found myself — no, *put* myself — in the exact same position. Certain I didn't want to end up like Blanche in thirty years, I looked forward even more to the job Louise had offered me.

23
Adrienne

Pleased with my shopping morning, I got off the bus on la place de la Fontaine, and sat at an outside Chez Dédé table. Centrally located, the bar was Sainte-Marie's source of gossip and zing. Despite the ugly interior décor — stuffed animal kills mounted on dark-wood walls — whole families flocked here after Sunday Mass for a catch-up. They perched on rickety chairs, around scuffed tables whose four feet never touched the ground simultaneously, women and children in a different section from the men.

But today, as was usual for mid-week, the only patrons of Chez Dédé, inside and out, were old men drinking, playing cards and smoking Gauloises, most of them dressed in the traditional *bleus*. I ignored their curious stares and raised eyebrows, obviously wondering what business a woman had at their bar.

Seven days after arriving at L'Auberge de Léa, my ankle was almost healed, and I'd taken a bus into Lyon earlier this morning, alighting in a different suburb from my flat. Running into Emile was unlikely, but still I'd been nervous, checking over my shoulder, as I sold a few of the gold coins.

When I'd spent the Carrefour grocery money, I'd used the gold money to buy toiletries — including a real toothbrush to replace that twig-thing from La Vallée du Bonheur — bras, knickers, socks and slips, I used the extra money to buy two cardigans, two shirts, a pair of those fashionable bell-bottom jeans, a coat, and shoes too, since it was getting chilly for the raggedy leather sandals.

Never had I been able to buy things for myself so easily. While Emile had always insisted I look my best for his work events, it was he who decided what dresses I bought, and how much I spent.

'Purchase only what is essential,' he always said. 'Though I'm certain my wife would never waste my hard-earned money, would she?'

Before I caught another bus home — for that's how I'd come to think of Sainte-Marie-du-Lac — I'd been tempted to turn up at the boarding school and demand to see my children, even knowing that was forbidden.

Six days I'd waited for word of them. Several times I'd itched to phone the school again, but was afraid of pestering that nice secretary — that's if I got the same one, rather than the first hoity-toity woman.

To lift my wilting spirits, I'd purchased some extras Emile would not have considered essential: fancy chocolate, several copies of *Cosmopolitan* magazine, a bottle of Chanel No. 5 and a pack of scented candles.

To the croon of pigeons pecking the ground for crumbs, I flicked through a copy of *Cosmopolitan*, sipping my coffee and dipping in squares of the creamy chocolate.

The summer swelter had vanished, and an early-autumn breeze drifted across the cobblestones. I tilted my head skyward, letting the lavender, thyme and rosemary-soaked breeze play across my face, bringing with it snippets of conversation as villagers chatted as they crossed the square between the bakery, chemist's, butcher's and post office.

I looked across at the bronze soldier statue, memorial to those villagers who'd perished in the two world wars. There was a list of martyrs too — brave citizens who'd fought and died for *La Résistance* against the Nazi occupation of France.

The coffee and chocolate finished, I headed away from la place de la Fontaine, my steps almost skipping. The guilt over leaving my husband still occasionally nagged at me, but the longer I stayed here, the easier it was to ignore those shards of remorse.

I was aware that it wasn't quite real though; that I was here under lies and false pretences. I'd always been a false person, eager to live up to what everybody, especially Emile, expected of me. How my husband wanted me to behave, and to *be*.

But as I glanced up at the imposing Saint Julien's bronze church bell chiming out the hour, I sensed that, right from *After the Supermarket*, a bell — invisible but tolling — had been guiding me back to Sainte-Marie-du-Lac for the chance to make this new life become real.

~

Since I was supposedly almost penniless, I whisked my shopping up to the attic as soon as I got back to the inn, Beau scampering up the stairs behind me. The ground-floor guest room was now occupied by a paying guest, and I no longer needed crutches, so I'd moved up to the attic yesterday.

The roof sloped down sharply on each side, so I could only stand upright in the middle, but the little attic had a wonderful, cosy feel. Amidst the old-fashioned, faded and peeling floral wallpaper, I felt I'd returned to a different era.

Through the tiny dormer window, I admired the majestic mountain and lake view and sank down onto the narrow bed. Beau whimpered and pawed at the bed.

'Come on then, but don't tell anyone I let you on the bed.'

The puppy bounced around like a wind-up toy, sniffing my shoulder bag. I moved it away from him, glancing around for a good hiding spot for MV's leather pouch.

As Beau finally settled for a nap, a rustling sound echoed across the ancient floorboards. Had I imagined it? No, there it was again — a faint but definite swish. Like the brush of a long skirt as its owner crossed the old parquetry.

Not that I'd believed a word of Juliette and Linda's talk, the whispering ghost lady immediately came to mind, and a chill scrambled down my spine. Another rustle, and floorboards creaking, one after the other. The skirt owner was walking toward me! My heart fluttered wildly, like some caged bird.

Ghosts? Really, Adrienne, you are ridiculous.

I hugged my goose-bumped arms around myself. The rustling stopped, as if the skirt-owner had simply popped in to let me know she was here. And to say hello. Or, I was simply chilly and imagining sounds. After all, the season had turned, with cooler evenings, and almost frosty mornings.

The attic had no wardrobe or dresser, but a wide rectangular space, cut into one wall, was lined with slightly bowed shelves. The same ancient floral paper as on the walls covered each shelf, much of it peeling away.

As I placed my new clothes, and the ones Léa had given me, on the shelves, I noticed that a spot in the corner of the bottom shelf looked thicker and bulkier than the rest of the shelving. I knelt down and slid a fingernail beneath a wad of wallpaper layers.

As I prised it away, I saw that what I'd thought were several paper layers was a niche, a bit shallower than the depth of a shoebox.

The perfect spot to stash a pouch of gold coins.

But as I removed the last paper layers, something else — what looked like a little notebook — already sat in the groove. The dust and its spine sewn with rough brown yarn told me it had been here a long time.

I plucked the notebook out, blew off the dust, and sat back on the bed. I shoved MV's pouch under the pillow — until I could find a better place — and gently opened the first, fragile page.

On the left-hand side, '*le journal de Suzanne*' was written in fountain-pen ink, and I recalled the girls' chatter.

... grandfather clock belonged to Victor's maman and papa, Suzanne and Jules Rossignol ... lived in this house during the Great War.

Suzanne Rossignol, Victor's mother and, no doubt, the ghost lady in the swishing skirt.

People have always written in journals, but why had Suzanne concealed hers in this groove? Obviously afraid of someone finding it.

... friendly, but frightened.

Léa and her family would surely find the journal when they renovated the attic, but I should let them know immediately, about such a valuable heirloom.

A cloud shifted, blocking the sun. The wind strengthened. A chill snaked through the cracked-open dormer window, cooling the nape of my neck, as I imagined Suzanne Rossignol up here over fifty years ago, the Great War raging across Europe. A chair scraped as she hunched over a rustic wooden desk, and I caught a whiff of burning candle as she wrote by the shadowy circle of candlelight.

I shifted my gaze to the right-hand page and Suzanne's first entry.

August 1914

I'm so excited — excited and nervous! Jules asked me to marry him, actually went down on one knee amidst the dusty sweet scent of the hay bales.

Jules Rossignol has been my friend since childhood, my only sweetheart, and I can hardly believe my gentle, mild-mannered fiancé is being mobilised, to fight a war on some far-flung battlefield. And all because a place nobody has heard of — Austria-Hungary — declared war on Serbia, another unheard-of place. And in full summer, right in the midst of our busy harvest!

Despite Jules already being in military service, I can't help wondering if he must go to war. Though I know the answer. All the wives and mothers of Sainte-Marie know, and we are all afraid.

Since the hated Germans declared war on us, all our men are to fight for France. Thankfully, though, the villagers are saying it will be over quickly — by Christmas at the latest — and my dear Jules will soon be with me again.

Jules says it may be tricky exchanging letters during a war, so I've decided to write all my thoughts in this journal, something I can show him when he's back home. My sweet husband will know then, how much I missed him.

The next week.

We are married! I am deliriously happy to be Madame Jules Rossignol. Many quick weddings, like ours, are happening in Sainte-Marie-du-Lac.

And, after we made tender love for the first time, I am hopeful that, by the time Jules comes home I'll know I'm carrying our child. A tiny miracle we made together.

The other day, a strange phenomenon happened in the sky. The moon covered up the sun and turned day into darkness. The villagers say it's an omen, a bleak premonition about this war, but I refuse to believe them. It must be over by Christmas.

As I closed the journal and took it downstairs to show Louise and Léa, Suzanne's words echoed my own excitement when I discovered I was pregnant.

'I already love you both,' I'd said, stroking the mound, unable to stop staring in the mirror at my swelling belly.

But that was a long time ago, when I'd been so vital to them; those years I'd been completely deluded about being a mother and a wife.

24
Adrienne

Five days later, and still no word from the twins, Louise told me she would be opening La Cuisine de Louise in two days, for the autumn season.

'And since your ankle is healed, Océane, you may begin work waiting tables and clearing away.'

My heart soared. Louise Bellefontaine wasn't an outwardly emotional person, but I couldn't stop myself from grabbing her in a hug.

'*Merci, merci!* You'll see, I won't disappoint you.'

'As I explained,' she said, backing away from me, 'the restaurant is open for the midday meal only, so for the rest of the day you'll be free to help with other auberge work, or do whatever you choose.' She wiped floury hands down her apron, and fiddled with the radio dial until the Jimi Hendrix song, *Castles Made of Sand*, came on.

'Maybe we could find you a boyfriend for your *free* time?' Léa said with a wink, from where she was chopping vegetables alongside Nelly. She nudged her friend, both of them giggling like teenagers, and I turned away to mask the guilty blush burning my cheeks.

'Well, since my ankle is better,' I said, keen to avoid the subject of boyfriends, and men in general, 'I think I'll stroll around the lake and see this Madonna statue.'

Unlike Blanche and Louise, who continually crossed themselves and discussed Père Châtaigne's sermons, I wasn't religious, but I was curious about this mysterious shrine.

'A superb idea.' Louise clapped her hands together as the Jimi Hendrix song ended and a newsreader's voice chimed in.

'... *song in memorial of American music legend, Jimi Hendrix, who died two days ago, September 18th, at the age of twenty-seven, reportedly from an overdose of sleeping pills ...*'

'Oh no, that's so sad,' Nelly said.

'How unhappy he must've been,' Léa said.

Many people at La Vallée du Bonheur would be grieving for Jimi Hendrix, and a stab of sadness pierced my heart for them. For Jimi Hendrix himself. And for all the lonely and sad people in the world.

From the doorway, a woman's voice cut into my melancholy.

'*Coucou*, Louise, I've come for my eggs and cheese.'

During the twelve days I'd been at the auberge, I'd witnessed several women coming to buy produce, and thought no more about her as she filled her basket. As Louise slipped the francs into her apron pocket, the woman threw me a curious stare.

'*Bonjour*, madame,' I said with a nod.

'*Bonjour* ... Océane, isn't it? I'm Marie Larue. I heard we had a newcomer in our village, and a new member of Louise's widows' circle.' She frowned at me. 'But that's strange, I'm *sure* I saw you the other day, in Lyon ... I'm known for *never* forgetting a face.'

I was silent for a moment, my heart fluttering, wondering if she'd seen me shopping, or selling stolen Napoléons.

'Oh y-yes, I was d-doing some sh-shopping,' I stuttered, turning away to mask the flush that bloomed in my cheeks.

As Louise accompanied her back across the courtyard, the Larue woman kept glancing over her shoulder at me, and frowning. But my angst was diverted when a tall, thin fellow about my age swaggered across the cobbles. With his long straggly hair worn in a loose ponytail, baggy trousers and a rumpled tie-dyed shirt, he looked like he belonged at La Vallée du Bonheur.

'I've come with your order, Madame Bellefontaine,' he said, and Louise introduced him to me as Thierry Marnier, her snail man for La Cuisine de Louise.

Nelly skittered outside, beaming. She kissed Thierry on the lips, took his hand and led him, and his snails, into the kitchen.

Banishing that village woman's suspicious looks from my mind, I crossed the cobblestoned courtyard, glancing up at the cheeky oak tree jay imitating Fifi the pheasant's *'eep, eep'* noise.

I set off along the path toward the Madonna, a breeze rippling the lake water into tufts off which the sun sparkled a lemony gold. The willow trees swayed like synchronised ballet dancers to an orchestra of wind and birdsong echoing across the water in a random harmony. A heron standing on coat-hanger legs in the reeds turned its face to me, then looked away as if saying, 'I never saw you.'

Even after almost two weeks here, this magnificent view still enchanted me — the snow cloaking the golden-haloed alps beyond, and the quiet, dense woods bordering the other side of the path. In this otherwise perfect landscape, I simply ignored that gaping dent of the plane crash.

Since my ankle had healed so quickly, it hadn't been such a bad sprain after all, but what a drama I'd made of it. I was embarrassed about the fuss they'd all made over me; how they'd made me feel like a princess recovering from some terrible injury.

I arrived at a fork where a smaller track led off deeper into the woods, and a twinge forced me to sit on a rock. I rubbed my ankle, and heard the yelp of a puppy and children's voices — Juliette and Linda, and Sonia and Elise Larue — and I recalled the girls' plans to play after school in the treehouse Juliette's father had built for them.

Drawn to the happy little voices, I turned down the narrow track, even though I sensed their joyful play would make me feel even more miserable about my own children.

In that pyramidal structure of boughs — built on the ground, rather than high in a tree — the girls were having a tea party, feeding treats to Belle and Beau, obviously their 'children'.

'Stop making so much noise,' Linda said, wagging a finger at the puppy. 'Or there'll be no biscuits for you.'

'Yes, you're giving us a headache, Beau,' Juliette chided.

Not wanting to disturb this lovely moment, I remained out of sight, imagining I was watching my own nine-year-old Antoine and Martine playing. Despondent, and my ankle still aching, I no longer felt like visiting the famous statue, and I shuffled back through the already-dying autumn leaves.

As I reached the inn, I spied Nelly and Thierry at the pergola table, sipping drinks from tall glasses — Louise's lemonade most likely. Theirry had thrown an arm casually across Nelly's shoulder, and they gazed lovingly at each other.

Seated on the opposite bench, Léa and the gendarme, Yves Rocamadour, were literally rubbing shoulders as they too, sipped lemonade. As they chatted and flirted, laughing at something one of them said, I envied the couples' easy banter and their love, for which I'd have exchanged the entire wealth of our Lyon apartment. If only I'd known, years ago, that all those objects weren't the answer to happiness.

Apart from right at the beginning, and those special moments here at lac du Héron before the twins were born, I couldn't recall ever truly enjoying Emile's company, like Nelly and Léa adored being with their boyfriends. And these past years, even my husband's mere presence had become a trial.

Loath to intrude on the love birds, I cut back along one side of the house, and slunk in via the back door.

~

The puppy followed me, leapt up onto the bed, and nosed at my shoulder bag, which I shoved beneath the pillow.

'No, Beau, leave it alone, though I bet that leather is *loaded* with enticing smells.'

Resting my ankle on a cushion, Beau curled up beside me, I thumbed through a copy of *Cosmopolitan*. I bet those beautiful models, Veruschka, Pattie Boyd, Peggy Moffitt and Twiggy never had to cope with the everyday grind. I couldn't imagine them tramping through the heat to Carrefour for groceries, or trying to please a demanding husband, or housecleaning and cooking without ever getting the slightest acknowledgement. How fabulous their lives sounded. Like my new life.

Why then didn't this new life seem so wonderful? In a short time, I'd found myself a happy and contented life. Even a job! Soon, I'd have a comfortable routine, a niche in the daily running of the auberge. So why were tears coursing down my cheeks? Why was my heart so heavy, my throat so tight?

Well, apart from still not being able to contact my children, I wasn't entirely carefree, like those *Cosmopolitan* models. The worry of my old life being discovered by these kind people, or Emile finding me and forcing me to return to that old life, hung around me like some starving, malevolent dog. The hungry dog never gave up — a constant reminder that all this was simply a fairytale that would, like most fairytales, come to a nasty end.

Disillusioned, I flung aside the magazine and plucked Suzanne's journal from its niche, eager to discover more about my ghostly friend.

When I'd showed the journal, and its hidden niche, to Louise and Léa, they'd both agreed — for once! — that the precious object should remain where I'd found it, until they could decide what to do with it.

'After all,' Louise said, 'it's been safe enough in the attic all these years.'

Technically, the journal was Victor's property, but both Louise and Léa doubted he'd understand its real value and be able to take proper care of it.

November 1914

During Mass this morning, the priest led us in prayer for our absent men, and for the poor souls who are forever gone. I prayed hard for you, my sweet Jules, as we all prayed for the safety of our husbands, sons, and fathers. Even Saint Julien's church itself prayed — the nave arching gracefully upward was, to me, like hands held together in prayer. The stained-glass windows glittered with colour, so welcome on these grey and foggy November days.

After Mass, I spent several hours at the bar with the other women, knitting socks for our brave soldiers, the children dashing about fashioning bayonets, rifles, and trenches out of anything they could find. We've developed a kinship, a closeness we didn't have before. As if, in the absence of our menfolk, the village has become our family.

We heard of the Germans' attack on Belgium, and that, with the British troops, our French army is trying to stop those despicable Huns, who are advancing to Ypres like fire-spitting dragons. I find it hard to believe they are killing innocent civilians standing in bread queues. That's not war, it's murder, and they are monsters!

We are all terrified that if the Germans get to Ypres, they'll cross the border and conquer us. Surely that can't be true.

We still remain hopeful the war will be over by Christmas — that right will win out over the might of the German war machine — but some are saying it won't be over by then, and I won't have you home for Yuletide, my dear Jules. How sad that makes me.

Despite my misery and my longing for you (and for a letter), I have exciting news. I'm certain that I am carrying our child. I'm well, though I was ill for the first weeks, and wished you were here to give me a hug and a cup of ginger tea. The nausea made it hard to get all the autumn work done, but every day I forced myself to get out the cart and harness up Daphne. And I'm thankful our sweet horse was too old to be taken off as a war horse, like most of them.

Anyway, the season's work is done. I've filled rows and rows of jars with vegetables — our tomatoes, peas and beans did well this season. And you'll return home to our cellar brimming with potatoes, turnips, apples and pears, and cherries and plums stewed in syrup or dried. It was a lot of work without you to joke around with Jules, though it did distract me from missing you.

The next day.

A letter from Jules has arrived, dated not long after he left Sainte-Marie. Never mind, old news is better than no news. I'm so excited my hands are shaking and I can barely open it, my heart melting at the sight of his familiar handwriting. At first, I skim his words, assuring myself he's alive and uninjured.

… no need to worry, sweet Suzanne … trenches now safer, deeper and better defended by steel, concrete and barbed wire than ever before … dug far below the earth's surface out of reach of the heaviest artillery.

… corporal took us up to the front line, pointed out the Hun trenches … no man's land … peeked into the periscope hoping to see one … not silly enough to stick his head up for me to shoot at … shared a cup of coffee and some chocolate and chatted about when we'll go over the top … can't wait to mow down those Huns.

Several days later, Jules' second letter arrives.

… we're the same colour as the mud … ha, ha, what better camouflage! Gilles looks like some clay creature with stars for eyes. My best friend has become everything to me, Suzanne, closer than the closest brother, and every time we go over the top and into another trench, all I search for is his twinkling stars.

I replaced Suzanne's journal in its groove as I caught the sound of Blanche's voice downstairs — sharp and agitated — as she spoke to Louise. I couldn't make out her words, but a foreboding sensation rose from the hollow of my belly, as if it could be linked to that other Madame Larue seeing me in Lyon.

25

Blanche

'My sister-in-law just told me she saw Océane in Lyon, selling gold coins!' Blanche frowned from where she sat at the auberge kitchen table, inhaling the heavy aroma of garlic, parsley and butter sauce. 'Could they be *my* Napoléons? That went missing the day Roger —'

'But how would Océane have come by your father's pouch?' Louise said. 'She wasn't even in Sainte-Marie when it went astray. No, no, it's likely a coincidence. Many people still favour gold over cash, and perhaps Océane simply has her own, and is not making that public knowledge, for fear of theft, or any other reason. Besides, in good Christian faith, we must accord Océane the benefit of the doubt.'

'You're probably right, as usual,' Blanche said, with a sigh. 'After all, well, they can't be my coins because Roger …'

Despite the shame and embarrassment, Blanche could no longer keep Roger's vile deed from her friend. Besides, as Clotilde said, what did it matter? Roger was dead and gone and — she hoped — rotting in Hell. She crossed herself for that godless thought and took a deep breath.

'Roger stole my gold,' Blanche blurted out, angry tears stinging her eyes. 'Took it to pay for that weekend jaunt with his secretary, though I still don't understand why he took *all* of it. Anyway, I don't care about him going off with that tramp, Brigitte, but I can't stop worrying about what became of the pouch.'

Her words rushed out in a jumble, like when Major Rocamadour had come to announce her husband's death. If she stopped now, she wouldn't have the courage to keep going. 'The only explanations are that the pouch is lost somewhere, forever, or it fell from the plane before the explosion, and someone found it, and *kept* it.'

'So maybe it's lying in the woods?' Louise said. 'Or in the lake, or somewhere else near the crash site? Did you telephone the Gendarmerie? Perhaps someone handed it in?'

'No, it wasn't handed in, so I'll likely never know what happened to it,' Blanche said with a sob. 'Although losing the gold is a financial blow, that pouch was my only remaining possession of papa's.'

'I'm so sorry, I know how you treasured it,' Louise said, patting Blanche's arm. 'Don't lose hope, it *may* turn up.' She poured two cups of tea and pushed one toward her friend.

'Before now,' Blanche said, after a sip of the tea. 'I'd never been brave enough to talk about my marriage ... how I accepted Roger's womanising.' She drew in a long breath. 'I couldn't have left him, couldn't bear the thought of living on my own, or being gossiped about. And, of course, divorce was always out of the question for us Catholics.' She glanced heavenward, making the sign of the cross again.

'This Brigitte wasn't the first, was she?' Louise said.

'So, you *did* know, you *and* Clotilde,' Blanche said, with a smile. 'Why am I not surprised? After all, Louise Bellefontaine knows about *everything* in Sainte-Marie.'

As she finished her tea, Blanche acknowledged that Clotilde had been right — the more she opened up about Roger, the more that heavy burden of secrecy lifted.

For all those years, Blanche had wanted to kick Roger out of her house. But, fearful of the village talk, she hadn't dared. Now she realised that the longer Roger putrefied in the church graveyard, the less she was worried what people thought, or said, of her. No longer having to fear enduring gossip was another burden off her shoulders, because nobody would speak badly about a widow. Widowhood was a humbling, revered kind of status, as if you'd done your bit for the war effort and, finally, you'd been demobilised.

26
Adrienne

Two days after the widows' circle, I started my first job, at La Cuisine de Louise. While Louise bustled about the kitchen finishing the *coq au vin*, Nelly, Léa and I cleaned the restaurant, and set the tables with white linen cloths and napkins, and polished silver cutlery.

Opening day was so busy, I didn't have a moment to fret about doing anything wrong. I was also thankful there was only *coq au vin* on the menu, and a small choice of *entrée* and dessert, which made it easier not to muck up orders.

'Don't forget to refill the water carafes,' Nelly said, she and Léa staying close, guiding me.

'You're doing great,' Léa kept encouraging me.

'More bread for that table, Océane,' Nelly said.

'Sorry, Mademoiselle, I dropped my fork —'

'I'll get you a clean one, monsieur,' I said with a smile.

I relaxed more as I served steaming plates of *coq au vin*, swanning across the polished parquetry floor, beneath those grand ceiling beams, amidst the old-fashioned sconce wall lights, and the watercolour paintings depicting local scenes.

'You did really well, Océane,' Léa said, once the last customers left, and we cleared away.

'You're a natural,' Nelly said with a smile as she swept the floor.

Even Louise beamed and said, 'Excellent work, Océane.'

As I washed crockery and cutlery, I almost laughed at the incongruity of my changed circumstances. How different this old-world charm, beauty, and elegant food was from the simple La Vallée du Bonheur campfire meals. And how different again, from my plush kitchen in Emile's flat. What a rainbow of changes, since that day *Before the Supermarket.*

If only I could see the twins; if only that starving dog shadow would leap off my shoulder and skitter away, this new, husband-less life would be perfect.

~

That evening we joined the auberge guests for dinner, savouring the succulent *coq au vin* leftovers. Afterwards, when the guests drifted away to their rooms, I bid everyone good night.

Nelly went off to her little cottage beside Victor's. Juliette, Louise and Léa trooped up to their bedrooms on the first floor, the older dog, Belle, following Juliette.

I trudged up to the attic, reached into the shelf groove, lifted out Suzanne's journal, and sank onto the bed. Beau settled beside me and I stroked the dog, soaking up the peace and solitude of my little room, the only noise coming from a moth fluttering around the bedside light.

'Don't you feel so close to the stars, Beau?' I stared through the dormer window into the inky blackness. One star twinkled brighter, as if winking at me, and Suzanne's long skirt rustled as she glided across the floorboards.

Another swish, and the boards beside the bed creaked, as if Suzanne was close to me. I closed my eyes and imagined her hand smoothing the high-waisted skirt over her pregnant belly. A mother getting in touch with her unborn child.

My nerves twitched as I sensed a presence — more comforting than frightening — beside me, as if she'd sat on the bed.

'How are you, Suzanne, not too sick?' I said, as if we were chatting now, rather than across six decades.

'A little nauseated,' she said. 'Chewing on ginger helps, but how are *you*?'

'Very happy to be a working woman, even though I never thought I wanted to work, all those years I was being Emile's housewife.'

I propped a pillow behind my back and opened Suzanne's journal to her next entry.

February 1915

Christmas came and went. The war is not over, and my beloved Jules is still far away. I try to stay hopeful, but at our knitting gatherings (our fingers are red and sore from knitting so many socks!) all we hear are horrifying stories of the trenches, and our soldiers staring, bayonets fixed and rigid, then racing forward, and falling like wheat beneath the scythe.

The next week.

Another letter from Jules ... Dieu merci, he's still alive! My heartbeat is skipping, though as I skim his words, it's obvious my dear husband's morale is low.

... mean, nipping, rain stinging like a wasp ... shells flying like that rain ... rifles hammering out bullets ... screams and moans and tearful cries ... Mummy! Mutti! Maman!

... trench stinks worse than a foul toilet ... I'm freezing ... uniforms more suited to a desert than these bitterly cold, sodden fields but so hot ... can barely breathe

... too scared to move. Go over the top and the Hun kills me, stay here and my own kill me.

Like me, all the women are working hard on the land, in shops and factories, doing what the men did before the war. At the same time, we must care for children and keep house, so, as eager as I am to meet our baby, I'm glad our little one is still inside me, safe and warm.

Several families have received the dreaded telegram — the Larue family have lost two cousins, and a son, Gilles — Jules' boyhood friend. Poor Jules must be devastated. I wish I could comfort him. If his hand could feel his baby kicking in my belly, I know he'd feel better.

Sudden terrors have begun to grip me. My heart clenches with fear and the blood rushes through my veins. I used to imagine that special people like Jules, and Gilles Larue, would be safe. But now I know that this ravenous war beast swallows whoever it wants. And there is no satisfying it.

Thankfully, it's winter and there aren't too many chores, as being with child does slow me down, but the midwife says our baby is growing well. He or she will come into the world (though what kind of world I wonder!) in spring.

The next week.

Another letter has arrived, and I am now sick with worry about Jules' morale, as he tells me about his lost friend.

... Gilles and me mending wire in no man's land, and heard that familiar crack. 'Gas!' I fixed on my mask, but Gilles was all shaky, trying not to let the cutters slip from his sweaty hands into the mud, and get his mask on at the same time. I smelt it, sickly, sweet, knew he had thirty seconds at most. The gas billowed in. I tried to pull up his mask for him, but Gilles fell into the mud, breathing in

that deadly gas. He rolled over in agony, and I couldn't help shouting at him not to leave me. But he did, Suzanne. My friend drowned in the mud, in the froth of his own blood.

I hate myself. I could've saved Gilles, if only I'd helped get his mask on more quickly.

My poor, sweet Jules. The more I hear of this war, the more I despair, the more helpless I feel. I'm becoming too afraid to sleep, my dreams filled with rat-infested, mud-filled trenches and barbed wire, bombs falling like gigantic raindrops, flying bullets and mulched up bodies. And Jules, standing amongst it all, in a blackened uniform, staring, but not seeing.

But all I can do, as I go about my daily chores, and sit by the fire at night with only my needlepoint for company, is pray and hope. And take comfort in the child growing within me.

'Poor Suzanne, what a terrible time to live through.' I closed her journal. 'I have children too, but you probably know that. Don't ghosts know everything?'

Careful not to disturb the sleeping puppy, I placed her journal back into its niche. 'And I can't help wondering — worrying! — that my children might be needing me. For what, though? They haven't needed me for some time now, but what if they *have*, and I haven't been there for them?'

Beau wriggled his warm little body closer.

'Do you think Antoine and Martine remembered those back-to-school dental and doctor's appointments I'd made before I …?'

Don't be silly, Adrienne, not a chance! I couldn't depend on them to recall anything, and Emile certainly wouldn't remember a single thing concerning the twins.

Had they even been home to the flat before starting their new school year?

A jabbing pain through my chest startled me, the nostalgia of my lost children cleaving my heart as painfully as one of those soldiers' bayonets.

I was exhausted, but my mind whirred too fast for sleep — fragmented thoughts of doing my best at the restaurant job, of worrying that I should try to find the owner of those gold coins, and whether that other Madame Larue did catch me selling them. All of that, and the overwhelming sadness for my children.

What if that nice school secretary never managed to get my message to them? In a last, desperate bid, I scrabbled around the attic for paper and a pen.

My dearest Martine and Antoine,

In case your father, or the school, didn't mention that I've been trying so hard to get in touch with you, here I am trying again.

Even though your father knows I'm alive and well, I wanted you to hear it from me.

I imagine you're wondering why I didn't return home that day in June? Well, I didn't know at first, but now I do have some idea and perhaps, if I'd known before, I could have tried to fix things.

I yearned to tell them that their father would never have listened to me. And if I'd complained about anything, I was terrified Emile would have certified me – – like one of his patients — as insane. It's in your blood, he'd said, and if you're cursed, there's nothing you can do about it, besides eventually be whisked away to some terrible asylum. But I didn't write a word of this, cautious not to say anything against their father. Their ally.

> *Anyway, I never planned to leave, but the notion must have been simmering for a long time and one day it just happened.*
>
> *I'm staying at this lovely inn where the people appreciate me. I have a job too.*
>
> *That said, I certainly haven't forgotten about you two — never could I forget about my twins — and it doesn't mean I no longer love you, because I will ALWAYS love you.*
>
> *I know it must be difficult, but I hope you can understand a little, and forgive me?*

Beau had woken, and was dragging MV's leather pouch from beneath my pillow.

'No, Beau, give it back.' I eased the pouch from the dog's mouth, clutched it in my lap as I took up my pen again, tempted to ask the twins if they missed me, or if they'd completely forgotten about their mother and were simply getting on with their lives.

> *I hope you're both enjoying your last year at high school, before you go out into the big working world.*
>
> *I'll include my phone number and address below, just in case the secretary didn't let you know.*
>
> *All my love forever,*
>
> *Maman.*

My eyelids drooped. I'd post the letter tomorrow. I turned off the light, snuggled into my cosy bed, curling an arm around Beau, and huddling into his soft warmth.

Sleep was my escape; a place I could ignore the terrifying thought that I *was* tarnished with the same crazy brush as my mother. And that perhaps my children really should be kept away from me.

~

The following morning, after Juliette skipped off to school and the guests drove away with cheery waves and promises to return to L'Auberge de Léa, I helped Nelly and Léa clean and make up their rooms.

On Louise's instructions, I fetched the basket filled with broccoli, carrots, and potatoes that Victor had gathered from the garden. I washed and cut the vegetables as Louise made a batch of goat's cheese, and Léa and Nelly peeled the apples Victor had brought from the orchard for apple stews, chutney and jam.

The four of us sang along to The Rolling Stones' *Honky Tonk Women* blaring from Louise's radio.

The jobs done, there was just enough time before La Cuisine de Louise opened, to hurry up to the *centre-ville* and posted the twins' letter.

On the way back down, as I passed Clotilde's home, she straightened up from her herbal patch.

'*Coucou*, Océane!' Her booming voice scared a bird off into screechy flight. 'I'm pleased to see that ankle is healed.'

'*Merci*, Clotilde, only the occasional twinge.'

'Feel free to pop in for a cup of tea,' she said, lumbering toward me, the blonde, grey-streaked hair hanging wild around her face. Clotilde wore her usual loose, flouncy caftan, colourful paste jewellery, scarlet lipstick, and thick eyeliner that extended from each lid into dramatic wings. 'And a chat if you ever need to get anything off your chest.'

'I know you recognised me from the day of the crash, when I came with Bambou,' I said. 'Thank you for keeping my secret. I wouldn't want everyone knowing about … about La Vallée du Bonheur.'

'Don't you fret, *chérie*,' Clotilde said with a wide smile. 'I'm the best secret keeper in Sainte-Marie.'

I smiled to myself, thinking Clotilde was possibly the *only* secret keeper in this village.

Obviously a trustworthy confidante, Clotilde could perhaps make sense of the dark cloud dogging my mind. I was tempted to blurt out my whole sorry story to her, but I didn't say anything because I needed to work this out myself. It was time Adrienne Chevalier — Océane – – made her own, responsible and logical decisions.

27

Blanche

'I've found your father's pouch of gold coins,' Louise said, the second Blanche answered her trilling phone.

Blanche's heart skipped beats, her fingers tightening into a claw around the receiver.

'Where?'

'Beau was playing with it,' Louise said. 'But don't worry, the puppy hasn't chewed it up, like the fate of so many of our socks.'

'So it must've been at the auberge?' Blanche said. 'Did Océane have it all this time?' She caught Louise's sharp breath and sensed her friend's hesitation.

'Beau was dragging it down the stairs ... from the attic.'

'So it *was* Océane. She *did* find it after the crash. But why did she hang onto it? The nerve of her ... the cheek!' Blanche inhaled a sharp breath, hot with the rising rage. 'I'm coming over this minute, not only to retrieve my papa's leather bag, but to confront that girl.'

'But how could Océane have known the pouch belonged to you?' Louise said.

'Well, I suppose she couldn't,' Blanche said, though the blood still boiled in her veins. 'But she should've handed it over to the gendarmes, like any *honest* person ... not like the common thief that she is!'

'Océane's out, up in the village,' Louise said.

'But you'll ask her to leave the auberge right now, won't you, Louise? To go quietly, without a fuss?'

'Calm yourself, Blanche. Let's see what Océane has to say first,' Louise said.

'I'm still coming over right now,' Blanche said. 'I'll wait for the girl with you.'

28
Adrienne

When I got back to the inn, Blanche was in the kitchen, looking furious, as if the steam hissing from Louise's pressure cooker might pour from her ears. Then I saw it — MV's leather pouch sitting on the bench.

So my suspicions had been right. The pouch had belonged to one of those plane passengers and, by the look on Blanche's face, it had likely been her husband.

'I can explain.' My voice shook as I glanced nervously from Blanche to Louise, wishing that hissing vapour would suck me deep into that enormous pressure cooker. 'I found it near the crash site, but I didn't know it belonged to your husband.'

'You know my husband died in that crash, so surely you must've had an idea it belonged to him? Anyway, it wasn't Roger's, it's *mine*,' Blanche snapped. 'Inherited from my dear papa ... Michel Vidal. *MV*,' she emphasised, as if I hadn't understood. 'Why didn't you hand it in to the Gendarmerie?' She shook her fist at me, and I reeled backwards, out of reach of her angry spittle. 'Besides, that dog had it in his mouth, he could've destroyed it!'

'I'm so sorry, truly I had no idea who it belonged —' I started, but Blanche cut me off again.

'You not only held onto my valuable possession without telling anyone, but you've been *selling* my gold.'

Blanche's red face contorted, her voice quaking. 'How *could* you? After Louise was kind enough to take you in when you were widowed and injured ... to give you a roof over your head *and* a job.'

'I barely had any money, Blanche, before I found those coins, but as soon as I start earning, I promise I'll repay —'

'Enough of your feeble excuses, I can't bear to hear another word from you.' Blanche swiped the pouch from the bench, and stomped from the kitchen. 'And I hope that the next time I come here,' she said, throwing me a black glare, 'you will be long gone.'

'I'll repay you every franc ... somehow, eventually,' I pleaded, scampering across the courtyard after her. 'I'm *really* sorry.'

Blanche held up a hand in a dismissing wave, refusing to look around at me.

'Best if you leave Blanche be for a while,' Louise said. 'Let her calm down.'

'No, no! I feel so terrible about this,' I said, hurrying after her. 'I have to try and get her to understand and forgive me.'

29

Blanche

Blanche hurried home, clasping her papa's pouch against her heaving chest, the rage settling in her rigid shoulder muscles. The panic — that pesky agoraphobia — had risen its ugly head again. With every step, her chest tightened so much she feared it would explode, and her heart thumped as fast as a runaway train.

Océane followed her along the lake-front path with a trail of pathetic sorries and excuses and, as much as Blanche yearned to yell at her again, she focussed on simply getting home, closing the door on the outside world, and collapsing onto her sofa with a calming brew.

The pain flaring in her arthritic knee, the panic threatening to overwhelm her, Blanche was about to stumble through her front door when she noticed that straggly, unwashed hippie, Bambou, strolling from Clotilde's house toward his Combi van parked out the front.

'Océane!' he called, smiling at the girl, who veered toward him. And from the way they kissed, it was obvious the two knew each other *very* well.

Blanche paused on her doorstep, ears burning. Intrigued, her heart still thwacking against her chest, she scurried inside, watching and listening from behind her cracked-open door.

'I saw your van,' Océane said, 'and guessed you'd come to Clotilde's for supplies.'

'How cool to see you,' Bambou said. 'I was so sad when you left La Vallée du Bonheur without even an *au revoir*.'

Océane was at La Vallée du Bonheur!

Blanche pressed a palm over her mouth to muffle her gasp.

'At first, I didn't realise you were upset because you saw me with Jasmin and Fleur,' Bambou went on. 'I thought you knew none of us was sworn to the one sexual partner.'

Sexual partner? Blanche almost fainted, her fingertips gripping the doorframe holding her upright.

'Oh I quickly worked that out,' Océane said. 'But I'd already fallen a little in love with you, Bambou, and didn't want to share you. But I'd never even heard of sex in groups, let alone *seen* it … I was shocked.'

The more Blanche understood what she was hearing, the more horrified she became. She had to keep that hand across her lips to stop herself from shouting her disgust at them.

'I'm so sorry I drove you away,' Bambou said, taking Océane's hands.

'It's all right, I'm fine now. I've been staying at L'Auberge de Léa … such a lovely inn.'

'Ah yes, you did mention that lac du Héron held a special place in your heart.'

'It did,' Océane said. 'But now … well, something's happened. It was my fault, and I don't think I can stay here any longer.'

'Why not come back to La Vallée du Bonheur? You know everyone's welcome, whatever's happened.' Bambou touched a long, earth-stained finger to her cheek. 'No one would ever have questioned you about your past,' he went on, 'but when I picked you up back in

June, you were in such a state, I did wonder what had happened, and figured you were running from *something*.'

His finger trailed down Océane's shoulder. 'I never asked you, because it wasn't my business, but the next day I heard on the radio about the wife of a psychiatrist who'd vanished. A woman who matched your description, named Adrienne Chevalier.'

'And I'd told you my real name … before I became Océane,' she said. 'Well, even though I probably can't stay here, I'm not sure about La Vallée du Bonheur. But I *definitely* can't go home to my husband, I could never go back to my life *Before the Supermarket*.'

Blanche inhaled a sharp breath.

Husband? So this Océane — Adrienne — is married. And she committed adultery. She's even more abominable than I thought!

Blanche couldn't stop frowning, trying to recall why this Adrienne Chevalier was so familiar. Then she remembered. She'd seen her at Clotilde's, with the scruffy Bambou, the day of the plane crash. Only a glimpse, but it was definitely her. So, she'd lied about her name too.

Blanche itched to storm back outside and confront Océane about 'Adrienne Chevalier', but she closed her front door, and leaned against it, swallowing down the foul acidy taste, and trying to calm her racing pulse.

Once she got her breath back, she shuffled into her kitchen, placed the leather pouch on her own bench, and made herself that calming brew.

As Blanche sat on her sofa, sipping the tea, a thought struck her. If news about a disappearing woman had been on the radio, it would surely have appeared in the newspaper. Gulping down her tea so quickly it burned her throat, Blanche lurched upright, and rifled through the stack of newspapers she stored in an old trunk beside the hearth for winter kindling.

Bambou mentioned picking her up in June.

It took Blanche no time to find the story about Madame Adrienne Chevalier, wife of psychiatrist, Dr Emile Chevalier — and mother of twins! — who vanished from a Carrefour supermarket.

Groaning with the pain shooting through her knee when she heaved herself upright, Blanche limped over to the telephone and dialled the number of L'Auberge de Léa.

~

'She's not only a thief, but a liar too!' Blanche cried, as soon as Louise picked up the receiver. 'Her name's not Océane. It's Adrienne Chevalier, and she's no widow. She's married with *twins*.'

'And who, pray, is Adrienne Chevalier?' Louise asked.

'You don't recall that housewife who vanished from Carrefour back in June? Left behind a trolley full of groceries?'

'No, should I?' Louise said.

'Well, no, there was only the one newspaper story about her disappearance. Since she was never mentioned again, I — everyone I guess — assumed she'd been found, or returned home of her own will. But she didn't go home.' Barely stopping for breath, Blanche told Louise everything she'd heard.

'Don't you recall she let slip her husband's name, Emile, at the widows' circle?' Blanche went on. 'I *knew* I'd seen her before. She came to Clotilde's with that La Vallée du Bonheur hippie who looks like your snail man — that I-don't-care, unwashed look.' She took a shuddery breath. 'And I have a good mind to find this Dr Emile Chevalier. It can't be that hard to locate a well-known psychiatrist in Lyon. And I'll tell him *exactly* where his wife disappeared to and what she got up to. *And* where she is now.' Another sharp breath. 'She tricked and cheated us,

Louise, with her tragic widow story, lying her way into our lives, stealing and then *selling* my gold. How dare she take us for idiots!'

'I understand your outrage,' Louise said, 'but you must calm yourself and think this through properly, or you'll give yourself a coronary.'

'Calm myself? You must be joking!'

'We are not aware of the state of her home life,' Louise said. 'One thing I have learned from years of widows' circle experience is that many women do not have ideal marriages, but are reluctant to speak of such things. Might I remind you of your tardy admissions about Roger? I'd have thought that you, Blanche, of all people, might understand that husbands are not always what they appear to outsiders, *non*?'

Blanche hesitated. 'Well, maybe, but —'

'There are two sides to every story,' Louise cut in. 'Perhaps, Océane, er, Adrienne was *forced* to flee her husband? Let's not jump to conclusions and see what she says first.'

30

Adrienne

'I hope you'll consider coming back to La Vallée du Bonheur,' Bambou said, as the Combi sputtered to life.

'I'll think about it,' I said, waving him off as the van rumbled away. I rubbed my arms, the skin still tingling from Bambou's caress. It seemed an age since I'd felt human touch and the scene with Blanche had left me so distraught and miserable that I'd been tempted to jump in the van and go back to La Vallée du Bonheur.

But returning with Bambou would be going backwards, and since making the break from Emile, I wanted only to move forward.

Besides, I only had half an hour to try and resolve things with Blanche before my restaurant shift. I strode up to her door and knocked. No answer, but I knew she was inside; I'd glimpsed her scurrying through her gate when Bambou was leaving Clotilde's.

'Please Blanche, talk to me.'

'Stop your pathetic begging, *Adrienne*.' Blanche's shaky voice came from inside. 'I overhead everything, and I refuse to listen to another word from the most self-centred and disgusting woman I've ever met. Don't you think we *all* get fed up with our husbands? But we don't *all* slink away and behave like unmarried *sluts*.'

Her hurtful accusations cut deep. 'Just give me a chance to explain what living with my husband was like, Blanche.'

'Go away, *tramp*, and don't ever bother me again.'

'Okay, I'll leave, but know that I'm so sorry. If I'd known the gold coins belonged to you, I'd have given them back straight away.'

When Blanche didn't reply, I turned and trudged back to the inn, wondering how I was going to manage to smile and be chirpy through the restaurant shift.

~

Nobody mentioned the leather pouch, or Adrienne Chevalier, over lunchtime. Louise mustn't have said anything to Léa and Nelly, and I was grateful for her professionalism, not disrupting work with personal issues. But from her sideways glances, I sensed she'd seek me out later.

Exhausted from the scene with Blanche and the waitressing, once we closed up that afternoon, I headed up to my attic haven.

'I've made of a terrible mess of everything,' I said, slumping on the bed and opening Suzanne's journal. 'And I have no idea what to do about it.'

But once I read about my ghostly friend's troubles, I felt ashamed for complaining about my own insignificant problems.

December 1915

After Jules' terrible news about his poor friend, Gilles Larue, I heard nothing from him until today, ten months later. But with all my work and a baby to care for, I haven't had a moment before now to write in my journal.

I did write to Jules about the birth of his son, Victor, in May, but he never answered, and I fear Gilles' death has badly affected him.

But, thank Dieu, my Jules is alive! Though, reading his words, I sense that my husband's mind has gone. Surely it's only temporary — the grief of losing his good friend in this terrible war? Once Jules is home, he'll recover. He simply needs time.

… fighting not only the army of Huns, but armies of rats … red-eyed and evil-looking like the Germans. They ooze from the mud, fat and sluggish from feeding on the meat left hooked in the barbed wire coils — bits of men who, only moments before, I smoked and drank coffee and joked with. But don't worry, Suzanne, I'm used to this, and I'm fine.

All that tells me is my dear Jules is far from fine; that he's simply sparing me the gory details I'm hearing, more and more, as we continue knitting socks and scarves, up in the village: stories of the severed limbs and sliced-off faces of men scattered across the mud, of their innards hanging from their uniforms like obscene medals.

I write back to Jules with mundane details of everyday life — how the naked trees shiver in the cold, clinging to their dying leaves as if to let go would mean defeat. And how the fog rises over the hills in the purple glow of morning, muffling ordinary noises into distant echoes. I tell him about the swifts screaming high in the sky, darting like arrows, gone when autumn came, before the swallows and the house martins.

I tell Jules all of this, rather than about the strange ways and look of Victor, our eight-month-old boy who is so different from the other village children. And I don't say Victor is slower than them, or that he doesn't smile or coo at me, or that my mind keeps returning, warily, to Victor's birth, and the midwife's unease about the cord around his neck.

Besides, I'm sure our darling boy will be fine, and that Jules will love Victor, however he is.

Two months later.

On a bleak morning in 1916, a telegraph boy knocked on our door.

My heart stopped. This is it, I told myself as I stared at the telegraph boy, smart in his uniform, his bicycle propped against the wall.

I waited till he left to open the telegram. Then I closed the front door, one shaking hand holding the envelope, the other clamped over my thundering heart.

High heels clunking on the stairs jarred me from Suzanne's words, and I looked up to Louise standing in the attic doorway. Immaculately dressed as always, with a touch of face powder, the ash-blonde chignon neat and unyielding at the nape of her neck, she stared at me, arms folded across her chest.

'Can we speak for a moment, Océane? Or should I say, Adrienne?'

~

I looked down at the quilted bedspread. 'You know everything?'

Louise nodded, explaining how Blanche had overheard my conversation with Bambou.

'I'm so sorry, Louise. I'd have eventually confessed that I'm not a widow, but I was afraid you'd ask me to leave the auberge if you knew I'd abandoned my husband.' I fiddled with the quilt, bunching it into my fist, then letting it go. 'I love it here, and … and I have nowhere else to go.' I grasped the quilt again. '*Mon Dieu*, Blanche must think I'm the worst person on earth.'

'I'm afraid she is quite vexed with you,' Louise said. 'And I thought it best to warn you that she's threatened to contact your husband and inform him of, well, of everything that's happened since you left your home. I, however, maintain that we should hear your side of the story first —'

'Contact *Emile*? No, she can't do that! Please, you *must* talk Blanche out of it.' I swiped away the tears that had sprung to my eyes. 'You don't know what living with Emile was like, and if he finds out where I am, he'll march in here and order me home.'

Louise stepped into the tiny attic room, unfolded her arms, and sat on the end of the bed.

'Tell me, then. Help me understand, Adrienne.'

I took a shaky breath. 'I had everything — healthy children, a wealthy and handsome husband, and a beautiful home filled with expensive things. But now I've realised all those objects aren't important; that people, love and affection are worth much more.'

I tried to explain Emile's mind games, the constant ridicule and criticism, as well as the twins' scorn. 'When I disappeared, not one of them could describe me properly to the authorities — my height, eye or hair colour. That's how much notice my family took of me.' I released the scrunched wad of quilt.

'But I never planned to leave them. Like I'd never have kept that leather pouch if I'd known it was Blanche's. I shouldn't have sold those gold coins, but —'

Louise held up a hand. 'Let's forget the Napoléons for now. You know I am a practising Catholic who believes in honouring one's wedding vows, however, seeing my son happy with his girlfriend, and Léa content with Yves Rocamadour, I have accepted that sometimes we make poor choices, and that nowadays, divorce can rectify those poor choices. But could you not have discussed your husband's poor attitude with him before things got so out of hand?'

'Emile would never discuss anything. His stupid wife is barely worth *talking* to.' I shook my head. '*Before the Supermarket*, I had no idea his behaviour was so bad. Though I suppose, since I *did* leave, I must have suspected that something wasn't right. But I assumed all marriages were like that … that the way he treated me was completely normal.'

I gripped the bunched-up bedspread again. 'At La Vallée du Bonheur, I saw people could be happy; that everyday life didn't have to be a struggle. It could be fun even! My life was never *fun* — not with Emile, and certainly not as a child.' I inhaled deeply.

'Then, here at the auberge, all of you were so friendly and kind straightaway. It's been so … so *blissful*.'

'I understand, and I sympathise,' Louise said. 'However, I believe that now you have understood all of this, you must contact your husband — if Blanche has not already done so — and attempt to talk with him. And there are your children to consider.'

'My children no longer need me. In fact, they despise me nowadays.' I took a trembly breath.

'You may believe your twins no longer need you, Océ — Adrienne, but children always need their mother, though in different ways. And you cannot flee this situation forever. You and your husband must resolve the issues, one way or another.' She gave me a quick smile, which surprised me, and patted my arm.

'Right, I'll leave you to try and speak about things with your husband, and after that, we'll deal with the problem of Blanche's gold coins. If you care to discuss anything further, I shall be in the kitchen.'

Her heels click-clacked back downstairs and I stared into the silence. Right from the moment I met Louise Bellefontaine, she'd struck me as a bit bossy and overbearing. But now I knew that underneath that firm, cool exterior lurked a kind-hearted woman. Not to mention a superb chef.

My heart still beat fast though, with the fear that Louise would throw me out of the inn, or Emile would come here and demand I return home. I glanced around the attic, perhaps for the last time. How I would miss this cosy sanctuary.

'Besides losing my first job, I'll be so sad to lose my new friends, especially you, Suzanne.'

How terribly lonely I would be once again. And, for a moment, I wished I was religious, so I could pray to, or beg, Louise's God that Blanche did not find Emile.

31
Adrienne

The following morning, I woke in an unsettled kind of limbo, as if some great tornado was brewing, about to sweep in and snatch the attic off the top of the inn. And me with it.

Last night at dinner, Léa and Nelly hadn't acted any differently toward me, so Louise must still not have mentioned Adrienne Chevalier. Not yet.

I peered through the attic window at the raw, bleak weather, mist dancing across the Monts du Lyonnais, fine rain puckering the lake water. Most of the leaves were turning scarlet, gold or mustard and dead ones shrouded the lakeshore.

I smiled and waved at Léa and Belle, on their way back from walking Juliette to school. Apparently, the little girl was no longer allowed to walk to school on her own since the terrible event everyone refuses to talk about.

But the smile quickly dropped from my lips as a car emerged from the mist, and pulled up outside the auberge. Emile's Citroën. My heart stopped, then galloped out of control. So, Blanche had found my husband, and he hadn't wasted a moment — the next morning! — coming for me.

'*Merde et merde,*' I cursed as Emile stepped outside, adjusting his stylish suede fedora lower across his brow.

What to do? Run again?

The only place to run was back to La Vallée du Bonheur, and Blanche would tell Emile that's where I'd most likely gone. Besides, at this point, as Emile strode toward the door, the puppy yapping at his heels, Belle's guarded gaze following the approaching stranger, there was no avoiding my husband.

'I have nothing to apologise for, Suzanne,' I said, as if spelling it out to my ghostly friend would convince me. 'He's been mistreating me for years. I'd had enough and left him, simple as that.'

And perhaps Louise was right. Emile and I needed to resolve this situation, so best I got it over with. Even so, I descended those two flights of stairs as if I were Queen Marie Antoinette on her way to *Madame La Guillotine*. Or 'the widow', as some had nicknamed the device.

Along the ground-floor hallway, on the tail of a heavenly pumpkin soup aroma, I caught whispers from the kitchen. They'd all seen the Citroën, and Louise, assuming — rightly — that Blanche had found Emile, must be telling Léa and Nelly who Océane was.

I didn't want Emile to come inside. L'Auberge de Léa was my sanctuary, so I opened the door before he had a chance to knock.

I stepped outside, meeting Emile's gaze, the chill wind slicing straight through me, tiny, cold raindrops piercing my cheeks.

'So that woman who phoned was telling the truth,' Emile said. 'You *are* here.' As always, his voice was calm, but Belle let out a quiet growl, sensing the brewing undercurrent of tension.

'Yes, you've found me, Emile, but I'm not coming home.' I tried to mask the tremble that shook my body. 'And all I want is your permission to see my children.'

'Antoine and Martine don't want to speak to you, Adrienne. They're confused. We all are. None of us understand why you left. And now you're telling me you don't even *want* to come home?' Emile shook his head. 'I don't understand. You can't deny that I've given you everything a wife could wish for?'

'No, I can't deny that but, as I already told you, possessions don't make for a loving marriage, and I refuse to accept your behaviour —'

'After those first few days,' Emile cut in, as if I hadn't spoken, 'when the authorities and the boarding school assured me that my wife had not met with foul play, I was so relieved.' With a small smile, he placed a palm over his heart. 'And I truly thought you'd come home of your own accord. Once you got this silly idea out of your head, you'd come to your senses. You'd come back to where you belong.'

Belle growled, the puppy yapping and dashing around Emile in mad circles, and I sensed them all watching and listening behind the cracked-open steamy kitchen window.

Emile seemed then, to notice my changed appearance — the slimmer silhouette, the longer, ungroomed hair, the loose, floral-patterned shirt beneath my cardigan.

'So, you finally lost that Michelin tyre then,' he said, reaching out and placing a gloved hand on my waist. Rather than being pleased for me, Emile seemed disappointed that I'd managed, without his help, to look like I'd wanted to for so long. I pulled away, and Belle crept closer.

Emile threw the dogs a nervous glance. 'Are those hounds dangerous?'

'They can be,' I said, 'if they dislike someone.'

'Can't you tie them up?'

I shrugged, making no move to tie them up. 'I slimmed down at La Vallée du Bonheur. I'm guessing

Blanche Larue told you that's where I ended up — a place where nobody feels alone or taken for granted.'

Emile took a step closer, fixed me with a frosty glare, though his voice remained calm. 'Oh yes, the Larue woman told me everything. I can certainly imagine it is *lovely*, fucking every man in sight.'

'No, Emile! It wasn't like —'

'And I'm surprised you're still wearing *that*.' He pointed to my wedding ring, his mouth arching into a pout.

'That's not how it was,' I said, obviously not mentioning that I'd removed my ring at La Vallée du Bonheur. I hugged my arms around myself, but the wind gusts snarled straight through the thin cardigan.

'You do know that adultery is a crime, don't you?' Emile said, voice turning as icy as the wind, 'and I could have you imprisoned?'

I did know this, though I'd never heard of anyone actually being gaoled for adultery. Probably just another of Emile's threats to frighten me.

'Why not ask me for a divorce, Emile? Since I'm a lowlife adulteress, wouldn't that be the best —'

'When that Larue woman told me everything,' Emile cut in again, 'I decided I'd overlook your adulterous behaviour. No point ruining our family with the stigma of divorce, is there? Besides, I don't want a divorce, I simply want you to forget this ridiculous carry on and come home, and we'll get on with things.' He waved an arm, Rolex watch flashing from beneath his coat sleeve. 'So go and get your things, I'll wait for you in the car.'

'I don't *have* to come back.'

'Not technically,' Emile said, 'but morally you do, because that's where you belong.' His face crumpled, as if he might actually cry. 'Come on, *ma chérie*, I need you.'

I almost felt sorry for him, but Suzanne's ghostly voice spurred me on and I swallowed hard.

'I don't belong to you, Emile, and I have a new life now, and a job.' I wasn't sure that would be the case for much longer, but it suited me to say so.

'But they won't want you here,' Emile said, as if, as usual, he'd read my thoughts. 'Now they know you lied, said I was *dead,* and that you abandoned your husband and children to become some hippie *slut*. Oh and apparently, you're a thief too … some story about gold I couldn't understand, the Larue woman was blabbering so.'

'Whatever happens here at the inn, I'm still not coming back to you.' I hunched over, shivering out of control, my body numb against the biting wind.

Emile's eyes narrowed, a vein in his temple twitching like a throbbing insect trapped beneath his skin — the only sign of the anger raging beneath his unruffled surface.

'You're telling me you're leaving me and our children *forever?*'

'Our children aren't even at home any longer. As you keep reminding me, Antoine and Martine are almost adults and can manage very well without their mother. But how *are* they, Emile? And why are you still refusing to let me speak to them?'

'Because your actions show me you are insane, Adrienne. I've always feared this might happen, after your mother. You need help, *chérie*, and I can get you the right treatment.' He touched my arm and, once more, I pulled away. 'How remiss of me not to realise my wife was in need of psychiatric therapy. After all, I am one of Lyon's best psychiatrists.'

'I don't need therapy,' I said through chattering teeth. 'I just want you to leave me alone, and to see my children.'

'I doubt Antoine and Martine will *ever* want to see you again,' Emile said, 'after you abandoned us like that.'

'I did not *abandon* ...' I sighed. What was the point of trying to make him see my side?

He lurched at me and kissed my lips. Not a caring kiss, but a mark of possession, and I stumbled backwards, almost tripping over the quivering Belle.

'Your real problem, Adrienne, is that you don't know how good you've got it. You never had to work because I handed you everything on a silver platter.'

'You never *allowed* me to work. You wanted me to stay home and run the perfect household ... to be the perfect wife.'

Emile shook his head and all I could do was stare at him, more dismayed, frustrated and confused than ever. I imagined him telling his mother.

Right from the start I told you that girl would be trouble — with a mother like that — so get rid of the whore right now and find someone else. Plenty of women would give their right arm for you, Emile.

'I still want a divorce, and I still won't come home to you.'

'Oh yes, you will, Adrienne. In fact, you'll come right now. Enough of your silliness.' He grabbed my arm and shook it. 'Now stop fussing, I'm a busy doctor, with patients waiting to see me.'

A sharp voice cut through the mist.

'*Monsieur*, release your wife this minute. And please leave the auberge grounds immediately. On your own.' A fierce-looking Louise jabbed her wooden spoon at Emile.

'Or we'll call the gendarmes,' Léa said, she and Nelly hovering behind Louise.

'Who do you think you are, barging in here, uninvited, and harassing this woman?' Louise said.

'Because this woman is my *wife*,' Emile said, through clenched teeth, obviously struggling to keep his temper. He studied that circle of dark glares and must have felt defeated, because he turned away.

We all stood there, huddled in a tight arc, watching him march back to his Citroën and fling open the door.

'You'll regret this, Adrienne. You won't get away with it, and you haven't heard the last from me.'

Against Belle's volley of barks, the Citroën roared off into the mist, tyres spinning in his angry wake.

~

Now he was gone, I let the tears flow as Nelly and Léa led me back into the warmth and comfort of the auberge.

'I'll brew some tea,' Nelly said.

Louise almost pushed me down onto the sofa.

'Such an *unpleasant* man,' she said, with a *tut-tut* tongue click.

'*Unpleasant?*' Léa scoffed. 'More like a pompous, manipulating bully. I completely understand why you left him. Louise told us everything about Adrienne Chevalier.'

'It must've been hard,' Nelly said, placing the tray of cups and teapot on the coffee table, 'leaving the comfort of financial stability, with no idea what was ahead of you.'

'I've learned that wealth doesn't buy happiness,' I said, with a sniff, as Nelly poured the tea. 'Though it *can* buy you a lot of misery.' I stroked Noisette as she curled up on my lap.

'I left with only a small amount of grocery money,' I said. 'And I know it's no excuse, but that's why I held onto Blanche's gold. But I'll pay her back every last franc, if only she'll give me another chance.'

'Well, she *did* blabber your whereabouts to your husband,' Léa said. 'So I'd say Blanche Larue has got her revenge.'

'Blanche is a reasonable woman,' Louise said. 'Once she understands the truth about your husband, she'll calm down.'

I sipped the hot, sweet tea. 'I've never seen Emile mad like that. He's always so calm. People said how lucky I was to have such a calm, good-looking and rich husband.'

'But he considers you his *possession*,' Léa said, 'who is now refusing to be possessed.'

'Which would anger any bully,' Nelly said.

'Even though my ex-husband certainly wasn't a bully,' Léa said, 'Bruno was never keen on me being financially independent. He's more suited to Francine, who'd happily give up her job if Bruno asked her to be a stay-at-home housewife.' She glanced at her mother-in-law. 'While Yves is supportive of my auberge business.' She sipped her tea and gave a little shrug. 'Bruno and I were a terrible match, right from the beginning. Maybe like you and Emile?'

I nodded. 'If only I'd understood from the start that life with Emile was miserable, I might've avoided that awful Carrefour scene, and everything else that's happened since. Not that I regret coming to L'Auberge de Léa. This is the best thing that's ever happened to me.' I finished my tea. 'Though what if Emile's right, and I *have* inherited my mother's madness? Only a crazy woman would abandon such a comfortable life, right?'

'Don't be ridiculous,' Louise said, standing up and straightening her apron. 'You're as sane as the rest of us, Adrienne. Right, I must finish preparing the restaurant meal.'

~

As I bustled around La Cuisine de Louise that lunchtime, I realised that speaking face-to-face with Emile after such a long time, and after so much had happened, had left me shaken. But I also felt strangely elated — a glorious sense of new-found freedom, like a prisoner who's done her time, and is standing outside the gates. I was proud too, that I'd stood my ground and not caved in to Emile, as I would have done *Before the Supermarket*.

I did worry though, what Emile might do next, to try and win me back. Because my husband could not bear to lose.

32
Adrienne

Five days after Emile's unsettling visit, before I left my warm bed on that grey and drizzly morning, I took a moment to return to Suzanne's story. Tentatively, I opened her journal to the next entry, fearing that telegram boy had brought the tragic news so many dreaded during the Great War.

Summer 1916

My cheek is still red and smarting. Jules never hit me before the war, but now it seems I only have to say one word and he slaps me. I'm more afraid of him every day. I don't understand why he hates me, and the whole world. What has this war done to my soft and gentle Jules?

He's been home several months, which was the reason for the telegram: being sent home as he's no longer capable of combat. The field hospital could do nothing for Jules, so they sent him home. Not a physical injury — no lost limbs or legs full of shrapnel — but something they call war neurosis, though I have never heard of this névrose de guerre!

For so long, I feared I'd never see him again, that he was dead and rotting in some stinking trench. Only last week five Sainte-Marie homes closed their shutters because the family soldier — or soldiers — had been sacrificed for the cause. So I was excited about his homecoming, convinced that with my love and care, and playing with Victor, we'd surely beat this war neurosis.

But the moment I saw Jules, I sensed he was no longer the man I'd waved off almost two years ago. Still, I threw my arms around him and kissed him and welcomed him home. He jerked away, as if I were a stranger, frowned at Victor and said: 'What's wrong with that boy?'

Now he mostly glares at me or stares at nothing, walks around dazed, or slumps in a chair, jabbing his pipe and yelling at imaginary people. He won't even look at Victor, as if it was our poor boy's fault the cord got stuck around his neck. And that is what saddens me the most.

He's constantly exhausted, even though I cook hearty meals he loves ... mutton stews and apple pies. He's silent for hours, then speaks a few — mostly nonsense — words, in a stammery whisper. Then he gets nervy and finds any reason to beat me cruelly.

He can't — or won't — work, so rather than his homecoming easing my life, I struggle even more to milk the cows, muck out the barn straw, feed the animals and tend the kitchen garden. And care for our home, and Victor.

I want to know everything that happened in those trenches, but at the same time I don't, fearing it was so awful that he refuses to speak about it, keeping it locked inside his dark mind, for the next nightmare.

I yearn for the days we shared everything, but I sense they're gone forever, and I can't help asking myself: do I really want Jules home like this?

This morning, I put Victor on a blanket on the grass to kick in the sun while I threaded the washing through the mangle, then pegged it on the line. Jules sat on the ground, not looking at Victor, but watching me, though his vacant stare told me he wasn't seeing anything.

Why don't you play with your son? I suggested, taking the wooden clothes prop and pushing the forked end tight against the line.

Not my son, Jules mumbled, ignoring me straining to lift up the heavy wet washing.

You could help me then! I tried not to yell my frustration at him as I pushed the prop hard into the ground to secure it.

Propping is my job, he said. What was the point of me coming home if you're doing it?

He stared up at the washing flapping and cracking in the wind, squeezed his eyes shut and started up a horrible wailing.

The Hun ... c-coming for us. The Hun ... k-kill the Hun before they k-kill us ... t-trapped in the b-b-barbed wire.

And, as he rolled around on the ground, hands covering his eyes, panting to catch his breath, I saw that the fluttering washing — skirts and shifts, pillowcases and sheets, bloomers, breeches and socks — must, to Jules, resemble fragments of men and uniforms caught on barbed wire. The same images that wake him in a cold sweat from a nightmare, stammering so much he can't even tell me what it was about.

He staggered to his feet, glaring at Victor, a foot raised to kick our son. No, don't hurt my boy! So, instead, Jules kicked me in the shins and punched my face.

Stop your screaming, bitch! Don't you think I've heard enough screaming?

That was in the beginning. When I tried so hard. Before I gave up. The war has broken him and, locked as he is, inside that unbending mind, my dear Jules will never recover.

Though what is really wrong? Some villagers say there's nothing wrong, Jules is simply a coward, and I should think myself lucky he's home at all. They have even shunned me from the knitting circle.

But something is so terribly wrong.

~

Bitterly sorry for poor Suzanne, I replaced her journal in its niche, as a movement outside made me glance through the dormer window.

A van had pulled up in front of the inn. Not like Bambou's Combi, more a vehicle I imagined would transport prisoners to gaol. Thinking it was a delivery van, I hurried downstairs to the kitchen's enticing smell of freshly brewed coffee.

I squinted through the rain pelting the kitchen window, as two burly men dressed in white uniforms leapt out of the van. An uneasy feeling spread through me as the hefty men looked around them, as if wondering whether they were at the right place.

My unease peaked into full-blown dread as Emile's Citroën parked behind the van, and my husband stepped out and nodded at the — obviously familiar! — men.

'*Merde,* Emile again!' My voice shook.

Juliette was already at school. Nelly and Léa were scrubbing and peeling the potatoes Victor had plucked from their earthy beds and Louise had instructed me to slice the cleaned potatoes for her *gratin dauphinois*. But the breath snagged in my throat and I couldn't do a single thing.

'Whoever are those unpleasant-looking men?' Louise set aside her goat's cheese and wiped her milky hands on a cloth. 'And whatever is your husband doing back here, Adrienne?'

'Why are they wearing white uniforms?' Léa asked

'Well, whoever they are,' Nelly said, 'I wouldn't want to get on the wrong side of them.'

Petrified, I remained wordless, with an urgent desire to flee. I reeled backwards, into a corner of the kitchen.

'They've come to take me away!' I cried. 'Like when they took Maman to the asylum.'

Even as I knew it was ridiculous to think I could get away from Emile and these men, I cowered in the corner. But they were already pounding on the door. I sank onto my haunches, tugging the edges of my cardigan across my chest, my breaths fast and ragged.

'Don't be silly, Adrienne,' Louise said, striding toward the door. 'People cannot be committed without a very good reason.'

'Why can't they knock normally?' Léa said with a scowl. 'Instead of banging?'

'The nerve of them,' Nelly said, 'trying to scare us.'

'*Bonjour, mesdames*, Dr Chevalier here, please open the door immediately.' Emile's voice held that usual self-confident, commanding tone. 'Adrienne, I know you're in there, no point trying to run off *again*.'

Terrified, my body shaking, I didn't move, as Louise went to open the door.

'Who do you think you are?' she began, 'forcing your way —'

But they pushed past Louise, and the three of them were in the kitchen, looming over me.

'Ah, there you are, my love,' Emile said with a smile. 'Why are you cowering like a frightened child? Surely you're not afraid of your own husband? Up you get now, so these nurses can help you out to the van. We're taking you to a doctor who can help you.'

'D-doctor? W-where?' I stammered. 'N-no, I don't w-want to go with you. I d-don't need any h-help.'

'I'm afraid, *ma petite chérie*, you have no choice.' He took my hand, and at first, I thought it was a tender gesture. This was another of Emile's jokes that only he found funny, and soon he'd collapse into laughter, and ask me why, once again, I couldn't understand his humour. But it was no tender gesture; my husband was counting my pulse rate.

'As I suspected,' he said with a concerned frown. 'Your pulse is beating too fast and too strong. That's unhealthy. Now come along, Adrienne, no fuss, we'll take you to a place where you'll receive proper treatment.'

'Tre-treatment f-for *what*?' I stammered as the nurses grabbed my arms and dragged me upright and into the hallway. One of them had silvery-grey, slicked-back hair, and his cold steel-grey eyes penetrated right to my core. The other one didn't look at me.

'No, I won't go!' I screamed, trying to pull away. 'How can you do this to me, Emile? Your wife, the mother of your children?'

'Wife? Mother?' Emile raised his eyebrows as if truly perplexed. 'You've been neither of those lately, have you?'

'Release Adrienne this minute,' Louise said. 'What right have you to do this?'

They only held me tighter. Fingertips digging into my flesh, I already felt bruises flowering.

'Oh, but I have every right, madame,' Emile said calmly. 'Every right to commit my wife to treat her insanity. So, I would advise you to stop interfering and allow us to leave quietly.'

'No, please don't take me away,' I yelled. 'I'm not mad … I'm not … I'm not!'

'Commit Adrienne for *insanity*?' Louise barked. 'But there's nothing insane about your wife's mind.'

'Well, madame, can you give me one *sane* reason why a woman turns her back on her family and the best apartment in Lyon?' Emile said. 'Why a *sane* woman leaves a full shopping trolley in a supermarket, and wafts off to some hippie camp? And why, when her husband finally finds her — worried sick out of his mind — that *sane* woman refuses to return to her home?'

'Adrienne may not have acted entirely rationally, but she had her reasons, and she is quite sane,' Louise said. 'And I find it hard to believe you can simply haul a person away and lock them up.'

'I never mentioned *locking her up*, madame,' Emile said, his voice still frustratingly calm. 'I simply want to commit Adrienne for a short time, to see a doctor and get the right treatment. She'll be far better off at L'Hôpital Sainte-Dymphna.'

'You're taking me to Sainte-Dymphna's? Where my mother *died*?' I could hardly believe it. Any second, I'd wake from this nightmare.

'Your mother's death was simply an unfortunate accident,' Emile said.

'Sainte-Dymphna's is an *asylum*,' Louise said, making the sign of the cross. 'How could you do this to your wife, Dr Chevalier?'

'Believe me, madame, this is the hardest, most heartbreaking decision I've ever had to make. But I am committing Adrienne to Sainte-Dymphna's as I believe she is a danger to herself, to me and to our children. My wife's behaviour has proved to me that she is of unsound mind.' He looked at me. 'I love you, Adrienne, but to see you in this state is too painful for me.'

'I don't understand, Emile,' I said, still trapped in the nurses' grip. 'If you want me to come home with you, why are you sending me to Sainte-Dymphna's?'

Not that I'll ever agree to come home, I wanted to add.

'Yes,' Louise said. 'If Adrienne is locked up in that *asylum*, how can she come home and be that wife and mother again?'

'Adrienne is ill right now,' Emile said, 'but she'll get treatment, then she'll see the error of her ways, and understand where her rightful place is. And then, she'll be released home to me.'

'I can understand you feel betrayed, humiliated even, that I left without a word, but that wasn't my intention.' I said. 'Though even if I'd known I was going to leave and tried to discuss it, you'd never have listened to me, would you?'

'Stop babbling please, Adrienne.' He nodded to the nurses. 'Let's go.'

They dragged me to the door. I kicked my legs out and sank onto the floor, but they hauled me upright.

'No, Emile. No!' I gulped in a deep breath. 'I need my shoulder bag,' I said, in a last, desperate attempt.

'You won't need anything,' one nurse said in a gravelly cigarette-voice. 'The hospital will provide everything.'

'Even her *toothbrush*?' Nelly asked.

'Yes, even a *toothbrush*,' the other, silver-haired nurse said, with a sneer. 'It might not be a new one, and she might have to share with a few others, but a *toothbrush* all the same.'

'Poor Adrienne, how unfair this all is! We know you're not mad,' Léa said, wringing her hands through a tea towel. 'I'm going straight to Yves to see if the gendarmes can help.'

'*Merci*,' I said, though I doubted even Major Rocamadour could overrule Dr Emile Chevalier. Once more, I tried to break away, but the nurses' grip held.

Nelly reappeared, holding my shoulder bag. 'I've put in your toothbrush and hairbrush,' she said, glaring at the nurses, who begrudgingly allowed her to loop it over my shoulder.

'Please, Emile no!' I shrieked again.

Emile sighed. 'Please stop this, *chérie*, you're making it hard for all of us.'

I glared at him. 'I hate you for this.'

'Right, don't say I didn't warn you,' Emile said, drawing up a syringeful of liquid from a vial he pulled from his pocket. 'Now stay still, you'll feel better soon.'

I felt a sharp prick in my upper arm.

The edges of my vision blurred, and as they hauled me away from the inn, the rain stabbed my face like a thousand needles.

The voices around me got smaller, fainter, and faded to a whisper. The creeping blackness smothered me. Then nothing.

33

Blanche

'They took her to the *asylum?*' Blanche hauled another log onto her blazing fire as Louise sat on the sofa, rubbing her hands before the flames.

Blanche poured out two cupfuls from her teapot, her horror rising as Louise explained how they'd dragged off Adrienne to L'Hôpital Sainte-Dymphna.

'It's no wonder she ran off from that obnoxious man,' Louise said, as they sipped the tea. 'She's truly repentant about the gold coins, and determined to repay you every single franc.'

'*Mon Dieu*, how could I have done something so terrible?' Blanche fought back a sob. 'The girl may have thieved and lied but she's not *mad*.'

'Don't be too hard on yourself. You weren't aware of Adrienne's home situation, and couldn't have known how diabolical the husband truly is ... or what he'd do.'

'Instead of trying to get revenge, and controlling my anger, I should have admired Adrienne for leaving a husband like that,' Blanche said. 'I should have followed her example, and left my own husband, years ago.' She waved an arm. '*Quelle imbécile* I was. Poor Adrienne ... we should go and see if, somehow, we can we get her back.'

'I doubt Sainte-Dymphna's allows visitors,' Louise said. 'Especially not in the beginning.'

'How long do you think they'll keep her?' Blanche said. 'And won't they release her when they realise she's quite sane?'

'Well, her husband, the *eminent* Dr Emile Chevalier, seems convinced his wife is suffering from an unstable mind,' Louise said. 'Though he also wants Adrienne back home with him, so perhaps she won't be at Sainte-Dymphna's for long. After all, this is the twentieth century, no longer the Middle Ages!'

Part II

September – December 1970

Adrienne

~

34

The van jerking to a stop dragged me from my groggy sleep, and the first thing I remembered was the needle prick.

How dare my husband sedate me without my permission?

I blinked, pushed the tangle of hair from my eyes and, from where I was lying on the back seat, eased into a sitting position. I stared through the window at a rundown, sprawling stone building, moss and ivy crawling across its ancient walls.

The building loomed even more miserable in this dark and brooding weather, surrounded by trees and fields as far as I could see. Not a single house, farm or village. As if this place — L'Hôpital Sainte-Dymphna I assumed — was stuck out here in its very own world.

I turned around to see Emile's Citroën parking in front of the hospital gates. My husband got out and marched toward the van, frowning.

'Where are we?' I asked the nurses. 'I thought we'd be going into Lyon, isn't that where all the hospitals are?' My father had never taken me to visit my mother — no children allowed, he'd said — though I'd imagined she was in a hospital in the city.

'They built Sainte-Dymphna's way out here so you nutcases wouldn't disturb the city people,' the gravelly voiced nurse said, as they both got out of the van and he opened the back door. 'Come on, out you get, you're not the only patient we have to deal with.'

When I made no move to climb out, the silver-haired nurse grabbed my arm, and dragged me out. It was pointless trying to shrug off his grip, so I just scowled at Emile, standing beside us, his gaze averted.

'Can't you even look at me, Emile? What a coward you are. You know this isn't right. You must know!'

Still, he refused to look at me, which only frustrated me more, that tiny, niggling voice in the back of my mind worrying at me like a persistent fly.

You are insane, Adrienne, like your mother.

The rain had stopped, but the ground was still damp, and, my shoulder bag bumping against my side, the nurses forced me to step through every puddle as they hauled me across the gravelled driveway toward the sentinel-like stone pillars flanking the gate. The north wind bit and cut through my flesh, and I shivered.

'Why do you have to hold me so tightly, as if I were some dangerous criminal?' I said. 'You're hurting my arms, and it's not as if there's anywhere to run to, is there?'

The nurses laughed. Not in humour, but in mirth, at my helplessness, and their grip was so tight I couldn't even turn my head to glance back at my husband.

They nudged me through the gates, and by the time we reached a flight of uneven stone steps leading up to the great wooden door of that forbidding building, my shoes were soaked, my feet were numb and my teeth chattered uncontrollably.

The nurses opened the door and, as they shoved me inside, I gagged on the stench of piss, bleach, and something like stale cooking fat mixed with overcooked vegetables. I swallowed back the foul, acid-tasting liquid that flooded my throat.

Another nurse, wearing the same white uniform, appeared clutching a clipboard.

'*Bonjour*, Madame Chevalier, I'm Nurse Durand, and I'll be admitting you.'

'*Admitting* me? No, this is a mistake, I'm not *staying*. Once the doctor sees me, and gives me some pills, or something I'll be going hom —'

Nurse Durand's smug laugh cut me off. 'That's what they all say, now come with me.' The burly nurses still gripping me, I had no choice but to follow her, nausea rising with every step along that long corridor of shiny lino.

Not mad, not insane.

I had to keep telling myself this; had to convince myself that Emile was wrong, and I wasn't like my mother. I swivelled around to plead, one last time, with Emile not to leave me in this stinky, frightening place.

'Emile, *please*, you can't —'

But my husband had vanished, and beneath the nurses' powerful hold and intimidating stares, there was nothing I could do but keep following Nurse Durand.

Windowless rooms with closed doors flanked one side of the corridor. On the other side, each room had a small, wired window against which was pressed a gruesome, anguished-looking face. As we passed them, fists banged against the window, mouths opening in silent screams and pleas. Goose bumps scrambled across the nape of my neck, and I wanted to scream too.

Mon Dieu, *what kind of place is this?*

As Nurse Durand led me into one of the rooms, the nurses released me and, wordlessly, left us. She sat behind a desk, on which she placed her clipboard, and pointed at the other chair.

'Sit down, Madame Chevalier. Now, are you able to tell me your full name, date of birth, address, and the names of your husband and children?'

'Of course I can tell you all that,' I said, with a scowl. 'But I refuse to tell you anything because I refuse to stay here!' I remained standing, my hands clenching into fists, which I yearned to shake at her.

Nurse Durand gave me a bored look. 'If I had a franc for every time a patient said that to me over the years, I'd be rich enough to give up this crap job and escape this shithole.' She took a tied-up bundle from a pile on a shelf behind her and thrust it at me. 'Here's your Admission Bundle.'

'*Admission Bundle*? But I told you I'm not stay —'

Nurse Durand rolled her eyes. 'So you keep saying.'

I flicked through the clothes: baggy and stained knickers with worn-out elastic, two pairs of holey socks, two misshapen grey shifts, a once-white — now beige — nightdress, a threadbare cardigan, and a coat that stank of mothballs. All these garments, piled on top of two starched white-grey bed sheets, and a rubber sheet, revolted me.

I wrinkled my nose. 'I can't wear any of these things, they look like they've been boiled and disinfected to death, and not fit for anyone to wear.'

'That's correct,' Nurse Durand said, in the same bored voice. 'All the hospital garments are washed at a high temperature to ensure that every trace of food, snot, urine, faeces, vomit, sputum, and semen are removed.'

'Quelle horreur!' I cried, feeling ill again just thinking about all those disgusting bodily fluids on things I was meant to wear. 'Can't I keep my own clothes?'

'You may keep your own shoes, and bra, since we have no communal bras. But that's all, it's much easier if every patient wears the hospital-issue garments.'

'Well, I certainly won't be needing this rubber sheet, Nurse Durand, I *never* wet the bed. And besides, once I see the doctor, and get some pills, I'll be going home. When can I see the doctor?'

'Dr Lacoste will see you shortly,' she said. 'And rubber sheets are standard procedure, whether or not the patient is incontinent. Now come with me.'

Nurse Durand led me back down that bleak corridor, and I was filled with renewed horror and dismay, as she led me into a vast and dark wood-panelled room with an overwhelming smell of antiseptic.

Old and saggy leather sofas and armchairs, dusty bookshelves and half-dead potted plants were randomly placed around the room. Besides the plants, there was no other decoration — no paintings, no ornaments, no flowers in vases. So different from the homely decor of Léa's auberge, and the fresh, aromatic flowers Louise always kept in vases. Not to mention her tantalising kitchen aromas.

Oh, why can't I be back at L'Auberge de Léa?

'This is the Day Room,' Nurse Durand said, 'where you are free to relax, read a book, chat with other patients or watch television.'

I looked around that cavernous space at the dozens of shabby people wandering around aimlessly, muttering to themselves as they stared at nothing, or dozing, threads of drool dangling from their mouth.

A skinny, hunched-over old man, who looked blind, was shakily feeling his way toward a cluster of armchairs. He bumped into a chair in which a male nurse was sitting, thumbing through a magazine. The nurse jumped up and hit the old man across the back of his head.

'Watch where you're going, old fool,' he yelled, as the man fell backwards, slid across the floor and banged into another chair.

The poor old soul kept trying, in vain, to clutch onto something to pull himself upright, and I went to help him, but Nurse Durand lay a hand on my arm. 'Don't even think about it, Madame Chevalier.'

'But …'

I could hardly believe her callousness, though the old man did finally get up, find a chair and slump down into it.

I imagined my mother in this room, sitting in one of the rickety armchairs, rocking herself back and forth, back and forth.

Stop rocking, Maman, stop it, please!

She keeps rocking, staring straight through her invisible daughter. I'm here, Maman. Please look at me.

Though I soon understood that when the madness leached into Maman's brain, and warped it, she could no longer look at, or take care of, me. And once more I asked myself if that same insanity had wormed itself into my brain.

No! Don't think like that. I am not mad. But I must be. Emile says so.

From that hideous throng of patients, a woman marched toward me, jerking me from my thoughts of Maman, and Emile. She was about to walk straight into me, but stopped right before me, her bloodshot eyes, one of which was swollen with a purple bruise, peering into mine.

'You're pretty, I love you,' she said. 'Got a Gauloises for me?'

'N-no,' I stammered, reeling away from her brown, crooked teeth and rancid breath; and from her fingertips, lips and the tip of her nose, that were black, like they'd been burnt.

'Bitch, I hate you.' She coughed like a wild dog, and poked out her tongue. The tip of that too, was black.

'Off you trot, Janine, don't bother the new patient,' Nurse Durand said, shooing away the woman.

'Don't worry about Janine,' Nurse Durand said to me, 'she's harmless.'

'But why the bruise, and the black fingers and nose?'

'Janine's always calling the other patients bitch or bastard, so sometimes they have to punch her in the face to shut her up.' Nurse Durand laughed as if that was a great joke. 'And the burns are from smoking *really* small cigarette butts.'

I followed her back out into the corridor, vowing I wouldn't spend a single moment in that gruesome Day Room.

~

'Here we are,' Nurse Durand announced as we reached a green-tiled bathroom, with just one high-sided tub in the middle. 'Take off your clothes, Madame Chevalier.'

'*All* of them?' I glanced at the door, which she made no move to shut.

'You prefer a bath in your clothes?'

'But I don't need a bath, I'll be going home as soon as I see the doc —'

'Standard procedure, now take everything off.'

'I need the toilet first,' I said.

Nurse Durand sighed as she took a great bunch of keys from her pocket and unlocked another room leading off from the bathroom.

'We keep toilet areas locked for safety reasons,' she said, as I went inside, dismayed to see that none of the cubicles had doors. 'We unlock them for ten minutes every three hours throughout the day. If you request the toilet outside these times, you'll be refused.'

'What if I'm busting, and can't wait?' I said, hovering over one of the foul toilet seats, and wishing Nurse Durand would at least turn away. But she carried on looking at me, and smirking.

'You'll do what everyone else does — piss or shit on the spot.'

'*Mon Dieu*, what a place this is. Thankfully, I won't be staying,' I said peeling off my clothes as Nurse Durand turned on the bath taps, and added a capful of what smelled like disinfectant. 'And I don't need a bath.'

'I advise you to make the most of it,' Nurse Durand said, 'because you'll never get another bath, they're reserved for admissions. It'll be showers from here on in.'

'I keep telling you, I'm not staying.' I was sobbing now, tears coursing down my cheeks, but her dark stare forced me to climb into that water, so hot it burned my skin.

'When c-can I go h-home?' I sobbed, as she scrubbed my body with soap so harsh it numbed me, and left my skin red raw.

'*Oh là là*, I've lost count of the number of times people have asked me that question. You'll go home when you've recovered.'

'I'm not mad.'

Ignoring me, she pointed to my Admission Bundle, perched on a chair. 'Now, out you get, dry yourself and put on a dress.'

'When will I see the doctor?'

Nurse Durand bent her head and checked her fob watch. 'Your appointment is right now, in fact.'

35

Nurse Durand left me standing in the doorway of an office lined, like the Day Room, in dark wood panels.

'*Bonjour*, Madame Chevalier, I'm Dr Lacoste. Please, take a seat.' He motioned to two chairs behind the wide desk, his warm smile revealing straight white teeth. What looked like framed medical certificates hung from the wall behind where the doctor stood.

I dumped my Admission Bundle on one chair and sat on the edge of the other.

'So, Madame Chevalier, first of all, how are you? And why do you believe you are here at Sainte-Dymphna's?' Another smile, and his face immediately struck me as familiar.

Do I know him from somewhere?

I couldn't stop staring, trying to remember if I'd seen this doctor before, or whether he simply reminded me of a handsome movie star.

'If you really want to know, I'm feeling annoyed, Dr Lacoste. And angry! Because my husband drugged me and forced me here. He tells me I'm mad, but I don't *feel* crazy, so maybe you could give me some pills, or something, and let me go?'

Even if Emile was right, and I was suffering from Maman's madness, I could not stay in this hellhole where she'd died. But if I wanted Dr Lacoste to release me, I had to look as sane as possible, so I sat up straighter, battling down the sobs and the panic.

'Your husband *drugged* and *forced* you?'

'Yes, Emile brought me here against my will.' I fought to keep my voice calm. 'I suppose he told you the reason? That I left our home, last June?'

'*Oui*, your husband did inform me of the episode at Carrefour supermarket, and how you refuse to return to the family abode,' Dr Lacoste said. 'But I can assure you, Madame Chevalier, that you are here because your husband — an *esteemed* psychiatrist — is concerned about your sanity and your safety. He simply desires the best professional care for his wife. I'm also aware of your mother's mental health history, and, in my experience, since there is often a hereditar —'

'Just because my mother was mad, doesn't mean I am too.' I swallowed a sob.

But Dr Lacoste's indulgent, sympathetic smile — like you'd give a naïve child — told me he'd already decided I was insane. My shoulders sagged as I sank into the chair, flinging my arms into the air in desperation, knowing I wasn't getting out of Sainte-Dymphna's today, and perhaps not even tomorrow.

The soft, blue-eyed gaze fixed on me, Dr Lacoste leaned across the desk toward me, and tapped a silver pen on his notepad. 'Your husband has also confided in me about your unfortunate childhood. Can you tell me your earliest memory of that time, Madame Chevalier?'

'How can my childhood memories have anything to do with why my husband sent me here, Dr Lacoste?'

'Perhaps nothing, perhaps everything.' His familiar smile made me more certain than ever that I'd met this man before. But where? In any case, whether I knew him or not, Dr Lacoste appeared to know everything about me, so what did I have to lose in telling him the whole ugly truth? Besides, he seemed keen to understand and help me.

'My earliest memory is from about five or six years old, when my mother stopped talking and just lay in bed staring into space, or rocked in a chair. Eventually, when I was seven, my father had her committed to this asylum.'

I licked my dry lips and, from a jug on his desk, Dr Lacoste filled a glass with water. He pushed it toward me, and I gulped down the water.

'Then my father's mother moved in with us. Grandmère was a heartless old woman who barked orders at me to do housework and shopping.' I took a shaky breath. 'If she found a speck of dust, she'd whack me with her wooden spoon, and starve me the next day.'

'I'm sorry you experienced this, Madame Chevalier,' he said, scribbling on the notepad but not taking his gaze from me. 'Can you tell me anything more?'

I'd always been too embarrassed to talk about my miserable childhood, but Dr Lacoste's gentle manner relaxed me, and spilling everything to him seemed to shift the lead ball from my chest; the weight that had pressed down on me for as long as I could recall.

And I realised that his tall, lean figure, lovely blue eyes, and warm smile *did* remind me of someone. Not a movie star, but Bambou. Though the hair and clothes were vastly different. While Bambou looked scruffy and unwashed, Dr Lacoste was distinguished-looking, with neatly combed hair, and expensive, well-cut clothes, like Emile's.

'They'd send Maman home for a while, but she kept getting sent back here, until one time she never returned home.' I caught the wobble in my voice. 'An accident, they said.'

'You're doing very well,' Dr Lacoste said. 'Anything else you can tell me?' That concerned smile urged me to finish my story; to purge myself of those bad things that had rotted inside me over the years.

'As soon as Maman left, Grandmère started sending me to the shops with a list, and some francs wrapped in a handkerchief. I'd have to walk a long way down our street, then cross a busy road. The cars whizzing by terrified me, and my fingers stung from gripping that money-handkerchief so tightly.' He poured more water, and I drank again.

'Then I'd stand for hours in queues, sometimes for only stale bread. You remember the years of the German Occupation?'

'You were sent to do the family shopping at age *seven*?' he said.

I nodded. 'And I remember one thing clearly, Dr Lacoste. It was July 1944 and some resistance fighters had attacked Le Moulin à Vent, a café the Gestapo frequented. So for revenge, the Germans randomly shot five men, and Grandmère would make me walk past those hanging bodies every day ... said that would teach me never to resist *her*.'

I shivered as the image, and the smell, of rotting bodies left in the sun for all to see, flashed through my mind.

'I'm so sorry, Madame Chevalier, how horrific.'

'As I grew older,' I went on, 'I did question the relevance of that particular punishment of Grandmère's, but I've never forgotten that terrible sight.'

His handsome features creased in sympathy, and a thought struck me. Since Dr Lacoste looked so much like Bambou did he also *behave* like Bambou — having sex with every woman around, just for fun, but no commitment?

Why ever am I wondering if Dr Lacoste behaves like Bambou?

'Did your father or grandmother speak of your mother's illness, or her death?'

'Not a word, except to warn me never to speak about Maman's madness.' I ran a finger around the rim of the glass. 'Grandmère said if people knew, they'd assume I was mad too.' I met his gaze. 'Like my husband, and like you, Dr Lacoste.'

'Oh, that's not the case. I'm simply trying to form a complete picture of everything that's happened in your life, to help you as best I can, Madame Chevalier.'

'Okay well, most of my childhood memories are of Maman being ill, absent or *dead*, my father acting like I was invisible, and my grandmother treating me worse than a stray dog.' I slapped my palms on his desk. 'So, there you have it.'

'All of this goes some way to explaining your behaviour that day at Carrefour,' Dr Lacoste said. 'But that's only my opinion. Why do *you* believe you abandoned your husband and home? And then, once your husband found you, that you refused to return to that home?'

'I never planned to leave, and at first I didn't know why, though now I have some idea.'

Dr Lacoste nodded, scribbling more notes.

'I had to escape Papa and Grandmère, so I fell into marriage with Emile straight from school, and I just wasn't *armed* to be a proper adult.' I told him about my dismal life with Emile, my fingertip still circling the rim of the glass. 'Anyway, things must have been simmering inside me for some time *Before the Supermarket*, and something insignificant — the words of a silly child — simply made me snap.'

'*Oui, oui, très bien,* go on,' the doctor mumbled, still scribbling.

'So, surely you see I'm not crazy? Can't you just send me home and use your valuable time treating patients who really need your help?'

He rested the silver pen on his notepad, crossed his arms, and looked up, that deep blue gaze piercing mine.

'Sorry, Madame Chevalier, but I'm loath to release you immediately. And whilst I do not find you of unstable mind, I believe you are suffering from depression, perhaps stemming from your disturbed upbringing. But with the appropriate treatments I can help you overcome those childhood memories, so they no longer impact your adult life.'

While depression didn't sound good, it was definitely better than 'insane'. 'Would that explain my fatigue and misery before I left Emile?'

He nodded. 'It very well could.'

'What's this appropriate treatment, Dr Lacoste?'

'A combination of psychoanalysis and electroconvulsive therapy.'

'Electro *what*?' I frowned.

'ECT it's called. We place electrodes on your head and pass electric volts through your brain to induce a seizure.'

'Electric volts through my *brain*? A *seizure*!' My heart thudded hard. 'You must be *joking*? No, no, I do not want that!'

'Calm down, it's not as bad as it sounds.' That familiar smile again, somehow haunting. 'These days we give patients muscle relaxants and a general anaesthetic. You'll be asleep and won't feel a thing.'

Trembling with rage, fright, and desperation, I kept shaking my head.

'No, no, I won't let you electrify my brain!'

'I'm afraid it's not your decision. We are not required to obtain permission from detained patients. Besides, ECT works very well for depression and has also been known to eliminate long-term memories, such as those of your unfortunate childhood.' He nodded, as if convincing himself. '*Oui, oui,* ECT can be effective in cases such as yours, Madame Chevalier.'

'Cases such as mine? You mean for wives whose husbands want to punish them because they refuse to live under the thumb?'

Dr Lacoste came around to my side of the desk and gave my arm a friendly pat.

'Stop worrying, you'll be fine. Now it's time to settle into your dormitory. I'll be seeing you again right after your first ECT session.'

'Can my friends come and visit?' I asked. 'I already miss them.'

'No friends yet. Let's see how you feel soon.' He placed my Admission Bundle back into my arms and, a palm against the small of my back, gently guided me out of his office.

Nurse Durand magically reappeared, and I followed her back down that dreary corridor.

Surely this can't be real? I'm dreaming. Any second I'll wake from this terrible nightmare.

But the raw, ugly reality hit me like a hammer blow. Emile had not brought me to Sainte-Dymphna's simply for an appointment with a psychiatrist who'd send me home with some pills. No, I would be staying in this dreadful place. Sleeping here. Wearing these hideous garments. And having my brain jolted with electricity.

The despair, hopelessness and powerlessness of my situation was a physical pain — a knife slicing through my heart — as I saw my wonderful new auberge life swept away in a single stroke of Emile's malicious wand.

36

'Your new home!' Nurse Durand announced with spiteful glee, from the doorway of the dormitory.

I stared, in horror, at the rows of fifty or sixty metal-framed beds, a small locker separating each one. Thick bars obscured most of the light coming from two small windows and, like the rest of Sainte-Dymphna's, the dormitory stank of overcooked cabbage, bleach and excrement.

'Make your bed and put the rest of your Admission Bundle in your locker,' Nurse Durand said, pointing to one of the beds. 'Then it'll be lunchtime.'

My heart heavier, I dumped my Admission Bundle onto the bed and looked around the spartan dormitory. It was the middle of the day, but several women were lying on their beds, sleeping or staring into space.

From the bed beside mine, an old woman turned over to face me. With a groan, she pushed herself into a sitting position, her face collapsing in a labyrinth of wrinkles as she smiled.

'*Bonjour, chérie*, what's your name?'

'Adrienne Chevalier.'

'Lovely to meet you, Adrienne Chevalier, I'm Joséphine.' She thrust a thin, trembling hand at me, and didn't look or sound the least bit mad, and I shook the gnarly hand gently, afraid of crushing those fragile, bird-like bones. 'Don't look so miserable. Sainte-Dymphna's isn't that bad. You'll get used to it.'

'Not a chance,' I said, shoving my Admission Bundle into the locker. 'I hope to be released *very* soon. How long have you been here, Joséphine?'

'Twenty years.'

'*Mon Dieu*, you must be joking!'

'My problem is that I can't obey my husband,' Joséphine said. 'They sent me home once, but I still refused to obey his commands, so he ordered me back here.'

'*Obey* your husband?'

Joséphine nodded. 'I kept annoying him, so I had to come back.'

'Doesn't your husband know that wives no longer have to *obey* their husbands?' I said, silently wishing I'd followed my own advice and stood up to Emile years ago.

'But you must obey your husband if he's an important man — a general all of France depends on,' Joséphine said.

I frowned. 'All of France?'

'You can't disobey your husband if he's Napoléon Bonaparte.'

'*Napoléon Bonaparte?*' I stared at Joséphine. No hint of a smile or a wink.

'I'll probably die in here,' she went on. 'They almost guillotined me once, you know, back in the days of the revolution.'

'Don't worry, she's harmless,' a woman said from the bed on my other side, where she lay beside another woman flicking through a dog-eared magazine. Both of them looked around mid-forties, their hair cut so short it looked almost shaved.

'Joséphine might be a lunatic, but she wouldn't hurt a fly,' the other woman said. 'I'm Marcelle, by the way. *Salut*, Adrienne. The women smiled and sat up on the bed. 'And this is Yvonne, my girlfriend.'

'Pleased to meet you, Adrienne,' Yvonne said. 'Oh, and her name's not Joséphine, but she *has* been here for twenty years, apparently.'

'*Bonjour*,' I said warily, since these women also appeared quite sane.

I closed my locker and sat on the side of the narrow bed, facing Yvonne and Marcelle. 'How long have you two been here?'

'I don't remember exactly, but quite a few years now, isn't it Marcelle?' Yvonne said. 'But we don't want to go home anymore, this is our home now.'

'Oh! I hope I *never* call this place my home, and I can get out soon,' I said, explaining how and why my husband had sent me here. 'But since it looks as if I'm staying for a few days, I wish I had my things, besides my bag, bra and shoes, and my toothbrush, that is.'

'It's safer not to have any personal possessions,' Yvonne said. 'If another patient doesn't steal your stuff, the nursing staff will. It's one of their perks, probably their *only* perk in this hellhole.' She laughed.

'The nurses steal patients' pocket money and food treats that relatives bring in, and crockery, bed linen and towels … anything that's not screwed down,' Marcelle said.

'God forbid, what a terrible place,' I said, as the shabby woman, Janine, from the Day Room trudged into the dormitory.

Oh no, please leave me alone!

I averted my gaze from that black nose and lips, and bruised eye, but Janine came straight toward me.

'You're pretty. I love you. Got a Gauloises for me?'

I shook my head. 'I don't smoke.'

'Bitch, I hate you.' She flicked the blackened fingertips at me.

'Off you go, Janine,' Yvonne said, waving her away. 'We don't smoke, so you can leave us alone.'

'That one's a nuisance, and mad as a hatter, but harmless too,' Marcelle said. 'Better since the doc started her on chlorpromazine. Like so many on tranquillisers, she's much calmer, and only asks you for a smoke five times a day instead of twenty.'

'You know a lot about the patients *and* Sainte-Dymphna's,' I said, wondering if Yvonne and Marcelle might be here, like me, on false or weak pretences. 'And you don't seem, er ...'

'Off our rockers? Nutcases?' Yvonne laughed.

'I don't mean to be nosy,' I said, 'but why *are* you both here?'

'We've been friends since childhood,' Marcelle said, with a cheeky grin, 'but when our husbands found out we'd become *more* than friends, they sent us to Sainte-Dymphna's for aversion therapy.'

I frowned. '*More* than friends? Aversion therapy?'

'Marcelle and I don't want to ... we *can't* have sex with our husbands. We prefer women,' Yvonne said, clasping Marcelle's hand.

'You know, lesbians,' Marcelle said. 'And when our husbands caught us together, they gave us a choice — either be arrested, or admitted to Sainte-Dymphna's to be cured with aversion therapy.'

I thought of Clotilde, and her girlfriend, Bev, who I'd hoped to meet before I'd ended up here. Clotilde was happily quite sane, didn't care a bit about village gossip, and certainly wasn't in need of therapy. 'Did this aversion therapy *cure* you?'

'Well, it's been years since they stopped the therapy,' Yvonne said, 'and no matter how many images of naked women they showed us, while giving us electric shocks and drugs to make us vomit, we still can't bear the thought of sleeping with our husbands.'

'So, obviously,' Marcelle said, 'their aversion therapy was a failure.'

'Dr Lacoste is making me start ECT tomorrow,' I said. 'Is it as terrible as it sounds? What will they do to me, exactly?'

'ECT can be awful for some people and perfectly fine for others,' Yvonne said. 'Basically, once they put you to sleep, they lodge a rubber gag in your mouth, then place electrodes on jellied areas of your scalp. Then the doctor turns on the machine, which sends electric volts through your brain.'

'*Mon Dieu*, how gruesome!' The panic rose again.

'Don't worry,' Yvonne said, patting my arm. 'It wasn't that bad for us.'

'ECT generally goes without a hitch,' Marcelle said. 'They use it a lot here, not only for depression, but to treat homosexuals, like us.'

'And other *crimes*, like fiddling around with oneself,' Yvonne said with a cackle.

As I imagined electric shocks seizing up my brain, the dormitory stink caught in my throat. Trapped in the suffocating air of desperation, it was harder to breathe, and I couldn't quell the rising panic.

Yvonne and Marcelle sat on my bed, on either side of me, patting me on the back as I rocked and sobbed, and took great, heaving breaths.

Rocking and sobbing, like Maman.

No, no, stop! You're not like her. Dr Lacoste says you're not mad.

My chest was so tight that I could only gasp, and I had a sudden urge to charge outside into that cold autumn day, and gulp in lungfuls of fresh air. Shrugging off

Marcelle and Yvonne, I lurched upright, bolted from the dormitory, and sprinted down that long corridor.

~

'Madame Chevalier, running is useless, there's no escape!' I recognised Nurse Durand's voice but didn't glance behind me as I sped toward the front door.

I'd almost reached the door when I slipped on the polished lino and almost lost my footing. To regain my balance, I grabbed onto a passing lunch trolley. The trolley tipped over, and I jumped aside to avoid the trays and food cascading onto the floor.

'Madame Chevalier, what the *hell* are you doing?'

Nurse Durand again, but I barely stopped for breath, jumping over skidding cutlery, smashed crockery, and sludgy puddles of food and liquid.

I kept my gaze fixed on the door, panting hard.

Soon I'll be able to breathe. Soon I'll be free.

I grasped the door handle, twisted it. It didn't budge. I kept twisting, pulling, pushing, tugging. Still, it didn't give.

'No, no, no!' I screamed, sinking to the floor, still clutching the handle. In desperation, even as I knew it was useless, I dug my fingernails into the space between the door and the frame, trying to prise them apart.

'Help me, somebody help me. I can't breathe ... need to get outside. *Please!*'

Fingers pressed, deep and painful, into my shoulders, and I glanced up at the same two nurses who'd dragged me here from the auberge.

'*Oh là là*, such stupid and childish behaviour,' the silver-haired one with the steel-grey eyes said with a smirk. 'I'm surprised at you, Madame Chevalier ... a *doctor's* wife.'

'And look at the mess you've made,' said Gravel-voice. He nodded back along the corridor where staff were cleaning up the lunch wreckage. 'They'll charge you for all that breakage, you know.'

'Ouch, let go!' I cried, but they only tightened their grip, hauled me to my feet and dragged me back along the corridor. 'Stop, you're hurting me,' I wailed.

An emaciated, red-eyed woman with wild, straggly hair rushed at me.

'Shut up, crazy bitch,' she shrieked, slapping my face. 'Shut up, shut up!'

'*Dieu* have mercy, make her stop!' I screamed, as the nurses tried to fend her off and grip me at the same time.

'That's enough. Calm yourself, Paulette,' Silver-hair said.

They gave Paulette a great shove, and she stumbled backwards, slipping on a slimy patch of mashed carrots and peas. As she lay on the floor, Gravel-voice lifted a black boot and kicked her in the ribs. Paulette screamed, trying to cover her chest with her shaky hands, but he kept kicking.

'What do we have to do to teach you to behave, Paulette?'

Paulette kept screeching. The nurse kept kicking.

'Stop!' I shouted. 'Please, stop hurting her.'

Both of them were kicking Paulette now, her screams dying a little with each boot thud.

All the screeching and ruckus set off a general uproar, and the corridor quickly became bedlam, patients yelling and skittering in every direction.

'Now look what you've done,' Gravel-voice said, as they gave Paulette a last kick and she fell silent, lying still on the floor, curled up like a foetus.

Paulette might be quiet now, but the noise around had built to a deafening screech, and several nurses and other staff appeared, grabbing and restraining the more disturbed patients.

'*Merde*, is she dead? I sobbed. 'Have you killed Paulette?'

'Course she's not dead. What do you think we are, murderers?' Nurse Durand said. 'Orderlies, get over here now!' she yelled down the corridor, at the staff who were dealing with the unruly patients. 'And hold these women.'

Glaring at me, Nurse Durand swiped at hair strands that had come loose in the scuffle, and straightened her uniform.

The burly men — the orderlies I assumed — grabbed my arms and held me still.

'Let me go,' I cried, trying again to pull away.

I felt that same needle prick in my arm, and everything quickly faded to black.

37

A soft voice and a bright light woke me. 'Madame Chevalier? *Bonjour*, I'm Nurse Trudeau.'

'Where am I? What time is it?' I pushed myself up from where I was lying on a tiled floor, taking in the olive-green walls of a tiny room that contained nothing but a bucket in one corner. Not even a mattress. There was one high, tiny window, against which the wind beat and rattled its frame.

'It's an Isolation Room, and we have eight of them,' Nurse Trudeau said. 'To calm people. That's why they painted the walls this shade of green. It's meant to promote serenity, and decrease anxiety.'

'It makes me feel ill,' I said.

'You missed lunch, so maybe it's the hunger making you feel unwell?' the nurse said. 'Do you feel calm enough to have dinner with the other patients in the dining room?'

'Yes, I'm calm,' I said, surprised at her friendly voice and gentle manner — the first humane nurse I'd encountered here. 'And hungry,' I added, relieved to getting out of that prison box.

'I'm glad,' Nurse Trudeau said, 'because I'd have hated to see you stay in this Wet Room the entire night.'

'Wet Room? Didn't you call it an Isolation Room?'

She nodded. 'They're also called Wet Rooms because every morning they're hosed down ... and the patients in them.' She shook her head. 'It's disgraceful, I know, and something you want to avoid, especially at this chilly time of year.'

I shivered at the thought of being hosed down like some dirty, penned animal, as I followed Nurse Trudeau back out into the corridor, even more bleak at nightfall.

'Wait here while I get your friend, Paulette,' Nurse Trudeau said, unlocking the next door.

'She's not my friend,' I said, rubbing the bump on my head where Paulette had hit me.

As Nurse Trudeau opened Paulette's door, and flipped the light switch, I peered over her shoulder into a small room similar to the one I'd been in. But I immediately recoiled, bile surging into my throat. Fearing I'd throw up, I pressed a hand over my mouth as I gazed, in horror, at Paulette's naked and lifeless body hanging from the window bars.

'*Mon Dieu*!' Nurse Trudeau cried, hurrying to the window. 'Poor Paulette used her dress as a noose.'

'Oh no!' Tears sprang to my eyes. Paulette wasn't even old, only around my age. How tortured she must have been to believe that death was her only escape. Though, from what I'd experienced in only half a day at Sainte-Dymphna's, I could understand that.

As Nurse Trudeau shouted for help, both of us trying, in vain, to release Paulette from her fatal noose, the faraway voice of my father chimed in my head.

'Your mother's dead … died at Sainte-Dymphna's, never coming home.'

And Papa and Grandmère murmuring in whispers, so I'd caught only snatches of their conversation.

'… locked up … isolation.'

'Desperate …'

'… only escape.'

'… suicide, but as if they'd looped the noose …'

And the cold, terrible truth of my mother's death hit me — the day my heart was torn open in a wound that had never healed. Just like Paulette, my dear maman had taken her own life in one of these pitiless rooms. And, like Paulette, it would be recorded as 'death by suicide'. Just as Sainte-Dymphna's had killed Paulette, this pit of misery had also murdered Maman.

The staff swarming into Paulette's room took no notice of me as I sank to the floor, hugging my arms around my bent-up knees and rocking back and forth, sobbing for my lost mother. And my stolen childhood.

I cried for everything else I'd lost too — my family, my home, my friends, my new life. That dark cloud of loss overwhelmed me and never before had I felt so powerless, so desperate and helpless. And so alone.

As they wheeled away the gurney, I avoided looking at Paulette's sheeted body. All I saw, through the fingers covering my face, were wheels creaking over shiny lino. And I feared that if I didn't find a way out of here, Sainte-Dymphna's would drive me to a deathly escape, too.

~

'I hope you'll be all right after such a shock, Madame Chevalier,' Nurse Trudeau said, her hand on my arm as she led me into the dining room.

'Thank you,' I said, thinking I'd never be all right here, as I looked around at all those seated patients, dressed in the same faded and shapeless grey uniform — women in dresses, men in shirts and trousers. Many stared down at the table, shoulders hunched, or gazed into the distance, eyes glazed, expressions vacant.

'There you are Adrienne,' Marcelle said as I sat beside her and Yvonne.

'Are you better now?' Yvonne said, as the staff placed a bowl of foul-smelling soup in front of each patient, and baskets of bread in the middle of each table. 'We were worried, the way you panicked like that.'

'And after what's happened to poor Paulette,' Marcelle said. 'We heard, news travels like fire in here.'

'I'm okay,' I said. 'Well, sort of. I can't bear it at Sainte-Dymphna's and I don't know how I'm going to stay alive in here.'

'Stay alive?' Yvonne dipped a chunk of bread into her soup, but, as hungry as I was, the thought of swallowing that vile-smelling, chunky liquid made me feel ill again.

I told Yvonne and Marcelle how Maman had hanged herself from the bars, like Paulette. I couldn't stop the tears coursing down my cheeks; couldn't rid my mind of the vision of Paulette's staring, popped out eyes, and purple-grey skin.

'I'll never forget that image,' I said, rubbing my goose-bumped arms. 'As long as I live, I'll never get it out of my mind.'

'You must try not to dwell on it, *chérie*,' Yvonne said, placing a hunk of bread on my plate. 'Sadly, many patients die in here.'

'Not forgetting the ones the staff have *murdered* over the years,' Marcelle said. 'Accidents though, of course,' she said, raising her eyebrows.

'And despite all the measures they take to stop people killing themselves, many, like poor Paulette, find a way,' Yvonne said. 'Only the other week, a woman banged her head against a window until it smashed, then she thrust her head through the broken glass and slit her own throat.'

'How gruesome!' I gasped. 'How do people get that desperate?'

'Severe depression,' Yvonne said.

'Depression that even ECT and the doctor's fancy drugs can't fix,' Marcelle said. 'All they see is a bleak, dark and hopeless future.'

'That's so sad,' I said, thinking of Dr Lacoste's depression diagnosis. Rather than fight against it, I should simply accept his treatment, to avert my own bleak and hopeless future.

'It's cabbage again, always cabbage,' Yvonne said, nodding at my bowl, urging me to drink the soup. 'It's not as bad as it smells, and you need to keep up your strength.'

Some patients looked too spaced out to eat or drink, and nobody was encouraging, or helping, them. These people were thin, some skeletal. Several were eating normally, but for a few, it was some bizarre competition, each person trying to outdo the rest by quickly stuffing as much bread and soup as possible into their mouth. They kept an arm circled around their bowl, eyeing neighbours with suspicious glares.

Bread and soup splotches flew around the table, onto the floor, and over those grey garments. There was no conversation or chit-chat, just the sound of people noisily chewing bread and slurping soup, which made me feel even less like eating. But, in the end, I was starving, and wolfed down the bland soup with my eyes shut, imagining it was Louise Bellefontaine's aromatic and flavoursome vegetable soup.

Some patients who'd finished their supper stood up, and wandered around.

'Sit back down!' the nurses and orderlies shouted, pushing them back into their seats.

A woman with greasy black hair, who was sitting on the other side of me, pilfered another woman's bread.

I expected this other woman, who had red, tangled hair, to simply swipe back her bread but, without a word, she jumped up, lifted her chair and smashed it down onto the head of the black-haired woman, who screamed as blood spurted from her head, splattering red spots across the table.

I remained seated, mouth agape, rigid with horror, as the black-haired woman spun around to her assailant.

'You mad fucking bitch,' she said. 'They should lock you up with the crazies.'

Marcelle and Yvonne smirked at the irony of that, as those same two orderlies who'd restrained me hauled away the attacking woman. She kicked, fought, yelled and swore, but she was no match for the hulking men who carried her off as if she were a feather.

I inhaled deeply, trying to take all this in; to accept this madness.

38

'Out of bed, you lazy buggers.'

The following morning, from my dormitory bed, the commanding voices of those same two nurses — Gravel-voice and Silver-hair — startled me awake. I didn't even have the pleasure of that blurry instant between sleeping and waking, before I remembered, with utter dismay, where I was.

'Hurry up, nightdresses off and into the bathroom.'

The women were obviously used to this, as they all stripped naked without the slightest embarrassment.

Marcelle and Yvonne, who'd squeezed into the same narrow bed, rose together. Nobody batted an eyelid, and I thought how ironic it was that the very place they'd been sent to be cured of their homosexuality turned a blind eye to them openly sharing a bed.

On my other side, old Joséphine Bonaparte didn't budge, and I wondered if she might have died.

'Get up, crazy old bat.' Gravel-voice grabbed her arm, which clicked as he dragged her out of bed, and I feared he'd pulled that fragile limb out of its socket.

'*Putain!*' he cursed. 'Fucking bitch's pissed and shat the bed *again*.'

Then I smelled the faeces that lay nestled in a pool of pee in Joséphine's bed. The remains of last night's cabbage soup heaved in my stomach, acidy bile flooding my throat. I couldn't stop gagging, as the nurses used Joséphine's pillow and blanket to soak up the worst and stop the pee leaking onto the floor. I immediately understood the importance of that Admission Bundle rubber sheet.

'If only they'd remember to put Joséphine in a nappy *every* night,' Marcelle said.

'Lots of patients wet the bed,' Yvonne said to me, 'but unless it's really bad, like that, the nurses just make it up again, wet.'

My nostrils flared at the intense, foul ammonia stink as the naked line of women trudged toward the bathroom and toilet area.

By the time we all reached the bathroom, and stood before a vast, collective shower cubicle, Silver-hair was waiting, holding a thick hose.

'In you go, hurry up,' he snapped, as Gravel-voice turned on a tap, and Silver-hair directed the hose at us. Joséphine Bonaparte screamed, her old skin crumpling like a last season's plum.

An image of a Holocaust chamber flashed through my mind, and I almost expected gas to come from that hose. But it was cool water, and I was thankful for that at least. A great thick jet of it, which the nurse directed onto the naked, trembling cluster of us, all huddled in the centre of the cubicle. Some women screamed, others cried or sobbed, but most remained wordless. There was no soap, no proper body washing, and soon we were all shivering, our teeth chattering. Once again, I was struck dumb at the inhumanity of Sainte-Dymphna's.

'Get dressed now, and off to breakfast,' Gravel-voice commanded.

'Make sure to grab your own shoes,' Marcelle said, 'or someone else might take them.'

All the patients' shoes had been thrown into a pile and people were taking any old pair and shoving their feet into them, whether or not they fitted.

'Hurry up, or I'll lose my patience,' Gravel-voice said, 'and you know what happens when I lose my patience.' He winked at Silver-hair and they giggled like children. I wanted to slap their stupid, horrible faces.

Silver-hair pointed a finger at me. 'No breakfast for you. you're going to the ECT suite, so go back to your bed and wait there till the orderly comes for you.'

As I lay back on my bed, I wondered, again, how Sainte-Dymphna's dare call itself a hospital. Nobody seemed to be getting the right treatment or recovering, and nobody was treated humanely. We were like lepers, hidden away from the world with only the bare minimum to exist.

The thought of dashing off again crossed my mind, but there was no escape. So I waited on my bed, staring at the high ceiling, until an orderly came and wheeled me away on a gurney.

~

'Here we are, the ECT suite,' the orderly said, wheeling me into a tiny claustrophobic room with dark brown walls. A strange gassy odour curled up my nostrils, making me dizzy.

'*Bonjour*, Madame Chevalier. How are we this morning?' The handsome Dr Lacoste stood over me, smiling and clutching the lapels of his starched white coat.

'I'm frightened,' I said, my heart racing faster, my body shaking so much with fear I thought I'd fall onto the floor. 'So afraid!'

'Calm down, Madame Chev … Adrienne. Do you mind if I use your first name?'

I shrugged. 'Okay.'

'You're worrying for nothing, Adrienne. We do this all the time, and you'll feel better afterwards. Now, the anaesthetist will insert a needle into your vein, for the muscle relaxant and anaesthetic.'

As the anaesthetist patted the back of my hand, Dr Lacoste spoke to a nurse. 'Please apply the conducting jelly to her temples.' He turned his attention to a box-type object and fiddled with its switches and dials.

I felt the small prick in the back of my hand, and I lay still, staring at one of the ugly brown walls as the anxiety seeped from me.

Dr Lacoste turned back to me and said, in his gentle voice, 'Don't worry, Adrienne, I won't let anything happen to you,' and something flashed through my mind.

It was the way he said 'Adrienne' — the same way he'd said it, many years ago — and now his voice, as well as his face, was intensely familiar. The place from where I knew Dr Lacoste was edging its way up from the depths of my mind, and I forced myself to focus, struggling to propel the memory to the forefront.

Then I remembered — I *had* met Dr Lacoste before. And, as blackness descended, the shock of that memory, and what it might mean now, stunned me.

~

I woke to a mask covering my face, and a smiling Dr Lacoste looming over me. My entire body ached, and pebbles ricocheted about in my brain. A steel ridge pressed behind my eyes, and blood drummed at my temples.

'There you are, that wasn't too bad, was it? I'll remove this oxygen mask,' Dr Lacoste said with a smile.

'I have a headache.'

'I'm sorry, that side effect can't be avoided, but it won't last,' he said, dabbing a cloth to the drool on my chin. 'And, while some of your memories may be crystal clear, others may be a bit scrambled at first. But they'll likely improve, and your depressive feelings will lift.' He patted my arm. 'Now you have a nice rest for a few hours,

Adrienne,' he said, as the orderly wheeled away my gurney, 'and I'll see you tomorrow.'

… memories may be a bit scrambled at first.

That was certainly true. No matter how hard I concentrated, my mind was one great fog-filled haze, and I could barely remember my name. It was as if my brain had swelled, too big now to fit inside my skull, and was set to burst.

But, as I slid from the gurney back onto my own bed, one small thought niggled at me.

Some memories may be crystal clear …

I suspected it was my last thought that was pestering me; that important thing I'd recalled before they knocked me out, which I now desperately tried to remember.

As I lay there, the more afraid I became. But afraid of what? And the longer I focused on recovering that memory, the more vital it became that I *had* to remember it. I sensed it was highly important, perhaps something my life depended on.

… have a nice rest for a few hours, Adrienne … Adrienne.

Like an axe bludgeon to my already aching skull, it hit me. I *had* met Dr Xavier Lacoste at Emile's medical graduation ceremony.

He'd been as good-looking all those years ago as he was now. A handsome charmer, like Emile.

Ha, perhaps that's why I remember him!

At the after-ceremony party, he'd come to chat with Emile. He'd smiled, and shaken my hand, holding on a moment longer than normal. Then, as he spoke to Emile, his gaze kept straying to me — brief, surreptitious glances, and I felt again, the heat of the blush that had scrambled up my neck, and settled in my cheeks.

'I saw the way he looked at you,' Emile had said when Xavier Lacoste moved away from us. 'Be careful of that one, he's a dreadful flirt who uses women, then throws them aside like rotted meat.' He clinched my arm. 'Not that I don't trust you, Adrienne. You're certainly not the type to have an affair.'

Then, like revolving cogs that finally fall into their rightful notch, the awful truth clicked into place. I gasped out loud, and gripped the edges of my narrow bed, my pulse racing in my ears, my breaths quickening.

Emile still knows Xavier Lacoste, as a psychiatrist colleague now, rather than a university friend. My husband has planned all of this and asked his colleague to declare me insane!

But that made no sense. Emile wanted me home with him, so why would he commit me to this asylum, and ask a psychiatrist friend to treat me for insanity? And why ever would Dr Lacoste agree to such an evil plan?

But he'd said 'depression', not madness and, with an icy shiver, I sensed Emile was playing one of his mind games that I didn't understand; a mean trick that would only become obvious later.

I wanted to blurt out my suspicions to Dr Lacoste, but maybe I'd got it wrong, and there was no plan. Emile truly was convinced of my insanity, and it was simply a coincidence that his colleague worked at Sainte-Dymphna's.

It was all so confusing, especially amidst the muddy brain fog that obscured all rational thought.

But one thing was clear, if Emile and Dr Lacoste *were* working together — for whatever bizarre reason — my battle to get out of Sainte-Dymphna's was lost even before I'd marched off to war.

39

'Feeling better, Adrienne?' Yvonne asked at breakfast the following morning, as the staff placed baskets of toast in the middle of the table.

'Yes thanks, but still groggy, like I'm floating around in a never-ending dream.'

And it was true what Dr Lacoste had said after ECT, that some memories were like scrambled egg in my brain, whilst others were clearer than ever. Like remembering where I'd met him and wondering if he and Emile had planned to send me here together.

But I kept my conspiracy theory to myself. Even to Yvonne and Marcelle, that would sound crazy, and besides, I wasn't certain; still I couldn't understand Emile's reasoning to commit me here, when he wanted me home with him.

'*Oh là là,* here we go again,' Yvonne said with a sigh, nodding at Gauloises Janine.

Once again, the ruckus was over stolen food. Janine and another woman had reached for the last slice of toast, and when Janine grabbed it, the other woman tugged on a fistful of Janine's hair. As a chunk of her hair came out, Janine screamed, her bloodshot eyes filling with tears.

That set off other patients yelling and scurrying around the table, or rocking in their chairs, pulling at their own hair.

In one swift and skilled movement, the orderlies pulled the women apart. They smacked them both on the head, which sent them sprawling to the floor in a knot of thin, pale limbs and grey garments.

The orderlies then hurried about, grabbing the runaways and yelling, 'Shut up and sit back down!'

Amidst the commotion, another patient fell off her chair, taking her plate of toast and jam with her, splattering it over her dress and the floor.

'Oh no, what's wrong with her?' I said.

'She's about to have one of her seizures,' Yvonne said, as two nurses hurried over and held the woman's head and limbs.

'Happens all the time,' Marcelle said.

A third nurse — the nice Nurse Trudeau — placed a rubber gag between the woman's teeth.

'To stop her from biting her tongue,' Yvonne explained.

'Where are they taking her?' I asked, when the patient had come to her senses, and the nurses half-walked, half-carried her away.

'To the dormitory to recover,' Marcelle said. '*If* she recovers. Often she goes straight into another fit.'

After breakfast, as a line of patients received their medication, other people shuffled off to the Day Room. Some went to the Therapy Room or the Activities Room, neither of which appealed, so I returned to the dormitory with Yvonne and Marcelle, to take advantage of the ten minutes' toilet time. Ten minutes of relative peace.

When I came out of the toilet, Yvonne and Marcelle were wearing their coats and holding out mine.

'Fancy a walk?' Yvonne nodded at the barred window. 'Let's make the most of this rare bit of sun?'

'Great idea,' I said, threading my arms through the awful coat, hoping fresh air would clear my foggy brain.

We walked out of the dormitory, past the seizure patient who was curled up on her bed. She didn't seem to notice us, just stared into space with a faraway look.

'Poor thing,' I said. 'Can't they give her pills to stop the seizures?'

Yvonne shrugged. 'The medication doesn't work too well. She's got *status epilepticus*.'

'It'll probably kill her one day,' Marcelle said.

How matter-of-fact and resigned they both sounded, and I vowed I'd never get so used to Sainte-Dymphna's horrors.

~

An orderly counted us outside into the high-walled Airing Space, along with the other patients.

Just inside the high stone walls enclosing Sainte-Dymphna's — over which you couldn't glimpse a single thing — a ditch ran all the way around the Airing Space perimeter, preventing people even attempting to scale the wall. I almost laughed at how futile my pathetic escape attempt had been. But walking beside my new friends, our arms linked, the bracing autumn air nipping at my cheeks did energise me.

'*Pardon*,' I said, almost tripping over a crouched man, his blackened fingers plucking cigarette butts from the dirt and shoving them into the pocket of his threadbare coat. Wordlessly, he glanced up at me. His face was deathly pale, with the same burnt nose and lips as Janine, his hair a greasy mess sprouting in all directions.

'Exercise time for the long-term patients,' Yvonne said, nodding at an orderly leading a single file of men around the perimeter, all identical in their grey garments, and all taking short shuffling steps, heads bowed, shoulders hunched. 'They force them outside for an hour every morning, otherwise they'd get no exercise at all.'

'And rather than helping them recover,' I said, as the orderly slapped the legs of an old man who'd veered out of line, with a stick, 'the staff only add to their misery.'

'I wonder how many times they've walked around this Airing Space over the years?' I said. 'How many times have they felt sad at being separated from their families?'

'Some people have been here longer than you've been alive, Adrienne,' Marcelle said.

'And they barely feel *or* think,' Yvonne said, as we headed toward the trees and shrubs at the end of the Airing Space. 'Poor buggers have no relatives or friends to visit them, and all they have to think about is eating, drinking, sleeping, and wanking off.'

'They've become completely institutionalised,' Marcelle said.

We passed an old man curled up on a wooden bench seat in the foetal position, trousers hanging around his knees, a single tooth protruding from thin navy-coloured lips. He fixed his cloudy gaze on me, and I had to stop myself from retching at his foul stench of urine.

'One more sad case,' Marcelle said as we walked on.

'He's almost blind, and never had a single visitor in all the years we've been here,' Yvonne said. She glanced at Marcelle and they exchanged a loving look, arms tightening together, as if all they had in this world was each other. Which was likely true.

'But whatever is *wrong* with him? With *all* these patients?' I waved an arm at a tall, thin man who was talking to himself. His arms flapped wildly, spittle flying as he spoke louder and louder, until he was shouting at himself.

'He's one of the worst cases,' Yvonne said. 'You can't see from here, but each side of his head is indented from a lobotomy.'

'A *what*?'

'They don't do them anymore, too barbaric,' Marcelle said, 'but for the completely mad and violent ones, when nothing else worked, they'd drill holes in their skull and poke around in their brain. Basically, they'd steal their personality, then claim they were cured.'

'*Oh là là,*' I said, unable to stop shaking my head.

'But apparently he's a lot calmer now,' Marcelle said.

'Some patients are so deeply depressed,' Yvonne said, 'that they live in constant darkness. Others are tormented by voices inside their head. We also have your run of the mill schizophrenic, epileptic, Parkinson's and Huntington's disease, and general mental deficients like those unfortunate souls.' She nodded at a group of Mongoloids shuffling about the Airing Space.

'And that's not even counting us homosexuals,' Marcelle said, 'or the petty thieves, pathological liars and disobedient wives.'

'Like me,' I said, 'and Joséphine Bonaparte.'

'You're not the only wife whose husband sent her here for disobeying him,' Yvonne said, patting my arm with her free hand.

'And that won't change until women fight back, and defend ourselves against those men who boss us around,' I said, bitterly. 'Which isn't easy, since men are usually physically stronger, *and* earn the wages.'

I looked around the bleak grounds at all those soulless, abandoned patients who inhabited this isolated world within the real world. 'But can you both *want* to stay here? I don't understand.'

'For several reasons,' Yvonne said, 'starting with the fact that if Sainte-Dymphna's released us, we'd have no choice but to return to our husbands.'

'Then they'd have won,' Marcelle said, 'and we'd never give them that satisfaction.'

'Besides, we don't have the slightest *desire* to return to our husbands,' Yvonne said.

'We feel safe at Sainte-Dymphna's,' Marcelle said. 'It would be difficult for us to be together on the outside. And, in here, if you shut up and keep calm, the nurses and orderlies pretty much leave you alone.'

'The really disruptive patients are enough for them to cope with,' Yvonne said, 'so they don't bother us.'

While I understood Yvonne and Marcelle could feel freer at Sainte-Dymphna's, I was even more of a prisoner here than with Emile at the flat. And, *somehow*, I had to get out of this new gaol in which Emile had shackled me.

~

'Watch out, here comes Georges,' Yvonne said with a smile, as a boy from the Mongoloid dormitory waddled toward us.

'He's *very* affectionate,' Marcelle said.

'Most of the Mongoloids are starved of affection and crave love,' Yvonne said.

'She your new friend?' Georges said, pushing between Yvonne and Marcelle and linking arms with them. He looked over at me, and with the cutest grin said, 'You my friend too?'

'Sure,' I said, as we approached a cluster of trees near the bottom of the Airing Space, from where a squirrel scurried from branch to branch, gathering food for the coming winter.

'Yvonne and Marcelle are my mamans, and you can be too. Then I'll have three mamans. *Moi* lucky boy!'

Without waiting for an answer, Georges let go of Yvonne and Marcelle, and cuddled me so tightly I had to stop walking. His arms still gripping my waist, Georges swayed from side to side, his affection overwhelming me.

He suddenly let go, and rushed toward a clump of bushes, pointing and giggling at the grunting noises coming from behind a bush.

'*L'amour, l'amour!*' Georges chanted.

I peered closer and caught sight of a couple behind the bush, though their raw, lustful animal coupling was anything but 'love'. I didn't know if I was more shocked at what they were doing in hospital grounds, or that they weren't even trying to hide.

'Those two are at it all the time,' Yvonne said.

'And they're certainly not the only ones to get a bit of comfort from another patient,' Marcelle said with a wink at her girlfriend.

'That girl looks so young,' I said. 'What if she gets pregnant?'

'She won't,' Marcelle said. 'They tie the tubes of all the young girls on admission here. Without their permission of course; without them even knowing.'

'Surely that's illegal?' I said.

'A lot of what happens at Sainte-Dymphna's is illegal,' Yvonne said. 'But who'd listen if we complained?'

'And this place dares to call itself a hospital.' I shook my head at the incongruity, as the bell rang, loud and insistent, for lunch.

As we headed back, Georges skipping along beside us, I gazed up in dismay at the place Emile had forced me to call home: its long dank corridors, its ever-present stink, the claustrophobic ECT room, and vast dormitories — like some olden-day orphanage — and its barred windows behind which all kinds of grey-clothed humans were left to wither and die.

40

After lunch, on Nurse Durand's orders, I sat, once again, in Dr Lacoste's office.

'Ah there you are, Adrienne.' That same friendly smile disarmed me. 'I do hope you're feeling better after your first ECT session?' He came around to my side of his desk, face all serious and sympathetic, took my hand and patted the back of it.

'Not really,' I said. Despite his gentle touch, I wanted to tell him that after only two days at Sainte-Dymphna's my spirit was crushed, and I was already a pathetic version of the former Adrienne. 'I had a pleasant walk this morning, but I still ache all over from the ECT. I'm sleepy and my brain's foggy, though I do remember *some* things clearly.'

I met Dr Lacoste's gaze, wondering if he too, recalled meeting me at that medical graduation party. I itched to ask him if he and Emile were working together — for *whatever* far-fetched reason — but instinct still warned me to keep my suspicions to myself. For now.

'I don't think electric volts through my brain helped, and I can't go on in this place.' I forced my voice not to rise to a desperate shriek. '*Please*, Dr Lacoste, there must be another treatment?'

'You are an attractive and intelligent woman, Adrienne, and I don't like to see you so upset.' He turned back to his desk, on which sat a tray bearing a floral-patterned china teapot with two matching cups and saucers, and a plate of *Palmier* biscuits. 'All I want is for you to have the right treatment and get better. How about a cup of tea and a biscuit before we start?'

I nodded, and he poured out two cups, and slid one toward me, with two biscuits on the saucer.

I had to stop myself gulping down the strong aromatic tea, nothing like the dining room vats of tea and coffee that tasted like dishwater. Dr Lacoste must have his own supply of biscuits too, as the sweet and buttery pastry melted on my tongue. They'd never give patients such fancy biscuits.

'As I mentioned — as you yourself *theorised* — your desperate childhood did not arm you for adulthood,' he said, stroking his chin between thumb and forefinger. 'That's why you experienced that episode at Carrefour, and made a rash, perhaps unconscious, decision to leave your comfortable home — without telling your husband — and reside in a questionable hippie camp. Then you lived as a single woman at some countryside auberge, when you are, in reality, a married woman.'

He drank his tea and nibbled on a biscuit. A crumb caught in his moustache, and I had an urge to reach over his desk and brush it off.

'However, I will reconsider the ECT, but you intrigue me, Adrienne, and I truly believe I can help you.'

He set his cup on the saucer, got up again, and stood before me. 'We need to find the key to unlock what's happening in here,' he said, tapping a finger to my forehead, which might have been a normal touch, or perhaps flirting, like at the graduation party. I couldn't tell, but my pulse quickened beneath his touch, the heat rushing to my cheeks. 'Do you recall me mentioning psychoanalysis? Have you heard of the father of psychoanalysis, Sigmund Freud?'

'Y-yes,' I replied, hot and cold beneath his touch. 'S- something to do with dr-dreams?'

'Freud was an Austrian neurologist who encouraged patients to talk about their experiences, particularly childhood ones,' Dr Lacoste said. 'He believed a person's psychological problems are rooted in the unconscious mind, so that by making conscious your unconscious thoughts, you could deal with these problems, and thus recover.'

As complicated as that sounded, it made sense. It was true that my thoughts had never been clear, and it was true that I had abandoned my elegant home and a husband who provided me with everything. And I had to admit that those actions were far from sane.

'So, shall we give it a go, Adrienne?'

'*Très bien.* I've got nothing to lose, have I Dr Lacoste?'

'Excellent. Right, let's start with a relaxation session.' He nodded at the *chaise longue*. 'Come and lie down. We must create favourable relaxation conditions to bring those troubling childhood memories into your conscious mind, so we can deal with them.'

'Oh, all right.' I lay down as Dr Lacoste put on the gramophone and gentle music filled the room. 'Nice music,' I said, as he stood behind my head.

'Close your eyes, Adrienne. Breathe deeply and relax. Concentrate on the feel of my fingertips.'

The soft touch of those fingertips on my head made it both easy, and hard, to relax. No one had touched me since Bambou, and I had to stop myself from groaning; from wondering, yet again, whether this was normal, or that Emile had been telling the truth, and Dr Lacoste a terrible womaniser.

'*Oh là là.*'

'Hush,' he said, the fingertips massaging all over my head. 'Trust me Adrienne, relax, you're trembling.'

'Sorry.'

I did relax then. All warm and tingly, and burning inside.

I was disappointed when the massaging stopped and he said, 'You may open your eyes now.' I looked straight into his soft gaze, and his breath was warm and biscuit-sweet.

'How do you feel now, Adrienne? And you may sit up.'

'I'm more relaxed than I've felt in years, Dr Lacoste.' I sat up on the *chaise longue* and dangled my feet over the side. 'You know, I never realised my husband could do this to me — force me to come to Sainte-Dymphna's. And if I'd understood that marrying Emile meant I would *belong* to him, I'm not sure I'd have married.' I shook my head, still trying to shake the lingering ECT fog. 'Now I understand why some girls choose never to marry. I always thought that was what girls did — we left school, snagged the best possible husband, then had his babies and kept his home — but now I've seen that women can do *so* much more.'

Dr Lacoste smiled. 'True, but that would have been a terrible shame if you'd never married — a beautiful woman like you.'

Beautiful? Does he say that to all his patients, to make them feel warm and fuzzy?

'Psychoanalysis is a lengthy process, involving many sessions,' he went on. 'Do you think you could settle at Sainte-Dymphna's for the time it will take for you to recover?'

'Oh, I could never settle here, Dr Lacoste, but if there was no more ECT, I might be able to cope ... though only for a short while.' I met his stare. 'But then, after you've cured me with this psychoanalysis, you'll release me, right?'

'As I said, after the appropriate treatment, you will be released.' Dr Lacoste nodded and held up a forefinger. 'On one condition.'

'Condition?'

'The condition that you return home to your husband.'

I caught my breath, thoughts humming and ticking through my hazy mind.

'You'll only release me from Sainte-Dymphna's if I agree to return home to Emile?'

'Yes. Your husband advised me that, following treatment, he is prepared to take you home to continue your recovery in your own surroundings, which, as I'm sure you'll agree, would be far more pleasant than Sainte-Dymphna's.'

Like a jolting crack of thunder, I understood everything.

Emile had marched into L'Auberge de Léa and tried to force me to come home. And when that failed, he'd devised a plan to commit me to Sainte-Dymphna's, where his colleague would keep me detained for this psychoanalysis. Knowing that this dark pit would certainly break me down to the lowest human depths, I would then beg Dr Lacoste to release me. And, once Emile got me home, he'd have me under his watch, rather than out of his reach at the auberge. He believed that I would come to my senses — *silly, stupid Rien* — and everything would go back to how it was before.

I was convinced now that my husband *had* devised this diabolical scheme, though I still couldn't imagine why Dr Lacoste would agree to such a thing.

What if I do return to Emile, my only way out?

My husband couldn't keep me locked in the flat; couldn't watch over me constantly. I could, once again, run off. And the next time, I really would vanish. I'd become Anonymous Mademoiselle Océane, who Dr Emile Chevalier would never find.

But there was one glaring drawback — I could no longer hide at L'Auberge de Léa, the only place I wanted to be.

No, returning home to Emile wasn't the answer.

But now I'd understood my husband's cruel plan, I was determined to outwit him. Mulling over his — possibly *their* — deception, I felt ill, and might have passed out had I not been sitting. I blinked away the tears stinging my eyes and looked away from Dr Lacoste.

'Are you all right, Adrienne? You've gone quite pale. Another cup of tea, or something stronger? I have whiskey.' He opened his desk drawer.

'*Non, merci.* I'm fine.'

I might be confused, but I still believed it was safer to keep my suspicions to myself, rather than risk sounding like some paranoid crackpot.

The only thing I was certain of was that I had to somehow convince Dr Lacoste to release me back to L'Auberge de Léa, rather than to Emile.

41

I walked down the corridor after my appointment with Dr Lacoste, staring through the barred windows as the last rays of sunset lit the sky a bloodstained hue. It might be cold outside, with a prowling wind, but I yearned to be free, beneath that beautiful sky.

Besides the pleasure of escaping the asylum din, that crisp air might help me think more clearly over what Dr Lacoste had said about releasing me home to Emile. But patients weren't allowed into the Airing Space outside morning exercise.

I couldn't find Yvonne and Marcelle to ask their advice, and since there was nowhere to go until dinnertime, besides the depressing dormitory, I shuffled into the Day Room.

Patients wandered about like zombies. Some rocked back and forth in shabby armchairs, staring into space or chattering nonsense to themselves. Several couples, of both sexes, kissed and cuddled on the sofas. One woman was cramming soil from a potted plant into her mouth. Avoiding eye contact with anyone, I slunk across to a battered armchair, as far away as possible from the general commotion.

Georges, the Mongoloid boy, waddled over, clambered onto my lap, and circled his chubby arms around my neck.

'*Bonjour*, new Maman.' He planted a slobbery kiss on my cheek, and I had to stop myself from wiping it away.

'You're *so* heavy, Georges,' I said with a laugh. 'You'll squash me.'

'Wanna play a game, Adrienne?'

'What game?'

'Play with my *Snoopy l'astronaute*? He's in my locker,' he said, but made no move to get off my lap, or shift his weight.

After the Americans walked on the moon last year, Charlie Brown's famous dog had been made into NASA's Apollo mascot, and I recalled seeing Juliette and Linda playing with a *Snoopy l'astronaute* doll.

I couldn't imagine how Georges had got hold of one of these dolls in this place *and* kept it intact, but I nudged him off my lap.

'Go and fetch Snoopy, Georges, and I'll play with you soon.'

Yvonne and Marcelle had told me Georges was in his mid-thirties, an adult. Sadly, though, he would be an eternal child, unlike my children, who'd been lucky enough to be able to grow up normally.

Poor Georges would always need a mother to care for him — not that he got much motherly love at Sainte-Dymphna's, besides that from the rare caring people like Nurse Trudeau — but I was glad to give Georges a little affection, as I'd given my own children when they were little.

I didn't dare close my eyes, for fear of Georges plonking himself heavily back on my lap, or Janine bothering me for a Gauloises, so I watched the darkness fall outside, and conjured up my ghostly friend. More than ever, I yearned for Suzanne's comforting presence.

'How can I convince Dr Lacoste to send me home to the auberge?' I whispered, as Suzanne appeared in my mind, in her bonnet, a white shirt with a hint of lace tucked into her high-waisted skirt.

I frowned in concentration, trying to focus on Suzanne's words amidst the ECT fog that still shrouded me like a dour blanket. A buzz started up in my mind and I recalled Yvonne and Marcelle saying they wouldn't give their husbands the satisfaction of going home to them.

'I won't give Emile that pleasure either, Suzanne … won't give him the power to possess me again. But going home to him is my only way out of this miserable place.' Some yelling near the doorway startled me.

'Put on some clothes!' a nurse shouted at a withered old man who stood naked in the Day Room, his watery gaze vacant.

When the man didn't move, the nurse kicked him in the backside, and he collapsed to the ground.

'Get up! Go and get dressed, if you want any dinner.'

My heart ached for that poor old man as he struggled onto all fours. Thankfully, the lovely Nurse Trudeau helped him upright, and led the wobbly old man from the Day Room.

'*Mon Dieu*, Suzanne, you see how inhumanely they treat people? If only there were a few more decent ones, like Nurse Trudeau.' I looked away from the commotion and concentrated on my friend's silent words.

'Was Dr Lacoste flirting with you in his office?' Suzanne asked.

'Maybe, I can't be sure.'

'Remember, he *did* flirt with you all those years ago,' she reminded me with a wry smile.

Yes, I think *he did*.

And as Georges bounded toward me, grinning and clutching his *Snoopy l'astronaute*, the kernel of an idea filtered into my mind.

~

'*Another* appointment?' I said to Nurse Durand as she took me to Dr Lacoste's office three days later.

During that time, the ECT fog had vanished, and my mind was quite clear. And my plan defined.

'Rumour has it you've become Dr Lacoste's favourite patient,' Nurse Durand said, with a sarcastic wink as she tapped on his door.

As if he'd been waiting for me to arrive, the doctor opened the door immediately, and Nurse Durand waltzed away, shoes squeaking on the polished lino like crazed mice.

'*Bonjour*, Dr Lacoste,' I said, with a coy smile, in my best sing-song voice.

'*Bonjour* to you, Adrienne, and please call me Xavier. Only fair, isn't it?' With a small bow-like gesture, he waved an arm toward my usual chair, as if it were a queen's throne. 'Cup of tea and a biscuit before we start?'

'*Oui merci*, I'd love that, Dr Lac ... Xavier.' I clasped my hands in my lap and crossed my ankles. The proper lady.

'How are you feeling, Adrienne? Ready to continue the psychoanalysis?'

'I'm much better now that I'm in your office with you,' I said. 'And yes, I'm so looking forward to continuing our dream treatment, it's already helped *so* much.'

I sipped the delicious tea, and nibbled a single *Palmier* biscuit, rather than giving in to the urge to snatch the lot from the tin and cram them into my mouth.

Once we'd drunk our tea, he helped me hoist myself onto the *chaise longue* — not that I needed help — and I had to force my legs to stop trembling as his hand lingered, for an extra heartbeat, on my back.

Or am I simply imagining it?

Dr Lacoste — Xavier — began the session with the same soft music, and his fingertips massaging my head. I breathed easily, relaxing into his warm touch.

'How did you feel when your mother was committed to Sainte-Dymphna's, Adrienne?'

'Should I open my eyes, Dr … er, Xavier?'

'Best to keep them closed.'

I was glad of that. It was easier to relax if I could avoid that sexy gaze.

'I felt abandoned, lonely and lost, and Papa and Grandmère made me do all the household jobs.'

'Poor girl,' he soothed, and I was horrified to feel my nipples harden. God forbid, he didn't notice through the thin fabric of the shift! 'And how was it when your mother came home from Sainte-Dymphna's?'

'Once she'd been here, Maman never truly came home again, in her mind, I mean. She was *absent*, gazing into space like so many of the patients here, until the time she returned to Sainte-Dymphna's … and never came home.'

That deep sadness drenched me again, as I thought of Maman killing herself to escape both Sainte-Dymphna's and her sick mind. How desperately miserable she must have been.

'So, you can see why I wanted to escape that childhood? Why I jumped at the chance to marry Emile straight from school?'

'Yes, I do understand that,' he said. 'Now, can you tell me about any dreams you recall?'

One recurrent dream came to me immediately. 'When I was about eight, I'd dream of a horse-drawn carriage pulling up at our flat.' I smiled at the memory of that gilded white carriage, and the decorated horses stamping their feet, waiting for me. 'I glided toward the carriage door. I couldn't see the face of the man who opened it, only his hand, bearing glittery gold rings. My father and grandmother were chasing after me, shouting: "No, don't you dare leave, Adrienne," but I ignored them, and hopped in, and the horse would clop off to some lovely place — a sun-drenched beach in Greece, an olive grove in France, or a vineyard in Italy. The dream always ended there, and I'd wake up convinced I was going to live in this new place, happily ever after.'

'*D'accord*, that's good,' he mumbled. 'What about any recent, adult dreams?'

'One I *do* remember,' I said, 'because it was so awful, and I dreamt it over and over. My children had died. I don't know how, they were just lying on the ground, side by side, dead. They were only about five years old, not almost grown up, like they are now.'

'Your children are always young in this dream?'

'Yes, very young.'

'But now they're almost adults?'

I nodded, thinking about Georges, the eternal child, and it struck me then that Antoine and Martine *were* no longer children. They had been, but now they were not.

'Yes, almost adults,' I said, 'and they'd made it plainly clear to me I was still treating them as children, which I now see, had also made me miserable.'

Mon Dieu, the twins would soon be finished high school. My babies were heading off on their adult journey without me. Well, thanks to Emile and his fancy boarding school idea, they'd already left home, and I hadn't even been able to say a proper goodbye.

Tears stung my eyes as I grieved now, for those lost babies; the children who no longer needed me. How sad that never again would I feel the heady joy of clasping my little ones to my chest and soothing them.

Don't worry, everything's going to be all right, Maman's here.

I felt Xavier Lacoste's soothing pat on my arm.

'It's all right, Adrienne, let the tears come, *très bien.*'

As I lay there, eyes still shut, a light flashed deep in my mind, startling me with its brightness, and I heard Louise Bellefontaine's wise words.

... children always need their mother, though in different ways. Louise was right.

'But rather than grieving for my lost little ones,' I said, 'something so simple as your children growing away from you, I should be happy and grateful they've been able to grow up and embark on their adult lives. And I should be making a new life for myself — a life as the mother of young adults, don't you think, Xavier?'

'Yes, Adrienne, that's excellent. Such good progress in a short time, you may open your eyes now.'

I gazed up at his handsome features, and as he smiled at me, I had to stop myself from reaching up, and pressing my lips against his. As enticing as that was, I forced myself to resist. And to keep playing the game.

'Since I'm making progress,' I said, 'which I'm certain is down to your expert technique, would you allow my friends to visit me?'

'I'm sorry, not yet,' he said, with a sympathetic smile. 'We're at a critical point in your treatment, Adrienne, so it's best we avoid any outside influence from friends. But your family is permitted to visit.'

'So I can call my children?' I expected him to refuse, like all my previous pleas, to use a telephone.

'Certainly, go ahead.' He nodded at the telephone on his desk.

'*Merci beaucoup*, Xavier.' I flashed him a winning smile as I picked up the receiver and dialled my home number, steeling myself to plead, yet again, with Emile.

42

That Thursday morning, four long days after I'd phoned and spoken to Emile, my initial hope of the twins visiting me had faded.

'As I said before, I doubt they'll want to see you,' Emile had said. 'Anyway, I won't harp on about your childish behaviour, are you feeling better now, *chérie*? Can I have my wife back home, where she belongs?'

I almost blurted out my suspicions about his cruel plan, and my determination never to return to him, but it wasn't the moment to antagonise Emile.

'I'm much better thanks,' I'd said, quickly returning to the subject of the twins and, after much begging, Emile said he'd try and coax them to visit. 'But I can't promise you anything, Rien.'

Despite the bitter wind, I was about to head out into the Airing Space with Yvonne, Marcelle and Georges, when Nurse Durand called out, 'If you want to see your husband and children, you'd better come to the Visiting Room, Madame Chevalier.'

My children? My pulse raced and I could hardly believe they were actually here. What would I say to Emile? Accuse him of sending me to this dreadful place to break me down so I'd beg his colleague to send me home to be, once again, his prisoner?

I still had no proof of this, and I certainly couldn't make such a wild accusation in front of our children.

Besides, I'd never give my husband the smug satisfaction of seeing me in this shabby grey frock, my hair greasy and tangled. I'd never let him witness my suffering here at Sainte-Dymphna's.

'I'd love to see my children, Nurse Durand,' I said, straightening my wrinkled shift and smoothing down my hair, 'but I refuse to see my husband. Please tell him he can wait in the car.'

'Come with me then,' Nurse Durand said, raising her eyebrows, 'though why any child would want to visit a crazy mother in this nuthouse is beyond me.'

I shook with anger. 'Did you call me a crazy mother?' She smirked. 'You heard.'

'I came to Sainte-Dymphna's a sane person, Nurse Durand, and I'll leave that way. Anyway, my husband is the crazy one, not me.'

'But your husband's the one on the outside, *chérie*, isn't he?' Nurse Durand laughed like a hyena. I yearned to slap her face, but held my fisted hands by my sides as I followed her to the Visiting Room.

'I'm glad he's not *my* husband,' she went on. 'A husband who commits his wife to a place like this. *Oh là là*, don't look at me like that, Madame Chevalier, and don't blame yourself, lots of women marry the wrong man.'

As much as I hated Nurse Durand for pointing that out, it was true. Though I hoped I could eventually *unmarry* myself from that wrong man.

I banished Emile from my thoughts and concentrated on my children, excited, but nervous too, and fearful of the stories Emile had surely planted in their minds.

But I'm their mother. Surely, if I explain?

~

As I glimpsed them sitting at a table, a deep, gut-wrenching tear ripped through me. My heart exploding with joy, I rushed toward my darling children, spreading my arms wide to draw them into a hug.

'Oh look, here you are! I'm so happy to see you both … if you knew how much I've longed for this moment!'

The twins didn't leap upright and fall into my embrace, but remained motionless.

'Why don't you want to see Papa?' Martine snapped, her scowl so fierce it burned right to my core. 'Why did you make him wait in the car?' As always, Antoine avoided eye contact, and stared at the ground.

'Well, I didn't want … I can't see your father right now. Besides, I wanted to devote all my attention to you two.'

'*Devote* yourself to us?' she said, her lip hitching in scorn, not only at my words, but at my bedraggled and unkempt appearance too. 'After you *chose* to leave our family? Papa said you wanted nothing to do with us ever again.'

'It wasn't like that. I phoned your school *so* many times, trying to get messages to you, and a letter, trying to explain. You didn't receive anything?'

'Nothing,' Martine said. 'And Papa said there was no point coming to visit you, but we wanted to see for ourselves, didn't we, Antoine?' She nudged her brother. 'To see if what he said was true — that you *are* crazy — isn't that right, Antoine?'

Her brother gave a slight nod, still not looking at me. As usual, Martine was talking for both of them. Antoine hadn't changed a bit, saying nothing, gazing now at his hands.

'Did you *forget* you had a home and a family?' Martine hissed.

'I could never forget you,' I said.

'So that's why you went to Carrefour for groceries and never came home?' Martine's almond brown eyes — Emile's lovely eyes — widened the more she spoke, her face flushing scarlet. 'Is that why you waltzed off to some hippie camp and left poor Papa worried sick that you'd been injured or *killed*? And leaving your children as almost orphans?'

'But you and Antoine were no longer at home. Your father sent you away without consulting me. I'd never have agreed to boarding school ... I *never* wanted you out of the house.'

'Okay, I know you'd never have agreed to boarding school,' Martine said, her tone softening a little, 'but whatever terrible thing did Papa do to make you leave him?' She heaved a great sigh, her eyes shining with tears. I lay a tentative hand over hers, so glad when she didn't pull away.

How can I even begin to explain? How will I ever get through Emile's brainwashing?

'It wasn't any one thing, *mon amour*,' I said. 'It wasn't black and white, and I never planned to leave. I think it was something that built up over the past few years and it just ... just happened.' How pathetic that sounded.

'Once the police told us you were alive,' Martine went on, 'Papa said you needed some time and that you'd see sense, and come home. But you didn't!' She pulled her hand away from beneath mine and gnawed her fingernails. 'Then, when you *refused* to come home, he said you'd gone crazy — like your own mother — and he'd have to commit you to Sainte-Dymphna's.' She took a shaky breath and nudged her brother again, who gave a grunt. 'And that once you got the right treatment, you'd get better, and come home ... is that true?'

'I'm not mad, Martine. At one time, I thought I might be, but now I'm certain I'm quite sane. It's more like I lost my way and became *unhappy* somewhere along the journey of life. But I'm definitely going to recover, so please don't believe everything your father says.'

'Papa is the *psychiatrist*, isn't he?' Martine said. 'And you are ... you're what, Maman? No longer even a housewife. No, because you ran away from your house *and* your family. So what does that make you?'

'Well, I suppose that makes me ... nothing,' I said, recoiling at her venomous words, and cupping a palm to my chest against the stab of pain. 'Perhaps your father was right after all, calling me "Rien", but I couldn't bear it any longer, and I never found his nicknames funny.'

'Well, I suppose we didn't think they were funny either,' Martine said. 'Did we, Antoine?'

My son gave a quick nod.

'After all I did for him, for our family,' I went on, my voice shaky. 'You all just took me for granted. I never got the slightest conversation, nice word or chat, only sulky, pouty looks. Never a word of gratitude for always thinking of you, and never thinking of myself.'

Martine rolled her eyes. 'What did you want, a medal? All mothers do those things for their family, that's their *job*.'

'I know that,' I said. 'I didn't want any thanks for being a mother and a wife. I only wanted you all to treat me like a person, rather than a dog.'

Antoine stifled a yawn.

'Anyway, I know I've been treating you like children these last few years, when I should've been treating you as adults, so I'm sorry for that.'

'Lots of mothers can't bear to see their children grow up, Maman,' Martine said. 'I think that's pretty usual, but what I'm having trouble understanding is you leaving Papa without him having any idea why.'

The room fell silent, and I realised this discussion was pointless. I couldn't tell them the raw truth about their father; couldn't bad-mouth Emile too much, which would simply be pitting him against me. Besides, I didn't stand a chance against Emile's efficient indoctrination. Afraid they'd leave, I racked my brain for a safe subject.

'How's school going? Have you made any plans for university?'

'We didn't come here to talk about *school*,' Martine said with a fresh scowl.

Then why did you come, I wanted to ask, though I knew exactly why — they'd come to vent their anger at me for abandoning our home, and their father. Which I probably deserved. I'd just hoped they'd understand why, but as Martine jumped up, I knew that wouldn't happen. Not now.

'Come on, Antoine.' She grabbed her brother's arm. 'Let's get out of this hellhole and leave our mother to her new life.'

She threw me a last scowl as she stamped out of the Visting Room, Antoine plodding along in his sister's angry wake.

'No, don't go!' I cried out feebly. 'Please let me try and explain.'

But they were gone and, miserable and desperate, I lay my aching head on my arms, and sobbed. My heart was hollow — a dried up, useless husk.

43

'Should I try to speak to the twins again?' I said to Yvonne and Marcelle as we stepped out into the Airing Space that dreary mid-November morning. They'd been constantly in my thoughts since their harrowing visit over a month ago. 'Though I still don't know how to make them understand.'

The sun hadn't shone for weeks, the constant grey and watery sky only heightening the asylum's grim aura. The night frost silvered the ground, and the fine, misty rain was an invisible, constant damp. But the chilly outside air was preferable to that oppressive stink indoors.

'Don't worry too much, *chérie*,' Yvonne said, as we huddled together, arms linked, strolling down toward the far perimeter. 'Teenagers get angry at everything, and nothing is ever their fault.'

'I'm sure they'll eventually understand why you left their father,' Marcelle said. 'Once you get out of here, and they grow up a bit more.'

I nodded, shivering in my threadbare coat.

'And I'm betting your favourite doctor will release you *very* soon,' Yvonne said with a wink. 'If you can keep on that secret track to his heart.'

Here in the Airing Space, out of earshot, I'd been telling my friends about the 'Dr Lacoste plan', keeping them up to date with the progress of my twice-weekly psychoanalysis treatments, the chats and cups of tea, and my flirty ways.

'I *think* he has feelings for me,' I said. 'Though he remains professional, never touching me beyond what could be normal ... or might not be, I'm not certain. I keep hinting that something could happen between us if I got out of here, so I can only hope my friendly doctor is about to release me back to L'Auberge de Léa, rather than to Emile.'

In the meantime, though, while I contained my impatience waiting for Xavier Lacoste to succumb to his lust — if that was, indeed, the case — the weeks crawled by as I endured this despicable place.

Winter approached, each day colder and bleaker than the last, and structured around the same grim routine, the same lunatics doing the same crazy things, and the same, horrific treatment from most of the staff.

For many patients, life at L'Hôpital Sainte-Dymphna was savage and barbaric, with no sign of a cure. In the time I'd been here — almost two months — I'd never known anyone to be cured or released. Though I'd gathered that most patients weren't cured because there had never been anything wrong with them. Poor souls imprisoned against their will because they didn't conform to society's expectations.

And if you weren't insane before you arrived, you almost always became crazy if you stayed long enough. If you didn't die. And the so-called treatments they suffered, often for years, were simply making them stupefied and compliant, rather than curing them.

One of the worst places, the Maniacs dormitory, was littered with stained, hole-ridden mattresses, rubbish and excrement. And the patients were beyond filthy, not having been bathed in months.

Another dormitory was filled with old people, many of them war amputees. None of them ever had a visitor and they all just lay slumped in bed, waiting for death to creep in and relieve them of their misery.

Not a single day passed without some drama, often instigated by a nurse or orderly for their own entertainment, basking in their little slice of power over the patients. Most of them despised their job, and only the rare kind ones, like Nurse Trudeau, cared about us.

That naked old man who the nurse had kicked in the backside died from pneumonia, as did Joséphine Bonaparte, whose real name I never learned. Nobody shed a tear.

'How can you keep so sane and relatively happy?' I asked Yvonne and Marcelle, as I gazed around at the windblown trees, leafless and skeletal, mistletoe dangling like raggedy hair.

'We told you,' Yvonne said with a smile and a loving glance at her girlfriend. 'Because Marcelle and I are "allowed" to be together in here.'

'It's certainly no fancy hotel, but we're safer here than on the outside,' Marcelle said with a dramatic arm wave, 'where some bigot might stone us to death, or burn us at the stake!'

Yvonne laughed and kissed Marcelle's cheek. 'Marcelle loves to exaggerate, but it's true. Though attitudes *are* finally changing, so who knows, maybe we'll get out one day.'

Horrific as it was, I understood, but I suspected my friends had become what they'd explained to me as 'institutionalised'. I silently prayed that I'd never be here long enough for that.

~

December brought winter's icy hissing breath, the elegant white coat of snow outside belying Sainte-Dymphna's ugliness within.

During these darkening weeks, after over two months of psychoanalysis treatment, I sensed Dr Lacoste was more and more keen on me. Like with Bambou, I could almost *smell* the lust oozing from him, but still he kept his distance, only touching me for the head massages, and when he took my hand to help me off the *chaise longue*. Emile's words kept jangling in my mind.

… a dreadful flirt who uses women, then throws them aside like rotted meat.

If that was true, why wasn't he taking advantage of me, a woman who was almost throwing herself at him? A vulnerable patient who'd never dare complain?

Because, after all, Dr Xavier Lacoste still held the power. He still clutched the magic wand that could get me out of here. Or keep me imprisoned.

Sensing the moment had come today, I took my chance, and kept hold of his hand as he helped me off the *chaise longue* after our session.

'Such a pity,' I said. 'If you and I had met under different circumstances, perhaps we could've … you know?'

He dropped my hand like it had burned his skin, turned away and strode back to his desk. He gulped down a glass of water and scribbled on his notepad, refusing to meet my gaze.

'I do feel *so* much better, after all our dream sessions. Perhaps I'm ready to leave here now?'

He frowned and, for the first time, that veneer of confidence — that mask of power and self-importance – – slipped. He coughed and cleared his throat.

'So, you feel you're ready to go home to your husband, Adrienne?'

Tempted as I was to question his part — or not — in Emile's plan, I still resisted.

'I've told you how Emile treated me, and I thought you understood that I definitely *don't* want to go home to him ... I can't, Xavier, I just can't.'

He nodded. 'Oh, I do understand your reluctance *and* your reasons for not wanting to return home, but you know I am only permitted to release you to your husband.'

'But *you're* the doctor, Xavier. *You're* the boss, not Emile. Surely you can decide what's best for your patient? And if your patient is released back to her friend's auberge, rather than to her abusive husband, well then ...' I waved an arm outside. 'If your patient was simply a normal woman out there, she could invite anyone she liked to come and visit her, couldn't she?'

He kept his gaze low, but I caught the flush that crept around his neck, and settled in those dramatic cheekbones.

'Y-yes, I-I suppose you're right,' he stuttered, something I'd never heard him do.

'I'd love you to come and see how I'm getting on, Xavier. Yes, you *must* come as soon as I'm no longer a patient here. I'm certain my friends at the inn would have me back there. You know where it is, don't you ... in the village of Sainte-Marie-du Lac, on the shores of lac du Héron?'

He nodded, and mumbled, 'Yes, I know the place.'

~

That same afternoon, an orderly unlocked the great wooden front door, and I stepped tentatively outside, hugging my shoulder bag to my side.

Gasping at the icy cold, I descended those uneven stone steps, my legs shaking. Clutching the railing to stop myself stumbling, I kept glancing back over my shoulder.

How closely I'd been guarded inside, how tightly I'd been held, and how strange it was to be simply waltzing off a free woman, with nobody telling me what to do, wear or eat.

At the bottom of the steps, I focused on the tall sentinel-like stone pillars flanking the gate, and beyond, to Léa waiting for me in her car. But I'd learned that hope was so fragile, and could be crushed in a second, and I expected Nurse Durand to yell, with her wild cackle, 'Come back, it's only a joke, you're *never* getting out of here.' Or those white-uniformed, rough nurses who'd bought me here to grab me, and haul me back inside. That freedom was within my grasp seemed too good to be true, and I hardly dared believe it would truly happen.

In my rush to leave Sainte-Dymphna's, there'd only been time for a quick goodbye to Yvonne and Marcelle.

What a pity you're both forced to stay here. What a waste of your lives, I yearned to say to my friends, but there was no point. Over the years, Sainte-Dymphna's had become as much a part of Yvonne and Marcelle as they'd become a part of the asylum. Like so many other patients that society had forgotten — sweet Georges, annoying Janine, and poor, dead Paulette. Even the staff — smirky Nurse Durand, those rough male nurses, and most of the others — were simply cogs in that evil asylum wheel.

My pulse throbbed, and I shivered violently, not only from the bitter north wind howling down the gravelled driveway, almost obscuring the crunch of my shoes, but from the fear that all of this was simply another of Emile's humourless, malevolent jokes.

'Adrienne!' Startled, I froze.

Breathing hard, I swivelled around. Dr Lacoste — Xavier — was standing at the top of the steps, white coat billowing around his tall, lean body like sails in the wind.

'Good luck, Adrienne,' he said with a smile and a wave. 'I hope to see you soon.'

Part III

December 1970 – April 1971

Adrienne

~

44

'*Oh là là*, how *thin* you are, Adrienne. Don't they feed people at Sainte-Dymphna's?' Louise made the sign of the cross, her heels clattering across the cobblestones toward Léa's car. 'Fortunately, I whipped up a batch of crêpes as soon as you called to say the doctor was releasing you.' She took my arm as I got out of the car, and tugged me toward the inn.

It was a bizarre feeling to suddenly be cocooned in this cosy inn kitchen, Noisette miaowing and threading through my ankles. It felt strange, almost *forbidden*, to be savouring a fluffy crêpe slathered with cream and blackberry jam, rather than fighting with wild-haired, smelly people over the last slice of burnt toast.

'You look like you need feeding up,' Nelly said, placing a steaming mug of sweetened tea in front of me.

'Juliette and Linda will be so excited to see you're home,' Léa said, 'after school.'

Home. Yes, I really did have the sensation of coming home, because this inn was where I'd felt the most at home in my whole life — warm, welcomed and loved. As if I truly belonged. A home I had missed more than I could have imagined.

'You might have only worked a couple of shifts, but the restaurant customers have been asking after that lovely new waitress,' Louise said, busy making a batch of goat's cheese.

'I can't wait to get back to my job,' I said, unable to stop grinning, an almost alien sensation. 'And I'm ready to work right now.' I patted Belle, who was nudging my knee, and Beau — grown even bigger in two months — pawing at me and trying to leap onto my lap.

Louise wagged a milky finger at me. 'You must build up your strength before resuming your work. Have another crêpe.'

As I enjoyed another delicious crêpe, I wondered what Emile might do when he discovered his colleague had released me back to the auberge. And what of Xavier Lacoste's possible part in his plan? Though I was no longer worried about that, since I'd got my way and convinced him to send me back here. One tiny victory! And, as good-looking and sexy as I found the doctor, I doubted he'd actually come to the inn and pursue his lust for me. Besides, getting involved with another man was the furthest thing from my mind right now.

'I've heard they keep patients at Sainte-Dymphna's for *years*,' Léa said, setting out crêpes for Juliette and Linda for their after-school *goûter*. 'So how did you get released after only two months?'

'That's a bit complicated,' I said with a wry smile. 'I'll tell you sometime, but for now, suffice it to say that Emile Chevalier is not the only person who can play mind games.'

~

After the crêpes, I went upstairs, sat on the attic bed, and opened Suzanne's journal. But my heart sank as I read her next entry.

Spring 1917

The war drags on and nobody knows when it will end. Jules has been home for a year, and life with my broken husband only gets worse. On top of everything else, he now has ghastly leg pains which make him scream and unable to move for several moments. He trembles too, still barely talks, and spends hours kissing the rosary beads, or cursing them and flinging them across the room.

Between bouts of punching or kicking me, there is nothing. No glances, no eye blinks. He no longer even hears me. Though since I have learned more about this war neurosis, I know he hears shells — the only thing he's heard non-stop, since he went to war.

The healer-woman on the farm next door, Eugénie Bonnefille, tells me they no longer call these mind wounds 'la névrose de guerre', but 'shell shock'.

She says the young men went off to the war with glorious adventure in mind, certain it would be over by Christmas. But faced with indescribable horror, intense anxiety and ear-splitting bombardment from enemy shells, the troops quickly realised that instead of heroism, they had to draw on all their endurance simply to survive those terrible trenches. The exhaustion and unbearable strain from witnessing the violent death and mutilation of their comrades, worsened by lack of sleep and decent food, made their minds shut down in this kind of shock.

Eugénie has given me some calming and healing brews for when Jules wakes in the night, sweating and screaming at the ghosts of Germans he'd bayoneted coming back for revenge. Though none of her potions help much.

The village doctor has a far different opinion of Jules' shell shock, calling my husband a lunatic and a malingerer. He says he's a victim of his own weak nerves and likens him to a woman with hysteria. He tells me Jules' palpitations, breathlessness and chest pains are simply caused by the weight of his military knapsack; that there is nothing physically wrong, and he'll get over it in time.

I do not believe him for a moment, and I am terrified that one day my husband will go too far and actually murder me, leaving my little Victor motherless.

I am petrified too, for Victor, as Jules seems to hate him more every day, despising his darling little son for being simple, slow, and 'not right in the head', as people say.

And the worst news of all — I am, once again, with child. Not conceived in passion, but in a moment of violence as my husband held me down, and battered into me like some war machine killing the enemy.

I must wait for the right moment to tell Jules, if ever I tell him. And all I can do is hope and pray this child will be normal.

Three days later.

I told Jules about the baby. He stared at me without a word, then punched me hard in my belly, over and over. I kept pleading with him to stop, please, to have mercy. But, as ever, he didn't hear me.

The terrible pain and bleeding began almost immediately, and when the midwife came, she said my tiny baby had died inside me.

I am overcome with grief for this lost little life — the brother or sister Victor will never have, for the midwife told me that, after this, I'll never again be with child. She gave me some herbal concoction to get rid of it. But I don't want to be rid of it, I want my baby to still be alive and growing inside me.

The husband I once loved and respected, I now despise with the deepest, blackest hatred.

I am bereft, with no idea what to do about him. And, since the villagers harbour jealousy against me that Jules is home, while their loved ones are still out fighting on the front — perhaps being blown to bits this second! — I have no one to turn to.

The bleeding finally slows and the cramps recede, and I realise there is only one thing for me to do.

~

'Poor Suzanne, how utterly tragic!' I said to the empty attic, my heart aching for my ghostly friend and her lost baby. There was no time to read any further and, as I closed her journal, her words made me think, yet again, of the twins — the healthy children who'd come from my perfectly healthy, unbeaten womb. The womb that could have borne many more babies. However many I'd wanted, if those first two hadn't so completely overwhelmed me.

Emile had never hit me, but as I stared through the dormer window into the gloaming hour — that sinister moment between day and night — I understood my husband had been violent all the same. Not the same violence as Jules Rossignol, but sneaky and subtle, and nothing an outsider — not even our children — would notice. Yes, Emile's mind games had often been trickier to deal with than any straight punch.

It struck me just how violent and controlling husbands have always been, no matter what the era. And my friend's words only strengthened my resolve to remove myself from my husband's grasp, for good.

45

On the fourth evening after my return from the asylum, Louise clapped her hands together.

'Hurry up everyone, coats, boots and bonnets on,' she said, as Juliette and Linda placed candles along the auberge windowsills for the annual *fête des lumières*. Like most homes in Lyon and its surrounding villages, these little candles would light up the auberge late into the night.

'We don't want to miss the party, do we?' Nelly said, unhooking the girls' coats from the hallway rack. Léa clipped on the dogs' leashes and I grabbed the basket, filled with more candles and a thick blanket.

'I *adore* your coat, Léa,' I said, slipping into the warm and stylish red coat she'd lent me, so different from the ragged asylum coat. Wearing my own clothes — or rather mainly Léa's cast-offs — languishing in a hot shower or bath in privacy, and devouring Louise's delicious meals, were only a few of the joys in returning to the auberge.

'Dommy insists on making me a coat every year, to try out new patterns,' Léa said, 'so I've got far more than I could ever wear.'

'You're lucky to have a sister you're close to,' I said. 'I wish I'd had siblings. My grandmother always claimed Maman got sick because she was pregnant with me. Then she got *really* ill and couldn't have ...'

'You're right, I *am* lucky, but now you've got *three* sisters, Adrienne — me, Dommy and Nelly,' Léa said with a smile.

'And Linda and I have an extra aunt,' Juliette said, taking Belle's leash from her mother.

'Well, I'm lucky to have *all* of you,' Dommy said, helping Linda into her coat as we stepped out into the cold dusk light, an eerie mist hovering over the lake. 'Or I'd always be on my own, since my husband refuses to join in any village events.' She winked at her daughter. 'And since Linda prefers her cousin's company to mine.'

'I'll hold Beau,' Linda said, grasping his leash, as the excited little dog tugged against it.

Wrapped up against the frosty evening, we set off along the lac du Héron pathway, joining the other Sainte-Marie villagers tramping through the woods toward the statue of Our Lady, heroine of this wintry evening.

The light hesitated between dusk and darkness, the gold and orange-streaked grey sky struggling to illuminate the land. Autumn had stolen most of the tree leaves, and their branches sticking out at all angles reminded me of Suzanne's description of the trenches and no man's land that had stolen her husband's mind.

People walked in couples, arms linked or gloved hands entwined. Mothers carried toddlers and held the hands of older children. Léa walked with her gendarme boyfriend, Yves Rocamadour, alongside Nelly and her snail man, Thierry Marnier. While it warmed my heart to see these loving couples, a stab of loneliness pierced me. And while I'd rather be here alone than with Emile, a warm flush spread through me at the idea of walking hand-in-hand with my doctor friend, Xavier Lacoste.

I'd not heard from him since my release, so my instincts had been wrong, and he wasn't attracted to me. Perhaps Emile was right, and he simply wanted to take advantage of a frail patient. As much as that disappointed me, I knew I should trust the little voice of reason echoing through my mind.

You don't need another man.

Onward we threaded, darkness veiling the woods. The first snow had fallen several days ago and, in the luminescence, the track shone like a white dappled carpet. On one side of the pathway the willow trees hid the lake — dark, silent and mysterious witness to our pilgrimage — whilst on the other side, in flickering torchlight, the trees rose like rows of soldiers in brown uniform. It was a magical place where fairies or goblins might pop up at any moment.

The children skipped along, their giggles and twitters ringing out into that frosty air, while the adults hunched into their coats, catching up on the latest gossip.

Linda and Juliette walked behind us with the dogs, and with their friend, Clotilde Bonnefille. Her girlfriend, Bev, was still away in Belgium.

'*Woo, ooh, woo, ooh.*' The owl's hoot made me jump, and I grabbed Dommy's arm.

'Do you think there are ghosts in the woods tonight, Tatie Clotilde?' Linda asked.

'*Certainement, ma chérie,*' Clotilde said, her booming voice resonating through the trees. 'This is the kind of spooky night ghosts *adore.*'

'Yes, I can hear them!' Juliette cried, cupping a hand behind her ear.

'Please stop filling Juliette and Linda's minds with your rot, Madame Bonnefille,' Louise said, throwing Clotilde a scowl over her shoulder. 'That was simply an owl hooting.'

'But Tatie Clotilde says the echoes *could* be ghosts,' Juliette insisted. 'The ghosts of olden-day people whispering their stories to us, so they're never lost. Isn't that right, Tatie Clotilde?'

'*Oui, mes petites,*' Clotilde said, panting as her large, lumbering frame struggled to keep up with the others.

'And aren't we lucky those ghosts *are* keeping alive our stories and legends, so they're never lost?'

Is this why the ghost of Suzanne is telling me her story?

'And that's why you must welcome ghosts,' Clotilde said, 'rather than be afraid of them.'

'Madame Bonnefille, that is quite enough,' Louise barked, exhaling sharp breaths in bursts of vapour. 'And, as I've said, *countless* times,' she went on to Léa. 'I will never understand why you allow Juliette and Linda to spend time at her ... at that *coven*.'

Léa turned and winked at Clotilde. 'And as I've said *countless* times, Louise, if only you'd take off your blinkers, you'd see all the good Clotilde does for the villagers for all kinds of ailments — physical *and* spiritual.'

'Far better results than the doctor,' Nelly said.

'*Humpf!* Well, I suppose I must concede there is a grain of truth in that,' Louise said, as a scream rang out through the woods, setting a young child crying.

'Only a fox,' Dommy said with a laugh, pointing into the dark woods, to a pair of glowing green eyes.

The child's mother gathered him into her arms. 'Only the night creatures going about their business, *mon petit chou*, nothing to be afraid of.'

I smiled, recalling cuddling and comforting my young twins, and another cold wave of sadness made me shiver, as before us, the majestic white statue of the Virgin Mary rose into the darkness.

~

Luxuriant ferns arched over her marble body like living wreaths, and it was easy to believe the myth and magic that encompassed the imposing white statue.

As I stared at the proud face of the matriarch, I imagined I could truly hear Our Lady's cries, warning villagers about the dangerous whirlpool — a deep spring that sucked people and animals underwater by some kind of back pressure, though nobody truly knew how.

'She looks even taller in the dark,' Juliette said, as people spread blankets on the frosty ground. The blankets would quickly become damp, but Léa and Nelly had assured me we'd stay dry long enough to hear the mayor's Black Plague tale.

'She's tall enough to touch the stars,' Linda said, as the children stared up in awe, parents keeping wary eyes and hands on youngsters to stop them darting off toward the boggy swamp.

'You can't *touch* the stars, silly,' Juliette said, as people placed their lighted candles in special glasses.

'But we can pretend to,' Linda said, as the children made a circle of the little candle-glasses on the snowy ground around the Madonna. And in that aura of light at her feet, I could swear Our Lady was staring down at us and nodding her approval.

Since my release from the asylum, I'd not seen Blanche, but now I glimpsed her amidst the vast Larue clan, with her daughter, Anna, and her granddaughters. It seemed the only family members missing, besides her dead husband, Roger, were the one-hundred-year-old great grandparents. Léa had told me they attended most village events, but traipsing through the woods on a winter night was a bit much, though they'd be joining everyone at Chez Dédé afterwards for mulled wine.

As Blanche's granddaughters, Sonia and Elise, skipped across to join Juliette and Linda, Blanche made her way through the chattering crowd toward me. Hopping from one foot to the other to keep warm, I stiffened, unsure what she was going to say.

'*Bonsoir*, Adrienne.' Her smile was wary. 'I've been meaning to speak to you since Louise told me they'd released you. I wanted to say how sorry I am for contacting your husband.'

'My husband would have found me eventually,' I said, waving a hand. 'I couldn't keep running and hiding from him forever.'

'I've heard Sainte-Dymphna's is a shocking place?' she said.

I nodded. 'More awful than words can describe. But the psychoanalysis sessions did help me realise that life with my husband hadn't been happy, and now I can stand up for myself. Besides, as Louise said, I had to resolve things with Emile, though that hasn't quite happened yet. But being at Sainte-Dymphna's has made me truly appreciate all of this.' I nodded at the crowd, took Blanche's gloved hands and smiled at her. 'So perhaps you actually did me a favour, telling Emile where I was.'

I let her hands go. 'But what I want to know is can you forgive me for keeping your father's leather pouch and selling some of the gold? I'm *so* sorry, and I'll pay you back every franc.'

Blanche smiled. 'The money itself isn't that important. The pouch is the really precious object and, after all, I'm just thankful it wasn't lost forever.'

'Well, I still insist on paying you back.'

'Hush, everyone,' the mayor said into his megaphone. '*Un grand merci à tous* for joining me on this annual pilgrimage to honour our Madonna — our protector.' Louise and Blanche solemnly crossed themselves as a hush fell over the crowd. Even the children ceased chattering as the mayor's voice pealed out into the frosty night.

'Fellow Sainte-Marie villagers,' he began, 'on this star-studded night, I invite you all to accompany me on a voyage through Lyon's labyrinth of the ages. Let us begin in 58 BC, as Julius Caesar invades the Gaul city of

Lugdunum, the old name of Lyon. Our friend Julius digs an entrenched camp on Lugdunum hill then, feeling pleased with himself, the famous conqueror flings his cape into the river and leaves.' He waved an imaginary cape and the crowd clapped and cheered.

'Even today one can feel that euphoria sweeping across the stage of the Fourvière Gallo-Roman amphitheatre, *n'est-ce pas mes amis*?' He took a breath, gaze sweeping across the rapt crowd. 'Alas though, Roman roses spike ugly thorns and by the fourth century, decadence has reached its apex. Our city is in ruins! Then, rising from the Middle Ages' darkness, we are thrust into the greedy merchant city that Lyon has become,' he said. 'The upper bourgeoisie prospers and the people suffer!' He thrust a fist into the air.

'Then, in a cruel twist of fate, the Black Plague — reaching us via a Rhône River barge from Marseille — mercilessly solves this problem.' The mayor made a sweeping gesture at the white marble statue beside him. 'But miraculously, our Virgin Mary eradicates the plague from Lyon, and to mark our thanks and devotion, the people construct a beautiful basilica on Fourvière hill.'

He nodded at the crowd. 'And that is the reason, my friends, we gather every eighth of December, and light candles to thank our Madonna for saving the city of Lyon.'

The crowd clapped and cheered at the beaming mayor.

'Now, if everyone who would like to pray could kneel in front of our statue,' the mayor said, 'then we'll all meet back at Chez Dédé for some mulled wine to warm our hearts and souls.'

More cheers and applause.

'I'm not sure how much the Madonna actually had to do with ridding us of the plague,' Nelly said to our small circle.

Léa smiled. 'Probably not much, but it *does* make for a good story.'

'Or they're just here for the fun, like me,' I said, relishing the crowd's warmth in that December chill as we threaded back through the woods.

Back on la place de la Fontaine, everyone gathered at Chez Dédé, candles glowing on the windowsill of every shop and home bordering the square. Smaller lights glowed from the houses in the adjoining alleyways, so that the whole of Sainte-Marie-du-Lac resembled a light-swathed Christmas tree.

As I warmed myself with a cup of steaming mulled wine, Dédé explained to everyone how he made his *vin chaud* with red wine, spices, and oranges.

'Not bad,' Louise said, sipping her hot wine, 'though mine is far superior.'

As I glanced at Léa, rolling her eyes at her mother-in-law, I glimpsed the figure of a tall man strolling across the square, and almost choked on my *vin chaud*.

Dr Xavier Lacoste.

46

In his caramel-coloured scarf and well-cut coat, Xavier Lacoste was even more handsome than I recalled.

'*Oh là là*, that scarf is cashmere silk,' Dommy muttered to Léa. 'And the coat is definitely sheepskin.'

'*Bonsoir*, Adrienne,' he said, towering over me, like in his office. 'I thought — hoped — I'd find you out celebrating, and I just wanted to make sure you were all right since ... since your release.'

'I'm fine, thank you,' I said, aware of the stares, whispers and giggles springing up around us. A good-looking stranger amid a village gathering where everyone knew everybody was bound to cause a commotion, and the flush settled in my cheeks.

Dieu merci, Xavier didn't touch me but, as before, I sensed his animal lust. Or perhaps that was my own longing — the wild animal caged inside me.

'Who *is* he?' someone hissed.

'... no idea.'

'... movie star.'

'Let's chat somewhere quiet, Xavier.' I stood up and, clutching my hot wine, I beckoned him to follow me across the square to the bronze war memorial soldier statue. The snow-covered wreaths around the eleventh of November memorial celebration had long since perished, like those millions of poor men who'd given their lives – – or their minds, like Jules Rossignol — for our freedom.

'I've been waiting for your call, Adrienne, to invite me to this auberge of yours,' he said, as we sat on the bench seat beside the memorial. 'But since it's been four days, I thought I'd come and make sure you were all right.' He snaked an arm across the seat behind me, and I yearned to snuggle into his warmth. 'Is that okay? I mean, do you mind me coming here?'

'Well no,' I said. 'It's lovely to see you, but something's been worrying me since my first day in your office.'

'Oh?' He frowned. 'You know you can confide in me.'

'Right from the beginning, your face was familiar,' I said, 'but it took me a while to recall that I'd met you at Emile's medical graduation party. Do you remember me?'

Xavier relaxed his arm against my shoulder and took my hand in his free one. 'Oh yes, I remembered you as soon as Emile phoned me about committing you to Sainte-Dymphna's. Back then, I immediately found you attractive, kind of mysterious … so different from all those other doctor's wives and girlfriends. And I still find you intriguing, Adrienne, and I thought — well I sensed — those feelings were recipro —'

I let go of his hand. 'Wait, I have so many questions.' I took a breath, stared into those soft blue-grey eyes, and explained my husband's malicious plan. 'What I never figured out though, Xavier, is if you were part of that plan?'

'No, no! I had no idea that was your husband's intention, and I'm shocked and saddened to hear this.' He shook his head wildly, then exhaled deeply, vapour streaming into the cold air. 'I hadn't seen Emile Chevalier for years, but when your husband phoned me, claiming his wife was suffering from insanity and asking me to treat you, all I did was reassure him I'd do my best for you …

for a *colleague*.' He took another breath. 'I quickly understood that you were quite sane, that's why I agreed to stop the ECT after only one session. But you *did* have depression issues relating to your childhood, so I kept you there as I truly believed psychoanalysis could help.'

'And it did, Xavier, I'm more settled and happier than in my entire life.'

'Well I'm pleased to hear that. And you believe me that I had no part in your husband's ploy to get you home? And that I have genuine feelings for you?'

'Well, if you say so.' Though I still wasn't convinced. 'Anyway, at least suffering in that hellhole has made me know what I want.'

'Is spending time with me something you want?' he said, cupping a smooth leather glove beneath my chin. 'We could go to my place for a drink or something? My car's parked over in the churchyard.'

'I'm sorry, I can't.' I stared at the ground, the toe of my boot pushing around a lump of snow.

'I don't understand. In my office at Sainte-Dymphna's, you gave me every sign that you're attracted to me,' he said. 'That, like me, you wanted something more. But now — when we *can* have more — you push me away.' He inhaled a deep breath. 'Were you simply using me, Adrienne? Teasing me with veiled promises you had no intention of fulfilling? Was your sole intention to get me to release you back here, instead of home to your husband?'

'Yes.' I raised my gaze to his. 'Though I really did find you attractive … I still do.'

'So what's stopping you now you *are* back at the auberge, and not with Emile?' He shook his head, looking crestfallen.

'While I'm grateful for your help, I'm not ready to dive into another relationship. I need to sort out my doomed marriage first, then be on my own for a while.'

'A while? How long's a while, Adrienne? Should I wait, or give up now, and stop bothering you?'

'No.' My voice came out little more than a whisper. 'Please don't give up on me ... not yet.'

He reached down and kissed me on the cheek. Not a passionate lover's kiss, but the brief, sweet kiss of a friend.

'Can we be friends then?' he said. 'For now?'

'Yes, I'd love to have you as my friend.'

Almost numb from the cold, and eager to get back to my friends at Chez Dédé, I stood up.

'Come on, I'll walk you to your car.'

'Can I see you again?' he asked, as we slithered through the muddy slush to the carpark of Saint Julien's church, well away from the rowdy villagers and the music.

'I can't promise anything,' I said, as we reached his car. 'You understand?'

'Yes,' he said, with a smile, melodramatically slapping a palm over his heart, 'but I'll live in hope you'll change your mind.'

'Now you really do sound like a movie star,' I said, and when Xavier kissed me again, on the lips, beneath the towering old church, I gave in to my yearning, leaned into him and returned his passionate kiss.

'Whore. Adulteress. *Slut.*' The voice rang out into the icy darkness, and I jerked away from Xavier.

I spun around. Leaning against the door of his Citroën, arms folded across his chest, was my husband.

~

'I called Sainte-Dymphna's today, to speak to you about my wife,' Emile said to Xavier, 'but I was informed you'd released her *four* days ago.'

His voice remained, as ever, calm, but Emile's gritted teeth belied his struggle to hold his temper. 'I thought the deal was to send her home to me? So why is she back in Sainte-Marie-du-Lac? And what are you doing here, kissing *my wife?*'

'I'm not —' Xavier started.

Emile glared at me. 'You do realise he's using you, like he uses all women — patients who are too scared to complain, fearful of being treated even worse at Sainte-Dymphna's?' His breaths came out short and sharp.

'No, Emile, that's not true! I'd never use any woman —'

'I'm not something you make a deal over, Emile,' I cut in, the rage rising from my gut like a rush of disgusting vomit. 'I'm not some cow on the marketplace.' Unafraid of my husband now, I stepped toward him.

'And, just so you know, I figured out your vile trick. And *yes*, that hellhole almost did break me down, like it broke Maman, like it broke so many others. 'But, as you can see, Emile, I survived, and your nasty scheme backfired, since Xavier did not send me home to you.'

Emile glared at me. 'Whatever are you raving about, Rien?'

'Don't be a coward,' I said, refusing to rise to the nickname bait. 'Can't you admit what you did?'

Emile flung an arm toward Xavier. 'Well, I don't understand why you'd celebrate the light festival with *him*, a stranger?' he said, avoiding my question. 'You could've come home to Lyon and celebrated with your family.' He sounded dejected, almost defeated. 'We always had fun, didn't we, all four of us together?' His voice was pleading now.

'The pretty lights and candles might have mesmerised Antoine and Martine when they were young, but these past years they were just bored, and whinged at us for dragging them around,' I said. 'Besides, my children are no longer even at home and, thanks to your brainwashing, they despise me.' I ran my tongue across my dry lips. 'No, Emile, none of our family outings were pleasant. You all ignored, poked fun or scoffed at me. Can't you see that you don't understand how it was for me and why I left you?'

I took a trembly breath, determined not to let my voice crack. 'So please, can you leave me alone, because I'm *never* coming back to you? And since you believe I'm a whore, why not give me a divorce?'

Emile scowled. 'I've told you, I'll *never* divorce you. You are my *wife*. And you'll come home to me, not to *him*.'

'I will not,' I said, growing bolder. 'I'll never forgive you for cutting me off from my children and carting me off to that hellhole.'

'Well, from what I've just witnessed, Sainte-Dymphna's can't have been quite the hell you describe,' Emile said, with another glare at Xavier. 'I can only imagine what you and he got up to in there.'

'Nothing happened with your wife. I'd never take advantage of any patient … or *any* woman,' Xavier said, as Emile stepped toward me, arms raised.

I thought he was about to wrap those arms around me, and maybe even kiss me, so I went to take a step backwards. But instead, my husband casually wrapped his hands around my throat, pressing his fingertips against the back of my neck, thumbs digging into the notch in my throat.

'*Merde,* let go of her!' Xavier pushed between us, and peeled Emile's hands from my throat. 'Are you *mad*, Emile?'

I reeled backwards, clutching my throat and staring wide-eyed at Emile. Never had my husband physically threatened me, and the shock left me shocked and speechless.

'You'd better leave,' Xavier said to him. 'Or I'll call the gendarmes.'

'You won't get away with this, Adrienne,' Emile hissed, as he opened the Citroën door. 'You cannot humiliate me like this. *I won't have it.* You'll regret it ... you'll never see your children again, and I'll make sure they hate you forever.'

Once Emile sped away, Xavier wrapped an arm around me as he walked me, still shaken, back to the villagers on the square. But I no longer felt festive and was glad to see everyone heading home. After all, it was a school night.

'Are you sure you'll be all right? You're not afraid Emile will come back?' Xavier said. 'I'm more than happy to stay with you.'

'I doubt he'll come back tonight,' I said, 'but he *will* return sometime, and keep trying to persuade me to go back to him. You see what he's like? He thinks he owns me, and he'll never free me from my wifely shackles. But Emile would never truly strangle me, he was only trying to scare me.'

'Here's my home phone number, just in case,' Xavier said, pulling a small card from his pocket and scribbling a number on the back.

On the walk home to the inn with the others, I fended off the questions about the handsome stranger. Still too shocked and embarrassed, I couldn't bring myself to mention Emile's attack.

After all, perhaps it had been my fault. I'd provoked my husband by being over-friendly with another man. I might no longer want to be married to Emile, but I still was.

47

'Emile's so angry with me, he'll make things even worse with the twins ... if that's possible.' I said as Suzanne sat beside me on the attic bed, and I stroked Beau, who'd curled up beside me. 'I might never be going back to Emile, but I'm still powerless against him, which is *so* frustrating.'

'Frustrating?' Suzanne said. 'Not frightening? He *did* attempt to strangle you.'

'Oh no, the skin's not damaged, not even red or sore.' I rubbed the spot where Emile's fingers had pressed. 'I provoked him and he was trying to scare me.'

'You *provoked* him?' Suzanne said as I reached into the groove for her journal. 'I thought you'd learned, by now, that nothing Emile does is your fault?'

'Perhaps,' I said, suddenly cold and shivery, and as I snuggled under the covers, I was grateful for the bedside lamp's small circle of warmth. I opened the journal, realising with dismay that this was Suzanne's last entry.

1917

Despite his aggression, which is surely down to this terrible shell shock, I still love Jules, will always love him, though I have no choice but to send him away so that he might recover. And so that Victor and I will be safe.

Many more soldiers besides Jules are returning from the front with this shell shock, so I have told the gossiping villagers I'm trying to get the doctor to send Jules to Sainte-

Dymphna's Hospital, where I've heard they're starting treatments for shell shock. Even though the doctor still believes my husband is simply a shirker, I hope I can convince him.

Since tonight might be our last supper together, I've made Jules' favourite summer soup — cucumber, mint, lemon juice, and some seeds and leaves from those pretty purple bell-shaped flowers that the healer-woman, Eugénie, kindly gave me.

Outside, a brewing storm is rattling our windows. The trees wave their bony arms, groaning and sighing as if in pain, in the wind that whistles beneath the roof.

But inside, all is calm, and Victor is sleeping. I thought it best my boy not be around his father for our last meal together — no risk of antagonising or infuriating Jules, who could easily tip over his soup bowl, stand up on his shaky legs and swipe me across the face.

My husband spoons the soup into his mouth methodically, without too much of a tremble. As usual, he doesn't look at me, and for once I am glad of that.

I hate sending him away, but as he slurps his soup, I keep telling myself that I'm doing the right thing, the only thing. It's better for all of us.

My heart heavy, I closed Suzanne's journal on those, her last words, sensing that I'd no longer feel her attic presence. I would miss my ghostly friend, and I was frustrated too, not knowing if Jules harmed her, or if she managed to send him away for the shell shock treatment.

Perhaps Louise, Blanche, or even Clotilde, descendent of Suzanne's healer-woman neighbour, know what became of her and Jules.

48

In the days following the light festival, to quell my lingering angst about Emile returning, I'd kept busy around the auberge and La Cuisine de Louise. But four days later, he returned.

It was a chilly December Saturday morning. Nelly and Léa were preparing cabbage stuffed with mushrooms and chestnuts, while I rolled out pastry for a beef and spinach pie. The kitchen was filled with the aromatic smell of the macarons Louise was baking for her restaurant patrons and for this afternoon's widows' circle.

'Don't you girls let me forget to set aside some strawberry macarons for *mon petit macaron*,' Louise said. 'They're Juliette's favourites.'

At the sound of a car outside, I glanced up through the window, squinting through the fog. The smile slid from my lips at the sight of Emile's Citroën, my rolling pin clattering to the floor. My heart beat as erratically as a caged rat, and I pictured its tail flicking from side to side inside my chest.

'*Merde!* Won't Emile *ever* leave me alone?'

I'd told them about the scene with Xavier and Emile in the churchyard, but still hadn't mentioned my husband's hands around my throat. I was brushing it off as a simple threat, but deep down I knew Emile's behaviour was unacceptable, and I should have done something about it. But what? Moan to the gendarmes that my husband — a highly regarded psychiatrist — had put his hands around my throat for a few seconds? His fingers hadn't even pressed into my skin. I'd sound like a hysterical woman; a lunatic who should never have been released from the asylum.

'Shall I send him off?' Louise patted her sticky hands against her apron, as Emile marched across the cobblestones in his fancy camel-hair overcoat and fedora hat.

'Thank you, but I need to deal with my husband myself,' I said, as the inevitable rap came on the door.

'Be careful,' Nelly said.

'Don't forget how he forced you into that terrible asylum,' Léa said.

Glad the girls were out of sight, playing with the dogs in Juliette's bedroom upstairs, I opened the door, and stepped out on the doorstep.

'Why are you here, Emile?' I crossed my arms against the biting air. 'Didn't I ask you to leave me alone?'

Across the high wintry sky, clouds raced, tinged with the pinkish hue that heralded more snow. Trees sagging with snow dotted the fields like costumed scarecrows with deformed limbs dangling at unnatural angles.

'Besides, after your threats about my children, *and* threatening to strangle me, surely you can understand me not wanting to see you? Anyway, I'm busy, I'm about to go —'

'About to what?' Emile cut in, his upper lip hitching. 'Go and see your new lover, Xavier?' He took my hand, gloved fingertips pressing into the back of it. 'I warned you about him using women, didn't I? I'd hate to see you get hurt. I still love you, Adrienne, even after all of this.'

'I'm not going anywhere with Dr Lacoste,' I said, pulling my hand away. I didn't tell Emile I hadn't heard from Xavier since the light festival; that perhaps I'd never hear from him again, which made me both sad and a little relieved. 'I'm about to open up the restaurant for the midday meal … you know, part of my waitressing job. And whether or not you accept it, I consider myself separated from you, so what I do with my life is no longer your business.'

'It certainly *is* my business,' Emile said. 'When a man takes liberties with my wife.' A frown creased his brow, his voice softened, cracked a little, and I thought he might shed a tear. 'I simply don't understand why you don't want to come back to everything we have? So many women would jump at the chance. What more could you possibly have *here*?' He waved an arm across the old stone building and shrugged, as if truly perplexed. 'Is it this fashionable women's liberation thing?'

'You don't get it, do you?' I said, exasperated.

'Do not address me as if I'm an imbecile, Adrienne.'

Snowflakes fell, and I swallowed hard, shivering not only from the cold.

'Anyway, women's liberation or not, you are still my wife … the wife who should come home to where she belongs. It's that easy. What more is there for your brain to comprehend?'

'Please leave now, Emile. I'm busy, and freezing.'

'All I can deduce is that you manipulated Xavier Lacoste into releasing you here, instead of home to me,' he went on, this quiet way he spoke more menacing than any yelling. 'And I've a mind to take legal action against his unprofessional actions.'

'You were the one doing the manipulating, Emile, right from the start of our marriage. And even though you've poisoned the twins' minds against me, I'm hoping they'll eventually see the truth and forgive me. Because then, my new life will be complete and happy.'

I breathed hard, staring at him, the silence falling heavy between us. I glanced away, up at an eagle circling the lake, its wide, dark wingspan a sliver coiling around and around, above the steel-grey water.

'Please don't come here again, or call me, Emile.'

The snow fell harder, blanketing the world in white, blurring everything, like one of those impressionist paintings where nothing looked real.

'*Mon amour*!' he pleaded. '*Please*, you can't do this to —'

'Come along, Adrienne, it's time we left,' Louise's words cut off Emile's pleading, as she came out onto the doorstep, and threw my husband a dark stare. 'Or we'll be late for the widows' circle.'

The meeting at Blanche's wasn't scheduled until the end of the afternoon, after the midday meal, but I wasn't about to point that out.

'*Widows'* circle?' Emile's eyebrows shot up and disappeared beneath the brim of his hat. 'Adrienne's no widow, she's my *wife*.'

'*Mon Dieu*, we are certainly aware of *that*, Dr Chevalier.' Louise rolled her eyes as Léa and Nelly came outside and the four of us stood in an arc before Emile. 'But my circle is not only for widows, it's a gathering for all women.'

Emile shifted his sad-puppy gaze to me, tiny snowflakes settling like dandruff on the shoulders of his coat and hat.

'You wish you were a *widow*?' he said. 'How can you want your loving husband *dead*? Have you no pity?'

'Don't be ridiculous, Emile, of course I don't want you dead. Stop twisting things to make me sound like some unfeeling monster.'

'Please leave our premises, Dr Chevalier,' Louise said. 'Before I am obliged to call Major Rocamadour with a trespassing *and* harassment complaint.'

Emile stared around the semi-circle of us. We all stared back at him.

'I cannot agree to a divorce, Adrienne.' With a heave of his twitching shoulders, Emile swivelled around and marched back to his car. 'And you will *always* be my wife.'

~

By the time we closed the restaurant, it was after four o'clock when we got to Blanche's house for the widows' circle. Relieved to take the weight off my aching feet amidst her homely clutter and warm up before her blazing fireplace, I sank into the sofa between Nelly and Léa.

Blanche put on Serge Gainsbourg's *Initials B.B.* record, while Louise poured cups of tea and handed around the macarons.

The spicy tea warmed my insides, and we pulled out our knitting and crocheting, Gisèle and Jeanne — who I'd met at my first widows' circle — humming along to *Comic Strip*.

Louise had instructed us to fashion Christmas toys and clothes for the orphans, apart from the serious seamstress-businesswomen, that is. At the dining table, Dommy and Blanche's machines whirred madly as they worked on villagers' commissioned outfits for the Christmas festivities.

'Are you finally going to spill the beans about that handsome stranger who was ogling you at the light festival?' Léa said to me with a grin.

'The one Emile is so jealous of,' Nelly said. 'You've been cagey, dodging all our questions.'

I paused at the end of a crochet row. 'Dr Lacoste was my psychiatrist at Sainte-Dymphna's.'

'*Only* your psychiatrist?' Dommy said with an exaggerated wink. 'From the way he was looking at you, I'll bet my last thread of yarn this Dr Lacoste is more than that.'

'Well, he is, and he isn't,' I said with a smirk.

'Oh, so mysterious,' Blanche said, which made us giggle like schoolgirls.

I'd already told them about my grisly two months at Sainte-Dymphna's and now, against the whirr of machines, and the click of knitting needles, I explained Emile's devious idea to break me down, and how I had to convince Dr Lacoste to send me back to the auberge rather than to Emile.

'You *seduced* your psychiatrist?' Nelly shrieked with laughter, which set us all off again. Laughing along with them felt nice after Emile's harrowing visit. After everything.

'*Oh là là,* you've made me drop stitches,' Léa cried.

'Not quite,' I said. 'But with a bit of seductive teasing, Xavier agreed to send me back here. Though now he's keen to pursue things, that's why he came to the light festival.'

'And you don't want to *pursue* things?' Dommy said. 'After what I've heard about your husband, he'd send any woman into the arms of the handsome Dr Lacoste.'

'Xavier's attention flatters me, but I don't want to fall for another man, especially not a psychiatrist. I'm a bit reluctant, after everything I've been through with Emile.'

I glanced down, counting my crochet stitches to hide the blush as I thought how much I really was attracted to Xavier Lacoste, and how hard it had been to ignore his advances in the churchyard.

'I could have told Emile the truth,' I said, 'that nothing has happened with Xavier, but if Emile believes I *am* involved with someone else, he might stop trying to force me back to him.'

'Oh, I doubt your husband will ever leave you alone, Adrienne. That man will never relinquish his *possession*,' Louise said, holding up the little knitted cardigan. With a satisfied nod, she folded the completed garment onto one of the piles between Dommy and Blanche's sewing machines. 'And I would advise caution, attempting to make Emile jealous. From my experience, men like him are unpredictable.'

Blanche nodded, her machine needle jab-jabbing through the fabric. 'Still waters run deep, and all that.'

'Well, Emile's mind games no longer scare me,' I said, stopping myself from rubbing the spot on my neck. 'Though his threat of cutting me off from my children forever is a very dark cloud.'

Blanche snipped off a thread of yarn and waved a hand. 'Don't be too miserable about sulky teenagers. They're all the same.'

'My four pouted their way through the teenage years,' Gisèle said. 'With barely a word for their mother, except to complain.'

'Mine were the same,' Jeanne said. 'Then one day, they suddenly grew up into rational adults whose company I actually enjoy.'

'This is more than usual teenage behaviour,' I said. 'My husband has made them hate me.'

'You could always consult Clotilde,' Blanche said, snipping off stray cotton threads. 'My neighbour is an expert on many things, including pesky husbands and unruly children.'

'And while we're on the subject of Clotilde Bonnefille,' Louise said, placing a teddy bear into a basket of finished toys. 'I imagine it was that witch who advised you to turn your perfectly tidy home into this *pigsty*?'

Louise waved an arm across Blanche's living room at the teetering piles of magazines, the dirty glasses and mugs littering the mantlepiece, the scattering of ash and threads of kindling spread across the hearth, the mismatched, stained cushions and the dust-laden rugs.

'Blanche Larue used to take so much pride in her pristine home. Whatever happened?'

'This is the new rebel Blanche!' she cried, with a laugh, as she pinned a paper pattern to some silky fabric. 'And yes, Clotilde did advise me to run my home just the opposite from when Roger was alive. She said it's all part of the healing process.' Blanche spread her arms across the disordered room. 'And I love my mess!'

'You'll be burning your bra next!' Dommy said.

'And wearing a miniskirt and marching around with banners like those women who laid that wreath at the Arc de Triomphe,' Léa said.

'What wreath?' Blanche said.

'The one with the inscription everyone was talking about,' Nelly said. '"There is one person more unknown than the unknown soldier, his wife."'

'That's clever,' Gisèle said.

Jeanne nodded. 'And true.'

'While that might be so,' Blanche said, waving her scissors, 'I doubt I'd go that far, But I find it hard to believe how pathetic I was, putting up with Roger's terrible behaviour all those years.'

'My husband had affairs too,' Jeanne blurted out. 'I never told him I knew. Like you, Blanche, I couldn't bear the embarrassment of the pitying stares of the entire village, or of divorce. It was just easier to stay married and put up with it.'

'Not to mention that *other* gossip,' Gisèle said with a knowing nod. 'People thinking that all spinsters end up … you know.' She nodded toward Clotilde's home.

'*Mon Dieu*, how awful,' Jeanne said, 'people thinking you'd become one of those lesbians. Anyway, since my cheating husband died, I haven't missed ironing his shirts for a second, or washing his stinky clothes.'

'I love being able to cook whatever I feel like eating,' Gisèle said. 'Or not cooking at all. Not having to get his lunch on the table at exactly midday. And I certainly don't miss all that snoring and farting in bed.' She let out a high-pitched shriek.

Everyone, even Louise, exploded into giggles.

'Or pee dribbles on the toilet floor,' Jeanne cried, wrinkling her nose.

'And you know what?' Louise said. 'I actually enjoyed learning how to use a hammer, and other such implements.'

'And opening tight jar lids and fixing leaky taps,' Jeanne said.

'Now that Roger's dead, and the awful agoraphobia has vanished,' Blanche said, guiding her fabric beneath the juddering needle, 'life is so much easier. No more pretending, even to him, and to myself. No more scrubbing to make Roger's house sparkle, just the way he liked it.' She smiled at Dommy. 'I far more enjoy being a *business* partner ... now that's a real job.'

I'd never suspected Emile of having affairs, but I empathised with Blanche's feeling of being squashed — a slab of meat bashed over the years to tenderise it into the exact shape he wanted.

'I stayed in a bad marriage for a long time,' I said, 'though I didn't even realise it was bad. Now that's pathetic.'

'I was unhappy with my husband too,' Léa said. 'Bruno wasn't keen on me being independent.' She glanced at Louise, obviously not wanting to bad-mouth her golden boy. 'But when our parents died, and Dommy and I inherited some money, I turned Suzanne's old place into L'Auberge de Léa, and I no longer had to rely on my husband's income. The inn will never make me wealthy,' she went on, 'but Nelly, Louise and I manage to live off it, and I love it so much that I feel rich in other ways.'

'Another reason I don't want to dive into anything with Xavier Lacoste,' I said, turning around my crocheting for a new row of the baby bonnet. 'While I love my waitressing job, and appreciate you giving me this chance to work, Louise, I have an idea for my very own career.'

'What career?' Léa said.

'I'll tell you once it's organised,' I said with a wink. 'But even though I don't want a boyfriend or a husband right now, sometimes I do miss a love life. Emile might be flawed, but I do pine for those times he was gentle and loving. Because he *was* like that too.'

'I certainly don't miss sex,' Blanche said, flushing scarlet. 'Maybe kisses and cuddles, but nowadays I wonder why sex once seemed like such a big deal. You'll see,' she went on, as Léa and Nelly rolled their eyes at each other and smirked. 'When you hit the change of life, everything changes, not only your body shape.'

'Well, for now I'm enjoying being young,' Nelly said with a laugh, as she wound up a ball of lilac-coloured wool. 'And I'm super excited to announce that Thierry's asked me to marry him, next summer. We're buying a little cottage a bit further along the lakefront. I'll still be close to you all, and I'll still work at the auberge, as well as helping Thierry with his snail-breeding, and other projects.'

Louise clapped her hands, all of us grinning like mad cats. 'I'm sure I speak for all of us, Nelly, when I say I am overjoyed for you.'

'This calls for champagne!' Blanche cried, pushing aside her cut-out dress pattern. 'And I think there's a bottle in the cellar.' While Blanche hurried off, Louise rummaged through the kitchen cupboards for glasses.

'Wherever are her flutes? What terrible disorder, every size and style of glass all together on the same shelf,' she scolded. 'What complete disorder!'

Ignoring Louise's chides, Blanche popped the champagne cork, and filled the mismatching glasses. And, to Serge Gainsbourg belting out the lyrics of *Shu Ba du ba loo ba*, we all sang and toasted Nelly.

For the first time in years, pure joy erupted from me, the happiness that had been buried for so long bursting from me like those fizzing champagne bubbles.

Once the excitement died down, Louise, Nelly, Léa and I sloshed through the snow back to the auberge. Moonlight shimmered silvery across the lake, and I shivered with the cold, even more conscious of missing the warmth of human touch. Despite our talk of independence, I found myself dismayed at the thought of growing old alone.

49

The following weekend, on the Sunday morning before Christmas, Saint Julien's bell jangled, clear and insistent, signalling the end of Père Châtaigne's sermon. The congregation poured out onto the snowy square, Juliette and Linda and their friends, Sonia and Elise, their respective grandmothers, Louise and Blanche, following in their noisy wake.

At our market stall, Léa, Nelly and I rubbed our gloved hands and stamped our booted feet against the cold, as we sold Louise's gift-packaged produce: macarons, almond and honey biscuits, jams, pickles, liqueurs and terrines.

It had been eight days since I'd seen Emile, and he hadn't phoned the auberge, but I couldn't shrug off the sensation that my husband was lingering close by, watching, waiting to pounce and try to drag me back to him. I kept spinning around, expecting to see his face, but there was nothing. I didn't dare relax though and assume my persistent husband had given up on me.

'Who wants to bet Louise will have another go at me about no longer attending church?' Léa said, nodding at her mother-in-law chatting with Blanche outside Saint Julien's, and tugging Juliette's bonnet down over her ears.

I watched as Blanche touched Louise's arm, kissed her granddaughters and hurried off toward her dressmaking shop, she and Louise waving at the four girls skipping off to join the other children shrieking and flinging snowballs at each other.

'I used to go to church,' I said, 'but only to please my husband. Emile said it was the right thing to do; it was good for appearances. I'm so glad I no longer have to *do the right thing.*'

'I was a churchgoer too,' Léa said, as Nelly placed four jars of jam into a customer's basket, and stored the francs in the old biscuit tin. 'Because I didn't have the energy to fight Bruno *and* his mother. But since we separated, I don't feel I have to do a single thing to please Bruno's mother,' she said as Louise approached us, her beret pulled low.

'After what happened to me, when I got pregnant, I don't believe in *any* God,' Nelly said. 'You wouldn't catch me in church for all the gold in France.'

'Well, girls, you missed a lovely sermon from Père Châtaigne,' Louise said, taking up her place beside the money tin. 'And whilst I can overlook a normal Sunday, I sincerely hope you will accompany Blanche and me to midnight Mass on Christmas Eve?'

Obviously not a question, but none of us answered, and I think we were all glad of the sudden cluster of customers.

Beneath that cloudless sky — the deep blue of a morning glory, the distant sun trying vainly to cast a thread of warmth — it seemed the whole of Sainte-Marie was milling about the Christmas market, far larger than the usual weekly one. All the shops on the square were open too.

Silver and gold tinsel, red and green bells and bows, and wooden sleigh-pulling reindeer festooned the shops and houses bordering the narrow, cobblestoned alleys. Wreaths fashioned from pine cones, holly and ivy hung from doorways, and a festive carol — *Les anges dans nos campagnes* — bleated out from the town hall megaphone, to which people sang or hummed as they purchased local produce and perused the toys for gifts.

Yves Rocadamour and Thierry Marnier arrived, bearing hot chocolates for all of us. They kissed and hugged their respective girlfriends and, in that loving, festive moment, I once more felt so alone. It seemed everyone, besides me, was with loved ones, and sorrow overwhelmed me.

On impulse, I guzzled down the hot chocolate, excused myself from the stall, and hurried toward to the phone booth outside the post office.

Through Blanche and Dommy's shop window, decorated with a beautiful *crèche de Noël* scene, I glimpsed them at their machines, finishing last-minute Christmas garments. They glanced up, and we exchanged waves and smiles.

At the chemist shop, Dommy's husband, Paul Renard, was also busy, people lined up purchasing medicines for winter coughs, colds and runny noses.

The butcher shop was packed with villagers ordering meat, terrines and pâtes, and the queue at the Larue bakery snaked out onto the square. Hunched in coats, baskets over their arms, customers hopped about to keep warm. Louise had even conceded that the Yule logs made by the Larue bakers — related to Blanche, though I'd forgotten exactly how, since there were so many Larues — were *almost* as good as her own.

'Though nobody will ever match my superior *bûche de Noël*,' she'd said.

Dodging flying snowballs, I hurried into the phone booth as the megaphone thrummed out *Vive le vent*.

I fumbled in my purse for the card Xavier had given me, flipped it over, and dialled his home number. As I waited for him to answer, thoughts whizzed through my mind.

Why am I doing this?

I didn't want another relationship, and especially not with a psychiatrist.

Is it simply his animal magnetism making me want to be with him, simply a fling like Bambou with all his women?

'Hello, Xavier. It's me, Adrienne.'

'Oh? I didn't expect you to call … I thought you didn't want … oh never mind, I'm glad you did.'

'Everyone from the auberge will be out this evening,' I said, speaking quickly so as not to lose my nerve. 'Going into Lyon for *le marché de Noël*, and to watch a Christmas show. I'm supposed to go with them, but I could stay home if you wanted to come to the inn?'

'Are you inviting me over?' His voice was wary.

'Yes.'

I caught his short, sharp breath.

'Are you sure? What you said bef —'

'Yes, Xavier, I'm sure.'

~

'Best snowman ever!' Linda cried, choosing two blue buttons from one of her mother's sewing tins. She pressed the blue eyes into the snowman's face as Juliette set aside the shovel, and the four rugged-up girls stepped back to admire their masterpiece.

After the morning Christmas market, Blanche's granddaughters had come back to the auberge to play with Juliette and Linda before they all left for their evening in Lyon.

'Oh no, Beau!' Juliette screeched, as the dog nipped off the snowman's carrot-nose and dashed off down to the orchard's dormant fruit trees.

'Come back, bad doggy!' Linda shrieked, as the girls chased the puppy through the snowy auberge grounds.

Belle sat motionless beside the nose-less snowman, gazing judgementally at Beau as we all watched from the kitchen window, laughing until our sides hurt.

'I swear Beau is mocking those girls,' I said, dicing carrots for Louise's dish of garlic roasted carrots — minus the stolen snowman's nose.

La Cuisine de Louise was closed until the end of January, since people didn't feel like eating in a restaurant over Christmas. We were free at lunchtimes, but the auberge kitchen bustle and activity hadn't died down, as we helped Louise prepare her Christmas Eve feast. I dashed about, thankful to be busy, to avoid dwelling on Xavier's visit this evening.

To mask my nervousness and excitement — like a teenage girl on her first date — I concentrated on crushing garlic, and mixing it with parsley and butter. I basted the carrots, and sang along with the others to the radio, and Dean Martin's *Let it Snow! Let it Snow! Let it Snow!*

This festive food preparation was similar to what I'd always done at home, but this time I had no responsibility for the meal. If anything went wrong, no one would blame it on me, and for that reason alone, I could relax and enjoy it all. But I smiled to myself, thinking there was little risk anything would go wrong with Louise's cooking.

'You and your *friend* will have the place all to yourselves,' Léa said with a wink, when I announced I wouldn't be joining them for the Lyon outing.

'Don't do anything we wouldn't do,' Nelly said with a laugh, as she and Léa tore up baguette chunks, and chopped onions and Gruyère cheese for the soup that would warm everyone after tramping around the chilly city.

'Concentrate on that soup, you two, and stop acting like sixteen-year-olds,' Louise said as she prepared the old-fashioned vegetable, *le cardon*, which she informed me was a cousin of the artichoke. She frowned as icy air rushed down the hallway behind Victor and Yves Rocamadour, lugging inside a huge pine tree. Noisette scowled, gave an angry tail swish, sprang from her chair and leapt upstairs.

'*Oh là là, les garçons,* you're tramping slush *everywhere*,' Louise chided, as they dragged the tree into the living room.

'Sorry boss,' Victor said, not looking one bit sorry as he and Yves stomped off to fetch the boxes of decorations, leaving more slush in their wake.

'Girls, come in out of the cold,' Louise called through the kitchen window. 'Time for a hot chocolate and Christmas tree decorating. And don't leave that shovel lying on the ground for someone to trip over. Prop it back beside the door.'

Thierry Marnier arrived too, trooping in after the girls, and handing the snails to Louise for her *escargots à la bourguignonne*.

The gust of cold air set the fire spitting in the grate and hurling jagged shadows against the walls. As the girls hung the pine cones, holly and ivy they'd gathered, along with the artificial decorations, Louise came in bearing a tray of steaming mugs.

'*Voilà!*' she announced, setting the tray on the coffee table. 'Made from freshly melted chocolate, far superior to that watery stuff you had at the market this morning.'

On the sofa, beside me, Léa snuggled up to Yves. Louise sat in one armchair, while Nelly and Thierry squeezed into the other one. Against a backdrop of the girls' chatter and that cosy room filled with Christmas cushions and throws, I sipped the divine hot chocolate, the flames snapping and crackling in the hearth beneath the mantlepiece decorated with miniature wooden and porcelain figurines.

Warm and contented, I was surprised at the wave of sorrow that hit me. Christmas with Emile and the twins had mostly been a strained event, with botched food and the wrong presents, but I couldn't help pining for that special day with the family I'd always dreamed of.

Right back when I'd sprained my ankle, these people had made me feel part of their family. But at this special time, I was more conscious than ever of being the outsider perching on the rim of their nest. Flickers of joy alternated with misery as I remembered I didn't truly belong here.

As I stared, mesmerised, at the flames leaping about the hearth, licking and devouring the logs, my own fire kindled inside me. I imagined the feel of Xavier's body, his strong, clean and manly smell, his soft lips against mine.

I kept glancing at the grandfather clock, watching those minutes tick slowly by.

50

Like the steam in a pressure cooker straining against the lid to escape, we fell into each other's arms, Xavier pressing his lips to mine.

The more we kissed and touched, the quicker my heart beat, and the faster I melted, like a marshmallow over a campfire.

But still I kept intact my protective armour, not allowing any romantic notions to penetrate that steel wall. Tonight would simply be fun — a pleasurable moment like the people of La Vallée du Bonheur shared. He drew away, but kept hold of me.

'I've wanted this so badly, Adrienne.'

Smiling, I took his hand, and led him along the hallway, and up the staircase to my attic room.

The instant I closed the door, we wrenched off our clothes in a frenzy, fell onto the bed, and made love with every part of our minds and bodies. As he thrust deep inside me, my body arched up to his, my breaths choking gasps, whispering fiercely into his ear, 'Don't stop, please don't stop.'

And then, with the joy of too much pent-up emotion; too many passionless, lonely nights, I cried out with pleasure.

Afterwards, our damp bodies still melded, entwined in the sheets tangled around our bare legs, he said, 'I love you, Adrienne, and I wish we could spend the rest of our lives together.'

No, no, I'm not ready for this!

But at least now I believed Xavier's feelings for me were genuine.

'Let's see how things go,' I said, as he stroked damp hair strands from my cheek and kissed my brow. 'Even if I no longer feel married, I still am.'

'We'll somehow convince Emile to give you a divorce,' Xavier said, his silky breath moving the hairs on top of my head.

'Emile hates being defeated,' I said. 'He can't even bear losing at Scrabble and Monopoly.'

Xavier laughed, a deep catchy sound that made me laugh too, as we got dressed and slipped downstairs to the kitchen.

I heated the cheese and onion soup, while Xavier sliced up saucisson. I poured two glasses of red wine, and Xavier carried the tray into the living room.

Amidst Christmas decorations bathed in the soft glow of lights, we sat cross-legged on the rug in front of the still-flaming fire.

'I've been meaning to talk to you about the asylum,' I said, as we clinked glasses. 'I keep thinking about all those patients, so disturbed they'd never cope in the outside world, so they'll just wither and die in Sainte-Dymphna's.' The smooth wine slid down my throat. 'So many of them have been locked away for years on end without a good reason, and I don't understand how you could allow that?'

'I do concede the conditions are grim, Adrienne, but they *are* changing, albeit slowly. And if you'd known the asylums of the old days when I was starting out — the lobotomies, insulin comas, patients drugged to the eyeballs in straightjackets and far worse, you'd see things are better nowadays.' He sipped the wine. 'Though you're right, we still have a long way to go to improve mental health treatment.'

'Most of the staff are horrible, and some are downright *monsters*,' I said. 'Only a rare few, like Nurse Trudeau, care about the patients.'

'I know and, sadly, they encourage one another,' he said. 'Many of them hate their jobs, and take entertainment at the patients' expense. Most of it goes on behind my back. I'd never condone that kind of behaviour if I could catch them at it.'

'I could help change that attitude,' I said, 'if I became a psychiatric nurse. I'd be one of the caring ones.'

He raised his eyebrows. 'Oh, that's a wonderful idea, if that's what you truly want?'

'I want to help those helpless patients — Yvonne and Marcelle, and the other homosexuals who are no crazier than I am, the poor Mongoloids like Georges, who aren't sick at all, but who society has no clue how to deal with.'

Xavier was nodding and smiling, encouraging me to go on.

'I also want to do this for my mother, who I never really knew, because her mental illness was so badly treated ... or rather, not treated at all. Only if the staff change their attitude will the patients have a chance, and I want to be one of those nurses.'

'That's very noble of you,' Xavier said, as the grandfather clock chimed the hour. 'And I'll help you as much as I can.'

'It's getting late,' I said with a sigh, as we drained our bowls of delicious onion soup with the bubbly Gruyère cheese crust. 'They'll be home soon, so you'd better get going.'

'You're kicking me out already?' Xavier laughed as he stood up, and held out a hand to help me up. 'Can't we spend the whole night together?'

'Maybe another time. Besides, my attic bed is small, not to mention the smirks I'd get from Léa and Nelly, and Louise's disapproving frowns.'

'So let's go to my place?' Xavier said, as I unhooked his coat and scarf from the rack. 'What's stopping you … this new and fiercely independent Adrienne?'

'Oh well, why not?' I truly was enjoying Xavier's company, and he was right, there was no reason it had to stop now.

So my friends wouldn't worry, I left them a note and on the kitchen table. I wound my scarf around my neck, slipped into Léa's plush red coat, and grabbed my shoulder bag. Grinning at each other like teenagers, Xavier and I stepped out, hand-in-hand, into the clear, chilly night air.

A car door slammed, and I squinted through the fog, expecting to glimpse the blurred figures of everyone arriving home from Lyon. But that foggy darkness remained silent, like the heavy quiet pause between thunder booms, before a rain squall, which was strange, since they were a rowdy lot, especially the girls.

Footsteps — one set — crunched, slow and steady, across the snowy cobbles. I squinted again, through fog and darkness, my eyes finally adjusting to the hunched figure of Emile.

'*Merde!*' I grabbed Xavier's arm.

'Don't worry, Adrienne, I'm here.'

'I'm not worried, I can handle Emile.'

51

I flipped on the outside light switch and stared at Emile as he marched toward us, his glare dark as the night. I kept a grip on Xavier's arm.

'So, you're with *him* again?' Emile said. 'I came to ask if you wanted to come home for Christmas, but sadly for me — for our *family* — you seem to prefer —'

'Emile, I don't —'

Like a traffic gendarme, he held up a gloved hand, his smile cryptic, his calm voice belying a pleading edge. 'Don't worry, I won't try to force you — as if I'd ever do that! — I just want you to know you're welcome to come to your *real* home for Christmas. I'd love you to be there, and so would our children.'

I snorted. 'I doubt the twins would love to have me home, since you've poisoned their minds against me. Besides, didn't you threaten never to let me see them again?' I shook my head. 'I don't understand you, Emile.'

His offer *was* tempting though — another chance at explaining myself, and begging the twins' forgiveness, which would truly be the best gift.

'So the twins are home for Christmas?'

'Well no,' Emile said, 'they've gone on some skiing holiday with friends, but I'll be there, alone —'

'Oh well,' I said, 'your mother will be ecstatic to have you to herself, without your disappointment of a wife.'

'But you've always *loved* Christmas,' he said, stepping toward me.

'You must be joking, or blind,' I said. 'Don't you recall any of our family Christmases?'

'Of course I do. Whatever was wrong with them?'

Last year's Christmas Day rolled out through my mind. The twins were lying on the living-room floor, staring at the new television set, with some colour channels, that Emile had purchased as an early present. They didn't lift a finger to help prepare the meal or decorate the tree, and when I attempted to speak to them, Antoine grunted something incomprehensible, and Martine sighed heavily and rolled her eyes, as if I was such a nuisance for interrupting their show.

I'd trudged back to the kitchen, and prepared the vegetables to accompany the roasting capon. Emile sidled in after me and gave me a friendly pat on my backside.

'Oh, we're having that again?' he'd said. 'Same as *every* year. Can't you be a bit imaginative, Rien?'

And, once again, my entire marriage unfurled before me like some tattered old rug I should've got rid of years ago but couldn't bring myself to throw away — the humiliations, the embarrassments and resentments. That unbroken line of minor injuries that had melded into one great, gaping wound. I let go of Xavier's arm and wrapped my arms around myself, both from the chill outside and within.

'What's the point, Emile, if have to spell it out? I couldn't come home to you now any more than I could fly to the moon. I'm a different person. Can't you see a divorce is best for both of us ... for our family?' I inhaled a shaky breath.

'Best for our *family*?' Emile hissed. 'How dare you speak of *our family*, when all you want to do is to destroy it with your silliness?' He stamped closer to me, the calm and controlled aura vanishing.

'I'll never get over this *silliness*, Emile, because I don't love you anymore.'

'You're crazy!' Emile's gaze flickered from me to Xavier, and back. 'You're emotionally immature. I'll get custody of the children, and you'll never see them again. I can easily prove you're unfit to be a mother.' His eyes wide, Emile had a strange kind of hot energy about him. 'Do you really want that to happen?'

'Your nasty threats no longer scare me, Emile.'

'You're making a big mistake. You'll come crawling back when you realise how good you had it with me. But you'll find out the hard way, and I won't give you a single franc.'

'Emile, stop —' Xavier started.

'You keep out of this,' Emile snarled, pointing a finger at Xavier.

'I don't want money, or anything, from you,' I said.

Silence fell, the falling snowflakes muting everything around, making me feel separated from the real world — a silence so intense I heard the blood pumping in my ears, and my heart thudding against its cage of my chest. Emile shifted his stunned gaze between me and Xavier.

'Oh, I get it now. You've been fucking *my wife*, haven't you?' he said, amidst sharp clouds of vapour. 'I can *see* it in your eyes … I can *smell* the sex on you both. Filthy fucking adulterers!'

A breeze blew up, rippling the dark lake water and throwing flurries of snow all around us.

'Making love is the correct phrase, I believe,' Xavier said. 'And I love Adrienne.'

'So you might as well cut me loose now,' I said, 'and I'll forgive your diabolical plan of committing me to Sainte-Dymphna's.'

Emile fisted his gloved hands, mouth twitching as his anger exploded into a red-black rage. I'd never seen him like this, so unlike the self-controlled Emile I knew, and it scared me. My whole body quivered as I tried to remain calm. Calm and terrified.

Emile's gaze kept flickering between Xavier and me, as if he still couldn't believe what he was hearing.

'You *cannot* do this to me,' he said. 'I'm not some fool you can mock —'

'You should leave now, Emile,' Xavier said. 'Quietly, without a fuss.'

Emile didn't leave. He remained rooted to the snowy ground then, without a word or warning, my husband lurched at me.

Before I had time to jump aside, he grabbed each dangling end of my scarf and pulled them tight.

~

'Stop, Emile, stop!' I tried to say, but the words came out muffled as Emile tugged each scarf end, tightening it around my neck.

'If I can't have you, Adrienne, nobody else will!' he screeched. 'Especially not Xavier *putain* Lacoste. How *dare* you both make fun of me, laugh in my face?'

'Emile, stop right now!' Xavier shouted, trying to drag him away from me, which only tightened the scarf even more.

Emile ignored Xavier, shrugging him off, his fury focussed on me. On *killing* me.

The darkness blurred, my fingers grappling to stretch the wool from my neck as I struggled to breathe and break free.

My throat is closing up. Blood stagnates in my face. My head, about to explode. Can't breathe.

It seemed like minutes, but must've been only seconds, when Emile reeled backwards, his grip on my scarf loosening as he toppled over in a moaning heap. His fedora tumbled from his head, and a snow flurry carried the tumbling hat off over the cobblestones.

I gasped in noisy, rasping lungfuls of air, staring down at Emile flailing about on the snow, boots slipping as he tried to get up, then falling back onto the cold, hard ground.

'My back! You've damaged my back, my kidneys … I'll sue, you bastard,' Emile cried at Xavier and only then did I realise that, failing to prise Emile's hands from my scarf, Xavier had kneed my husband hard in his lower back.

Still panting hard into the freezing air, I kept staring at Emile, the chill and the shock paralysing me, still not believing what had happened. Before, it had only been a veiled, harmless threat, but this time I was convinced Emile had truly wanted to kill me.

Xavier was beside me, gathering me in his arms, neither of us paying any attention to Emile, still screeching about his sore back.

'Are you all right, Adrienne? Can you breathe properly? Did he hurt you? Oh, my poor love.'

As Xavier held me, I glanced over his shoulder, barely registering Emile's curses as he finally managed to stand upright.

And when my husband took a few wobbly steps, and grabbed the snow shovel from beside the door, still I didn't react. All I could do was scream into that silent night as, with a great, heaving sigh, Emile brought the shovel down onto Xavier's head.

Xavier's grip slid from me as he sank to the ground.

Still yelling, I knelt down on the snow beside him. 'Xavier, speak to me! Open your eyes!'

I drew in a sharp breath, gazing in horror at the crimson flower blooming from beneath his head.

52

The following morning, I stared out through the kitchen window, the shock and numbness still raw.

The sun rising across Mont Blanc illuminated the snowcapped peaks in lavender and pink hues, the light dazzling as it reflected off the snowy fields and the trees drooping beneath their white cloaks. I sensed I wasn't really here, but stuck in some faraway time and place, beyond those distant mountains.

But beneath the stupor and paralysis, a seam of sadness, gloom and — above all — fear, emerged.

Would Xavier wake from his coma? And if so, would his brain be permanently damaged?

The doctors couldn't give me any definite news last night, good or bad. 'You'll have to be patient, madame, it's a wait and see situation.'

For Xavier, while it wasn't the deep grief for a person you loved beyond reason — it had been too soon, and the wrong circumstances, for my love to blossom — I felt a deep affection for him, and now, sorrow and guilt. His life was hanging by threads, and that was partly my fault. The other part was Emile's doing, and the germ of a raw and terrible anger at my husband seeded.

I wanted to shriek out this profound wrath bottled inside me. If Xavier died, Emile would, in a bizarre twist of fate, have won our last battle. But if I started screaming, I'd never be able to stop.

Major Yves Rocamadour's blue Renault 4L with GENDARMERIE written on the side, pulled up outside the auberge. I knew he'd gone to fetch Martine and Antoine from their boarding school, and as the twins clambered from the car, my pulse quickened, and I wrung my hands, slick with sweat.

I tried to snap to my senses as, with great trepidation, I walked out into the whitened, blinding landscape to meet my children and the gendarme in his starched uniform, kepi and polished boots.

'Is it t-true, Maman, w-what Major Rocamadour is s-saying? I can't believe it,' Martine said, shaking and sobbing, her dark hair a tangle around her red, blotchy face. Antoine stood behind her, staring down at the cobblestones. 'Some story about Papa trying to strangle you, then bashing a man who saved you from him … I don't understand. Surely Major Rocamadour got it wrong? Tell me he got it wrong, Maman?'

'I'm sorry, *chérie*, it's the truth.' Though I couldn't believe it all either, certain I would never rid from my mind those terrible images of Emile clutching my scarf ends, intent on strangling me, then Xavier sprawled on the ground, the blood wreath around his head so dark against the white of the snow. And a panicked Emile, the colour bleached from his face, brow sweat-beaded, cursing, 'Oh *putain*, oh *merde*!' and bending over Xavier, trying to stem the seeping blood. In that terrible moment, I'd almost fainted with relief when everyone arrived home from Lyon.

Léa and Nelly had herded the girls inside, away from Emile hunched over Xavier's body, and Louise called the *pompiers*. Once the medics arrived and took over from Emile, Major Rocamadour handcuffed my husband and took him away. My shock was so profound in those hours after the tragedy, I hadn't thought about the twins. And I hadn't known the major had gone to break the news to them early this morning, or I'd have insisted on accompanying him.

'But *why* would Papa try to strangle you?' Martine sobbed. 'Just tell me *why*, Maman?'

I took her hand, relieved when she didn't pull away. Unlike his sister, my son wasn't crying, but from his lack of eye contact, it was obvious Antoine was ill at ease.

'What did you do to Papa, to make him do such a thing?' Martine cried, shaking my hand in frustration. 'And who is this man who *saved* you?

'Xavier Lacoste was my doctor at Sainte-Dymphna's.' I didn't want to tell the twins anything more and, thankfully, Martine was still too shocked to think to ask why my doctor had been at the auberge. That story would keep for another day, and I was relieved when Louise hurried outside toward us.

'Let's get you all inside, out of this cold,' she said, ushering us into the fire-warmed living room.

The twins sat on the sofa. I wanted to sit with them, to hug them tight, but still wary of Martine's suspicious stares, I perched on the edge of an armchair, well away from them.

The three of us sipped the coffee that Louise placed on the small table, though only Antoine ate the cookies. The room fell silent, and I tried once more to explain.

'You didn't see it — your father was an expert at hiding things — he ordered your school to forbid you to have any contact with me, which tore me to shreds. And the worst thing, he *almost* convinced me I was mad ... that I'd inherited my mother's mental illness. But I was never insane.'

'Papa did keep saying you'd gone mad, like your own mother,' Martine said. 'And since he's the psychiatrist, we naturally believed him, didn't we, Antoine?'

She nudged her brother, who shrugged, chomping through the cookies.

'We didn't know who, or what, to believe ... all the bad things he kept saying about you,' Martine sobbed, the coffee spilling from her shaking hand.

I told the twins how their father had unceremoniously drugged me and dragged me off to Sainte-Dymphna's, and how I'd suffered in that pit of hell.

'But Dr Lacoste convinced me there was no madness, just a bit of depression,' I said. 'So at least my time at that terrible place wasn't completely wasted.'

Rather than roll her eyes, as I expected, Martine nodded, with a flicker of understanding. 'Ok yes, Papa was sometimes mean to you, but he was still a good husband, and I can't believe he'd try to *kill* you. Surely you got that wrong, Maman?'

'You can't know how sad and shocked I am, Martine, to know that he really wanted me gone. Once I'd been on my own for a while,' I went on, 'I knew that to be happy, our marriage had to end. But your father wouldn't let me go ... he'd *never* have let me go. He'd rather have me dead than not his possession.'

'That's true, you *were* his possession,' Martine said. 'But he also gave you absolutely everything, didn't he? Bought all that nice stuff for you and the flat?'

I went and sat beside Martine, and took her hand, about to explain how objects were meaningless, but she moved away from me. A subtle but definite shift.

Louise brought in a breakfast of baguette, creamy butter and little bowls of her dandelion, quince, and redberry jams. She placed the tray on the coffee table and tip-toed — something she never did — back to the kitchen.

'So in the end, it seems our father is the mad one, not you?' Martine said, more tears gathering in her eyes.

'In the heat of the moment, people sometimes do things they never mean to,' I said. 'Things they'd *never* normally do.'

'We knew things had been strained between you and Papa for a long time,' Martine said, 'but we never thought it would come to this! Did we, Antoine?'

He shrugged again, shovelling bread and jam into his mouth.

'Neither did I,' I said, seeing, in that instant, that much of my children's attitude — and their absence from the flat on weekends and holidays — had been them detaching themselves from the uncomfortable situation between their parents. That, and simply being teenagers.

The front door opened, and a voice boomed down the hallway.

'Adrienne?' Clotilde swept into the living room in a flowing coat, so bright and colourful it almost blinded me. She held up a phial of green-coloured liquid. 'I've made a special potion for you. A simple brew for the shock and grief.' She beamed at Martine and Antoine. 'And these gorgeous young people must be your twins?'

'Madame Bonnefille!' Louise hurried in from the kitchen and scowled at Clotilde. 'We have Adrienne and her children's care in hand, and do not require your black magic. Besides, can't you knock on the door instead of always barging in?'

As much as Louise tried to force Clotilde, and her magic brew, to leave, she eventually gave up, sighing heavily, flinging her hands in the air and vanishing back to the kitchen.

Clotilde poured equal measures of her potion into three glasses of water and pushed one toward each of us. I didn't ask what it was, simply drank it down, eager to try anything to ease those raw and tender emotions — my sadness for Xavier, who might lose his life, or never properly recover, and for what Emile had done.

I hoped her potion would dampen down my anger too, for Emile, and the sorrow that our marriage had ended so unnecessarily badly. But I was relieved that, with a possible manslaughter or grievous bodily harm charge, my husband would be out of my life for good. I was sorry for the twins though; he was their father, after all.

'I never want to go back to the flat, Maman,' Martine said.

Antoine nodded his agreement, and Louise, who must have been listening, hurried into the living room.

'There is no question of anyone returning to Lyon,' she said, looking around the sorry arc of us. 'Since Nelly has become engaged, and will move into her new home with Thierry, their cottage will be free.' She waved an arm in the direction of the orchard and the two quaint white cottages. 'And you are all most welcome to stay there as long as you need. It's vital the three of you remain together during this most difficult of times.'

53

Three months after Emile's terrible attack on Xavier, I knelt beside Suzanne Rossignol's grave in the Sainte-Marie-du-Lac cemetery.

These graveyard chats with Suzanne were a great comfort after the shock of Emile's violence, and Xavier's terrible head injury. I took solace in the presence of my children too, and our life together at the auberge cottage.

Thankfully, Xavier had completely recovered, and I loved visiting him several times a week, and seeing him progressing from being unconscious to almost back to his kind, smart, and handsome self.

'I'm not asking for a commitment, Adrienne,' he'd said on my last visit. 'But tell me there's hope that you might one day love me as I love you.'

'There's hope,' I said, sitting beside him and taking his hand. 'I'm sorry I can't promise anything more right now. Too much has happened, and I'm not ready. Yet.'

'Thank you,' he'd said, with that dazzling smile that had disarmed me right from the beginning. He pulled me into his arms.

'Let's just take it one day at a time,' I said, hugging him back.

On this March morning, beneath a cornflower-blue sky, the sun warmed the vast village graveyard. The harsh winter frosts had thawed, and new grass spiked from the sun-warmed soil. Leaves unfurled on tree branches from which the spring chorus of birds twittered and shrieked, as if making up for months of silence.

All around me, optimistically adorned in short sleeves, people weeded family plots, removed last year's shrivelled chrysanthemums, and watered the flowers that had sprung from their cosy winter beds — irises, pansies, tulips and daffodils — the bulbs they'd thrust into the damp, dark earth last All Souls' Day.

Reluctant as I had been to leave the auberge attic, and Suzanne, to move into Nelly's vacated cottage, as the wise Louise Bellefontaine had said, it was vital the twins and I stayed together. And it was true, my children's new-found — though still wary — love and respect for me could, like these spring flowers, grow and flourish. The twins had needed this time with me, to see the difference between their mother then and now. The *After the Supermarket* mother. And they'd needed to come to terms with their absent father, and the shadow of a nasty trial hanging over him. But I missed my ghostly friend, so I'd started coming to the graveyard to speak with Suzanne.

'Only four more months and the twins are done with high school. Then, no doubt, they'll be leaving L'Auberge de Léa,' I said, pulling out weeds around Suzanne's headstone. 'I'll miss them, though I'm happy to see them setting off in their new adult lives.' I tugged on a stubborn root. 'Just as I have to find my own way now, as the mother of those adults.' I smiled to myself, certain that Suzanne was nodding at me across the decades.

'I'm so sorry about what happened to Jules in those dreadful trenches, and how he treated you,' I said, pouring water from one of the cemetery jugs onto the potted plants. 'Your story made me feel guilty for complaining about the asylum — my time in a different war trench. But I was disappointed you stopped writing, and I never found out if Jules was cured of the shell shock, and came to love you again. But I hope so.'

I half-expected Suzanne to whisper the end of her story to me, but she remained silent in her earthy bed. With a sigh, I touched two fingers to my lips, then to her tombstone.

I glanced around at the graves of the Sainte-Marie villagers I'd come to know and call friends. My gaze came to rest on Dommy and Lea's family plot and I ensured, as always when I came here, that the little blue teddy bear was sitting upright against the headstone of that tiny, sad grave.

'See you next week, Suzanne,' I said, nodding at the old priest, Père Châtaigne, hunched over a pair of secateurs as he tended the rose bushes.

I headed back across la place de la Fontaine, nodding and waving at people running errands, and calling out *bonjour* to Dédé, languidly cleaning his tables and chairs for the coming outdoors' season.

As I walked back down to the auberge, the Spring Goddess's magic wand that had broken the winter spell captivated me. The sun shone brightly over the fields, where ploughs had made stripes of deep ruts, now filled with light-reflecting water from the winter melt.

A rabbit scuttered across my path, tail bobbing in a white puff, as I strolled along the lac du Héron pathway. A light breeze rippled the lake water and swayed the scores of dandelions dotting the fields.

At the auberge, I waved to Antoine and Victor, working together down in the orchard amidst the cherry blossoms, all dressed up to parade their elegant white blooms.

'*Coucou*,' I called.

Amidst the new leaves of his old oak tree, the cheeky jay bird echoed back at me. '*Coucou.*'

Victor waved, and Antoine called back, '*Salut*, Maman.'

Yes, because my son spoke now — the boy who I'd often feared had gone mute. And deaf. Though Antoine spoke mostly to Victor. Both outcasts in their own way, they'd found common, comfortable ground in the auberge maintenance work, chatting like lifelong buddies as Antoine helped Victor on weekends and in the school holidays — preparing the soil in the kitchen garden, cutting and stacking next winter's wood, and repairing animal enclosures.

I smiled at the dogs barking as they dashed across the new grass, chasing the ball Linda and Juliette threw around, and I slipped inside, to where Martine was helping Louise prepare the guests' meal of *saucisson chaud* stuffed with pistachio nuts, and a lentil and goat-cheese salad.

I couldn't mask my pride at my daughter's new penchant for cuisine, relieved that she was finally interested in something beyond makeup and chatting with friends on the telephone.

'Your daughter will make an excellent chef once she's completed her studies,' Louise said, smiling at the floury-handed Martine, who blushed scarlet. 'If she continues to apply herself, I'll have stiff competition in the future.'

'Maybe I'll be good enough to cook for La Cuisine de Louise one day?' Martine said, blotting her hands on her apron. 'What a dream, to live beside this amazing lake and be your *sous-chef*.'

I was surprised, but pleased, that Martine would consider settling here. To have her, and possibly Antoine, living close by, was beyond my fanciest dream.

'Once you make friends at university, you surely you won't want to live with your boring old maman,' I said with a wink.

'Maybe not *with* you, Maman,' she said, rolling her eyes in that familiar teenage way, 'but close by, so one day I can offload your grandchildren.'

My heart soared as this new chapter of our lives unfolded. As those long and painful scenes with Emile faded, I acknowledged that the days of caring for my little children were gone, but that the three of us were still a family. And that family was a moving story, unfolding onward and forward, and the trick was to keep turning those pages; to keep welcoming the new chapters. And not to dwell on the what-ifs.

Epilogue
April 1971

A month later, only ten months since I left home — though it was a whole lifetime — we unpack our picnic lunch in the warm April sunshine.

Beneath a cerulean sky, and the newly budding trees, Louise, Blanche, Dommy, Léa, Nelly and I settle on the blanket on the soft lake-side grass. Luxuriant maidenhair ferns arch over the Virgin Mary, clusters of violets huddling around her marbled feet like tiny purple pilgrims.

Blanche and Dommy have taken a well-earned day off to join us. Their dressmaking business, *La Bonne Couture,* is thriving and they are working on several wedding and bridesmaid gowns for this summer, one of them Nelly's, which is Dommy and Blanche's gift to her.

I pass around plates and napkins, and Blanche and Louise serve out slices of quiche, terrine, and olive and grain bread. Léa and Nelly fill glasses with Louise's tangy lemonade, while Dommy slices up the crumble Martine made with last season's apples.

'I can't wait to see my finished dress,' Nelly says, licking quiche crumbs from her lips.

'I'm so happy for you,' Léa says, 'though I doubt I'll ever marry again. You know, once bitten ... But thankfully Bruno and I *are* divorcing, so we can both be with our new partners without too much village backstabbing.'

'Do you think you'll ever forgive Emile for what he did to you and Dr Lacoste?' Dommy asks. 'And for all those years you endured with him?'

'I try never to think about Emile,' I say with a heavy sigh, plucking daisies, and threading them into a halo. 'Holding on to all that bitterness, the regret and anger, is like holding your breath under that lake water.'

I glance down at the dangerous boggy patch before Our Lady, and glimpse an enormous fish gliding through between lily pads. There, and gone, like our lives could have been — Xavier's and mine. 'You end up drowning if you don't resurface … if you don't let go.'

'Yves thinks your husband might be sent to Sainte-Dymphna's,' Léa says, 'since he's pleading temporary insanity when he attacked Dr Lacoste.'

I settle the daisy chain on my head. 'Well, isn't that ironic?'

'Speaking of Sainte-Dymphna's, when do you start your psychiatric nurse training?' Nelly asks. 'How exciting!'

'Exciting, yes,' I say, plucking a buttercup and twirling it between my thumb and index finger. 'But nerve-racking too. I hope I'll be up to it … going back to that terrible place will be scary. I've never studied anything in my life, and I'll miss waitressing at La Cuisine de Louise.'

'Of course you'll be up to it,' Louise says. 'Be proud you'll be helping to make a difference to those poor souls.'

I nod. 'Let's hope that one day, Sainte-Dymphna's will be the best hospital around for mental health treatment.'

'Apparently, an extension was built onto the original Sainte-Dymphna's building for treating shell-shocked men, like Jules Rossignol,' Louise says. 'They were sent there for the countryside peace, though nobody really knew how to help those soldiers, and any treatment apparently only made them worse.'

'I don't know if you've read Suzanne's journal yet?' I say, gazing up at a perfect dark triangle of tiny birds flying overhead, 'but she wanted the doctor to send Jules there for treatment.' As they swing around, the sun lights up the birds, and when they turn again, they are, once more, dark.

'Louise and I didn't know Suzanne,' Blanche says. 'She was about fifteen years older than us. But we knew *of* her, and that her husband had been injured in the trenches … his mind was gone, they said.'

'Most families in Sainte-Marie still bear the scars of their menfolk who fought in the trenches,' Louise says, 'killed or maimed physically or mentally, or both.'

'So many of our poor boys never made it home,' Blanche says, 'including one of Roger's relatives, Gilles Larue, boyhood friend of Jules Rossignol. I recall Maman saying that Suzanne Rossignol was one of the lucky ones, because her husband made it home.'

'Not so lucky,' I say. 'In her journal, she says the shell shock transformed Jules into a violent monster. Suzanne feared he might actually *kill* her, and she was terrified that Victor would be left without his mother … without anyone.'

I shiver, and stop myself from rubbing my neck, a blade of fear stabbing my heart as I realise, yet again, how easily Emile could have succeeded.

'Frustratingly, Suzanne's journal entries stopped, and I never found out what happened to them,' I say, finishing the delicious crumble. 'And Jules' grave is not beside Suzanne's, so I wonder where he's buried?'

'Are we sure he returned from Sainte-Dymphna's?' Nelly says.

'Maybe Jules died there, and is buried at the asylum?' Léa says.

'Now that you mention it,' Louise says with a frown, 'I do not recall him returning to the village.'

'Nobody was sure he even *went* to Sainte-Dymphna's,' Blanche says. 'In fact, it's like the man completely vanished.'

'All we know is that Suzanne passed away about six years ago,' Louise says. 'Poor Victor found his mother dead in her armchair, and came running to tell my husband, who was our mayor at the time.'

'We never knew what she died from,' Blanche says. 'Natural causes, we assumed, though she'd only have been in her seventies. But since Jules never reappeared, and Suzanne was on her own for many years after the war, he most likely did not harm his wife.'

'I just hope things turned out all right for my ghostly friend,' I say, holding the buttercup beneath my chin as I lie back on the grass, soaking up the sun to the clatter of a bird's wings echoing across the lake. 'All these different echo theories ... what do you think the sounds really are?'

'A mixture of all the noises around us,' Blanche says, as the plop of a jumping fish punctuates the silence.

'And even, as Clotilde claims, the ghosts of our ancestors whispering the legends to us, so they're never lost,' Nelly says.

'There is that other theory,' Blanche says. 'That the lake echoes are the dying cries of that man whose skeleton the frogmen found last year.'

'One poor soul your Madonna forgot to save, eh, Louise?' Léa says with a sarcastic smirk. '*Tut-tut*, such a *lazy* Virgin Mary.'

'Léa, *must* you take Our Lady's name in vain?' Louise chides, she and Blanche crossing themselves.

'Man's skeleton?' I say. 'Who was he?'

Dommy shrugs. 'He was never identified.'

We all fall silent again as insects rustle beneath us, and a falcon flaps its wings overhead. The hovering bird swoops down and traps one of those insects and, as the raptor wings away, the breeze blows a chill down my spine.

I pluck a purple flower from a cluster of pretty, bell-shaped blossoms.

'Be careful,' Louise says. 'Foxglove can be fatal, especially the seeds and leaves. Well, so Clotilde claims. Apparently, her ancestors used it freely to do away with people ... which is probably true. That family is capable of *anything*.'

'So you'd better stop bad-mouthing Clotilde,' Léa says with a laugh. 'Or you might be next.'

'Well, if that woman would cease calling me "Loulou",' Louise says, 'I may even concede that she does possess a few of the most basic healing skills.'

As I drop the flower and wipe my hand on my shirt, Suzanne's words clang through my mind.

I've made Jules' favourite summer soup ... cucumber, mint, lemon juice ... seeds and leaves from those pretty purple, bell-shaped flowers.

'Isn't it called *la légitime défense*,' I ask, 'if you kill someone because they are endangering your own life?'

'I believe so,' Louise says, and from the way she looks at me, I am certain she knows why I ask. 'Anyway, as I always say, whatever we say, or think, in the widows' circle, remains in the widows' circle.' She nods up at the great imposing statue. 'Let's just pray that our Madonna is covering her ears.'

I gaze up at the marbled face of the Virgin Mary, seeing her as the passive symbol of all of us. She is every woman, knowing all our stories, aware of so much more than we mere humans.

And I wonder if lac du Héron has now given up all its secrets, or if Our Lady is holding onto other mysteries, close to her heart.

~END~

Message from Liza

I hope you enjoyed *Lake of Widows*, book 2 in *The Women of the Lake* French Historical trilogy. If you did, I would really appreciate it if you could spare a minute to leave a short review — even one line is enough — at the retailer where you purchased the book. Reviews make a huge difference to authors, in that they help books get discovered by other readers. Thank you so much, your review is really important!

If you would like to read about the Sainte-Marie-du-Lac women of the lake in book 1 of the trilogy, *Lake of Echoes*, here's the opening:

Lake of Echoes
1
July 1969
Léa

The snap of a twig. The rustle of leaves. A breath, stilled.

Someone is out there, watching me. I smell them, almost feel their tapered fingers reaching out to seize me.

I stare into the summer gloaming. Listening, waiting.

Another breath. Is that a muffled cough?

A sense of foreboding steals through me and my pulse quickens as I gather the plates from the guests' evening meal.

Clutching the crockery to my chest, I swivel away from the outside dining table, looking left, right, squinting through the twilight, searching for something tangible. But, as always, there is nothing.

Yet again I wonder, has my mind slipped, my thoughts turned wild? My gaze rests down on the lake shimmering gold beneath the silky moonlight. Is the sound only a drift of breeze across the water — a normal lake echo — and I simply perceive it as closer, louder, through this calm, silent night?

Is it only a rabbit, fox or deer straying from the woods? A badger on its night hunt?

I could try to convince myself it's just a busy night creature, only I've felt its presence in the daytime too. Four years ago, when Bruno and I bought this place to create L'Auberge de Léa, we'd heard the village rumour about ghostly echoes across the lake.

But the location of the old stone building on picturesque Lac du Héron, its unhampered view of Mont Blanc's snowy crown to the east and the Monts du Lyonnais hills to the west, were so sublime that I refused to dwell on the word *ghost*.

Besides, those echoes are merely the willow trees dancing in the wind, the herons calling to each other or, if you believe my mother-in-law, the Virgin Mary's warning cries.

I became distracted, busy renovating my inn, though I continued to be aware of an eerie spectre gliding across the water on a summer zephyr, floating down on a winter snowfall or lingering like a spring dew.

The presence was always more homely than frightening though and, over time, as my auberge thrived, the echoes melded into background noise.

I stopped noticing them altogether until this summer when they began again, more frequently. Around the auberge now, rather than across the lake. And somehow more disturbing.

Bruno never senses the slightest thing.

'The only phantoms around here are in your imagination, Léa,' my husband says, with a laugh that these days verges on a sneer.

I remind myself that I've hosted more guests than usual this summer. The extra work and the heat must be frazzling my brain, and these shadowy auras are purely hallucinations conjured from a fatigued mind.

'Don't be silly, there are no ghosts,' the stars say, winking down at me. I exhale a long breath and carry the plates into the kitchen.

Besides the faint hum from the living room, where Bruno is watching television, the inn is quiet. Tired from a day of boating on Lac du Héron, my guests have retired to their rooms. Exhausted from playing with her cousin, Linda, my daughter is asleep, and my mother-in-law is still not home. But Bruno's mother often stays out late with her widows' circle on these long summer nights chatting, playing bridge or dancing to Elvis, The Beatles and Johnny Hallyday.

I rinse dirty plates, dreading going back outside to gather the wine and water glasses. I want to take Belle with me — the ghostly presence never manifests when the dog is about — but Belle pattered upstairs with Juliette an hour ago, to sleep on my daughter's bed with her.

I could ask my husband to finish clearing the dinner table, but such requests are often met with a snappy retort.

Your inn, Léa ... you insisted on running it on your own.

Why can't Bruno understand how important this place is to me? That it wasn't simply a ballast steadying me on my own ground. A place from which I'd no longer have to rely on my husband for an income, like so many wives in Sainte-Marie-du-Lac. Apart from all of that, I'd hoped that establishing this lakeside inn would be a new start to my marriage. A path through the tunnel of our dark grief, out into the light. Back into those unclouded days Bruno and I once enjoyed.

But that was in the beginning.

With a sigh, I sidle back out to the table beneath the vine-covered pergola.

The moon lures my gaze and I still find it incredible that only days ago Apollo 11 landed on that mysterious, faraway place, and man walked where no man has walked before.

But my thoughts are torn from space travel as I glimpse it — a tall silhouette against the moon. There, then gone. I gasp, reel backward.

Hands trembling, I shove the glasses onto my tray. One of them falls and shatters. I don't stop to gather the shards, but hurry inside, dump the tray in the kitchen and lock the door.

Should I tell Bruno that this time I saw something real, almost palpable? No. Afraid of more mockery, I pad upstairs and creep into Juliette's bedroom.

In the luminescence, I see my daughter is asleep in her usual position — on her back, gleaming dark hair splayed across the pillow, arms flung above her head. Small, innocent, trusting. I plant a gentle kiss on her brow and pat the dog and cat curled on the end of her bed.

I cross to the window, reach out to close the shutters, and watch an owl waiting quietly on a high branch. In seconds, the *chouette* detects his prey. Down he glides, soundlessly, wings spreading over his victim.

And in the heat of that summer night, I shiver as his powerful claws imprison and slaughter the luckless creature.

~

Please go to *https://books2read.com/u/38PvEr*
to buy *Lake of Echoes.*

Liza's Newsletter

If you would like updates on the book I am currently writing, as well as all book-related news and promotions, why not subscribe to my very occasional newsletter? Don't worry, I would never share your email address with a third party.

I love hearing from readers and will answer all my newsletter replies. As a thank you for subscribing, I'll send you a free download of *Friends & Other Strangers*, my award-winning Australian short story collection.

Sign up on my website at *https://www.lizaperrat.com*

Author's Note

Lake of Widows is a work of fiction, a work that combines the actual with the invented. All incidents and dialogue and all characters, with the exception of some well-known historical figures, are products of the author's imagination and are not to be construed as real. Where real-life historical figures appear, the situations, incidents and dialogues concerning those persons are fictional and are not intended to depict actual events or to change the fictional nature of the work. In all other respects, any resemblance to persons living or dead is entirely coincidental. My fictional Lac du Héron bears no resemblance to the real Lac du Héron in the north of France.

Sainte-Dymphna's Hospital.
A few beta readers questioned the horrors I depicted at Sainte-Dymphna's asylum. As a young and impressionable student nurse back in 1980 (so even after this story is set!), I spent three months of my training at a psychiatric hospital (now closed down and supposedly haunted!) in New South Wales, Australia. I can attest that everything depicted in *Lake of Widows* actually happened — even worse — and some of those horrific images are still stuck in my mind over 40 years later. I asked some nursing friends about their memories of the place, and they agreed that things really were that terrible, and added some more of their own memories, which I've integrated into Sainte-Dymphna's.

Thankfully, mental health care has come a long way since then!

Acknowledgements

Many thanks to these generous people who gave their time and effort to make *Lake of Widows* a better story. To JD Smith for the cover design; Barbara Scott Emmett for her proofreading expertise; Olga Núñez Miret, Jan Patterson, Cindy Taylor, and Noela Tziarkas for checking for last typos; Catriona Troth for her fine structural editing skills; long-time nursing friends Margaret Reid, Deb Holdsworth and Catriona Wilson for their psychiatric hospital memories; Dr Norman James for his ongoing and much-appreciated comments on the asylum section and for suggesting the name, Sainte Dymphna (most frequently named patron saint of the mentally ill); pilot, Tom Vogel for his small aircraft crash information; Suzie Grogan for her shell shock expertise and her very informative book: *Shell Shocked Britain*; fellow authors and generous beta readers who read the different versions of this story: Sue Barnard, Marlene Brown, Vanessa Couchman, Jane Davis, Tricia Gilbey, Karen Inglis, Nancy Jardine, Gwenda Lansbury, Lorraine Mace, Ingrid Maitland, Jill Marsh, Karen Milner, Debora Prichard, Barbara Scott Emmett, Brenda Telford, Susan Van der Spuy, Marianne Vincent, Claire Whatley; Jill Marsh for working out how to integrate Blanche; Jean Gill for help with the title; Karen Inglis for her brilliant idea for the ending; my wonderful 'Sanctuary' author friends for help with the cover and blurb, as well as their ongoing support and encouragement.

Thanks, as always, to my wonderful husband for his infinite patience, support and encouragement.

And, most of all, thank you to my loyal readers who make writing such a joy!

Other Novels by Liza Perrat

French Historical Novels
(All standalones)

Spirit of Lost Angels
Book 1 in *The Bone Angel* trilogy
A Paris lunatic asylum. A woman imprisoned. Plunge into France on the brink of revolution.

Wolfsangel
Book 2 in *The Bone Angel* trilogy
France under Nazi Occupation. Lives colliding unpredictably. One woman's fatal choice.

Blood Rose Angel
Book 3 in *The Bone Angel* trilogy
1348. A bone-sculpted angel and the woman who wears it — heretic, Devil's servant or saint?

Lake of Echoes
Book 1 in *The Women of the Lake* trilogy
A vanished daughter. A failing marriage. A mother's life in ruins.

Australian Historical Novels
(all standalones)

The Silent Kookaburra
Embracing the social changes of 1970s Australia, against a backdrop of native fauna and flora, The Silent Kookaburra is a haunting exploration of the blessings, curses and tyranny of memory.

The Swooping Magpie
A heartbreaking drama of lost innocence, deceit and a scandal that shook Australia.

The Lost Blackbird
A poignant testament to child migrants who suffered unforgivable evil, *The Lost Blackbird* explores the power of family bonds and our desire to know who we are.

Australian Short Stories Collection

Friends & Other Strangers
An award-winning, eclectic collection of funny, shocking, heart-breaking and distinctly Australian short stories, each with its own message.

About the Author

Liza grew up in Wollongong, Australia, where she worked as a general nurse and midwife. She has now lived in rural France for thirty years, working as a medical translator, an editor and a novelist. For more information on Liza and her writing:

For occasional book news and a free copy of *Friends & Other Strangers*, Liza's award-winning Australian short story collection, sign-up on her website:
https://www.lizaperrat.com

Facebook:
https://www.facebook.com/Liza-Perrat-232382930192297

www.ingramcontent.com/pod-product-compliance
Lightning Source LLC
LaVergne TN
LVHW041743060526
838201LV00046B/888